Diana's Mourning

A PEOPLE'S HISTORY

JAMES THOMAS

UNIV

The Mass-Observation material © The Trustees of the Mass-Observation Archive, University of Sussex

British Library Cataloguing-in-Publication Data.
A catalogue record for this book is available from the British Library.

ISBN 0–7083–1753–7 paperback
       0–7083–1754–5 hardback

Typeset at the University of Wales Press
Printed in Great Britain by Dinefwr Press, Llandybïe

Diana's Mourning

Contents

Acknowledgements

I am conscious, as I write this, of the many debts I have run up during my brief academic career in general and this book in particular. Departmental colleagues and friends at Swansea, Bangor and latterly Cardiff have provided a friendly atmosphere both for work and play, while I would particularly like to thank Peter Stead, David Howell and Duncan Tanner for all their support and help. I am also grateful to Nancy Edwards for generously allowing me use of her office for a term last year in Bangor, and to Erin Stockhill for lending me her collection of Diana tapes. Thanks to Karin Wahl-Jorgensen, Matt Hills, Nick Couldry and the anonymous reader for their helpful comments in making this a much better or less bad book than it certainly would have been. My thanks to everyone at University of Wales Press, and especially Duncan Campbell and Ceinwen Jones, for their help in this book's production. Similar sentiments are extended to all the staff at the Mass-Observation archive. A particular debt is due to their archivist Dorothy Sheridan, without whom the collection probably would not be in existence, and to all those people who took the trouble to write about their experiences in September 1997 and make this book possible.

More personally, I owe a big thank you to Deborah Youngs for all her input into this book's intellectual development, not to mention her friendship. Writing this during a less than ideal situation of academic unemployment made me even more aware of the importance of my friends: especially visible during its course were, from north to south, Len, Bob, Jeff, Dark Skies, Lloydee, Lis and last, but certainly not least, Rakna. Their input into this book's contents was thankfully minimal, but their role in helping this book to be written could not have been more vital. Meanwhile, big thanks are due to my extended family for providing top-quality accommodation and even better entertainment on research trips to London and Brighton. Above all, my greatest debt, and one which I can never even begin to repay, goes to my parents, for the unlimited support and help they have given me in every way over the years. The good bits of this book are for them, the rest is for my friends.

James Thomas
Cardiff, August 2001

Introduction

Some might wonder whether there is much point in yet another analysis of the popular reaction that followed the death of Princess Diana on 31 August 1997. After all, her mourning generated more media coverage than any other event in world history, even the outbreak of the Second World War (Jack 1997) and was followed by a wave of popular analyses of her life and death. Amongst academia the pace was slower but the output has been no less remarkable. Until September 1997 the popular appeal of modern royalty was a largely neglected academic topic, deemed unworthy of serious enquiry, despite some important exceptions. Michael Billig, author of one of the most notable of these, recalled that the response of colleagues to his subject of research was a sort of amused, or bemused, tolerance: 'People would smile condescendingly when I told them what I was doing. It was considered a rather silly topic for an academic to apply his mind to' (Driscoll 1997). It was an attitude that distinguished historian Ben Pimlott encountered when he turned his attention to the subject. 'I hear you have been writing a biography of the Queen', said one colleague expecting a denial. 'But does it', puzzled the colleague pausing, 'does it count towards the Research Assessment Exercise?' (Swain 1998). Diana's mourning qualified, even if it did not destroy, these elitist dismissals of such a central feature of contemporary Britain. There followed a wave of conferences, half a dozen books and countless journal articles devoted to exploring the extraordinary popular response. Collectively they suggest that studying Diana's mourning, for want of a better phrase, has been done to death, buried under an avalanche of populist and academic analyses. Perhaps it is time to let it rest in peace?

My answer, somewhat predictably, would be no. Too much, perhaps, has been written on the subject, but not nearly enough attention, curiously, has been spent examining the popular reaction. Despite all the emphasis on the response of 'the people', there has actually been no detailed empirical examination of a popular response wrongly assumed to be self-evidently on public display in September 1997. As part I of this book explores, there is a popular myth of mourning, informed by both media and academic analysis, that the nation was united in tearful, adulatory grief in September 1997. This book goes on to demonstrate that this was far from being the case and that in actual fact there were proportionately few people – even mourners – reacting in the way that was widely emphasized in media coverage. It argues firstly that a majority of the country was not in deep grief after Diana's death, but it also demonstrates that the opinions and actions of those who did mourn were much more moderate, unemotional and rational than their increasingly negative popular image suggests. In so doing, one of its informing spirits has been a desire to rescue the popular reaction from what E. P. Thompson famously called 'the enormous condescension of posterity' (1991: 12). It aims to capture some of the individuality, complexity and diversity of a popular response that has been hidden 'under a large monolith called GRIEF' (Jack 1997: 17). More critically, as this suggests, it echoes the view of the great French historian Fernand Braudel's that 'the lesson' that history 'teaches is . . . not to think that those actors who make the most noise are the most authentic; there are other silent ones' (quoted in Couldry forthcoming).

In emphasizing the views of both the silent and noisy ones, this book begins, in part I, by exploring media and academic approaches to the Diana Event. Chapter 1 examines media coverage of the popular reaction, arguing that it emphasized, to the virtual exclusion of other interpretations, the unity, intensity and adulation of popular opinion. And despite the subsequent emergence of increasingly negative perceptions of the 'mass hysteria-like' response of 'the people', this image has endured largely unchallenged in the popular memory. Following on from this, chapter 2 argues that academic analyses have, for the most part, echoed the above interpretation, but have failed to offer much empirical evidence beyond media coverage to support this. It goes on to explain how this book seeks to rectify this by examining the strengths and weaknesses of the quantitative and qualitative opinion sources used, and in particular one key source, the 250 or so 'ordinary people' who recorded their views for the contemporary 'Mass-Observation' project.

Exploring this and other evidence, part II looks, across three chapters, at the key elements of the popular myth of mourning. It begins with an examination of complex and varied attitudes to Diana herself. One particular important theme here is the much-emphasized nature of Diana's 'ordinary' or 'one of us' appeal. While not ignoring this, this book argues that the princess's elite status remained highly prominent and served as the basis for scepticism about her extra/ordinariness. And in so far as there was one common sentiment among the diverse and mixed feelings visible, it was not popular support for Diana's rapid sanctification, but precisely the reverse, a hostility to this process, even among mourners.

Of course attitudes to Diana herself were only one element within popular attitudes, which often concentrated on the extraordinary week that followed. Chapter 4 offers a broad overview of popular experiences and suggests a lived experience of the mourning that was very different, and far less grief-stricken, from that widely emphasized in media coverage, even at the grieving 'high-points' on the day of the news and during the funeral. More specifically, chapter 5 goes on to argue that, far from being united in grief, popular attitudes were deeply divided across cultures of how people grieve in contemporary Britain. Most importantly, it stresses that, while some people did indeed feel loss over someone they regarded as like a friend, a larger majority considered it to be impossible – and quite possibly pathological – to feel so sad for someone who was ultimately a stranger. Even for those who did feel grief, the apparent nature of the popular reaction – of an un-British, 'wobbly bottom lip' in which everyone had to grieve and be seen to grieve – further served to divide opinion.

Linked up with these points, part III then examines three more specific themes of the mourning, beginning with the rather neglected but very important issue of nationalism. It suggests that British identities both drew people in towards the mourning but also alienated them in ways that combined marked continuities with the past with some very different responses. Indeed ultimately it stresses that Diana's mourning, far from serving as a basis for a new national identity, marked a serious challenge for most people to the idea of 'Britishness'. Replicating past patterns, chapter 8 then illustrates a marked gender difference in which women were collectively and individually much more upset than men. It suggests that despite feminist support for the 'progressive' nature of popular identities with Diana, female identification (when positive) was broadly conservative, and was particularly connected with Diana's role as a mother. At the same time it argues that one of the central themes, among women as well as men, was not support for the new 'feminine' emotionalism on display, but a strong suspicion against such irrational 'mass hysteria'. Chapter 8 then addresses a new theme in discussions of British royalty, that of sexuality. In particular it challenges the media and academic 'fairy story' that saw gays and lesbians united in mourning their 'queen of hearts'. It suggests, instead, a more complex, less reverential reaction in which sexual identity, both negative and positive, was only one aspect of gay and lesbian attitudes that closely replicated those found more generally.

As this suggests, in many ways, the themes discussed throughout this book are interlocking as it really seeks to explore two main questions across a range of themes – individual popular attitudes and broader perceptions of the popular response. One reason for the interest in the latter is that this book is not just an examination of popular responses but a critical exploration of media coverage and power. The role of the mass media is inextricably linked with the Diana Event, both in the way it was experienced and its power in shaping perceptions of the popular response. Of course Diana's mourning was far from being just a media event – three people died in a very real, very tragic accident and there was a highly visible social aspect to her mourning. But that said, it was primarily mediated, and illustrative of the way that the rise of the mass media has meant that 'the monarch's subjects . . . have gradually become an audience rather than the awe-struck onlookers of a traditional crowd' (Chaney 2001: 210). Most people consumed the Diana Event primarily through the media. Only a minority went to sign the books of condolences or place flowers and even they, for the most part, were following the mourning through media images of a woman known to them only through these media.

So on one level this book is not just a 'people's history' but an exploration of audience responses to media images, an approach to the study of media that has proved increasingly popular since the 1980s. Other scholars have, however, expressed concern that such an approach ignores both the content and the power of the media text and the need to set audience responses at their most 'micro' within a broader 'macro' examination of media and society and the complex interaction of the two (Morley 1997). Certainly this is the approach taken throughout this book, most notably in the first chapter that explores media images and part IV of the book, that returns the analysis full circle to examine the power of these messages. This explores the key role of media power in shaping popular perceptions of the mourning, as it examines the paradox that while proportionately few people responded in the way media coverage emphasized, the truth of these messages was widely accepted. It then goes on to suggest that the massive discrepancy between the opinions found in private and those displayed in public was the product of a media-generated 'spiral of silence'. A relentless and intolerant message that 'we are all mourning' meant that the non-mourning majority, lacking media and social sanction, retreated into private safety. Conversely the sentiments of a highly vocal, unrepresentative minority became elevated into the exclusive response of 'the people' by a media that not only misrepresented the full complexity and diversity of popular opinion, but actually prevented its public expression.

In seeking to explore these themes, this book draws on several academic perspectives. It began as, and remains in part, a work of contemporary media and social history, but has veered increasingly into media and cultural studies, while making occasional raids into the disciplines of political science, sociology, psychology and anthropology where their insights have been useful and my knowledge has allowed.

Doubtless this runs the risk of further exacerbating the general intellectual shortcomings of this book, and what follows is unlikely, perhaps rightly, to satisfy the purists in any area. But it is based on the hope that a pragmatic use of the expertise of a variety of disciplines can, for all its weaknesses, ensure a rather more comprehensive exploration than a 'pure' approach fixed within one tradition. Whether this is the case, however, ultimately remains for others to judge.

ଞ୦୯ଓ

1

The Myth of Mourning

I hate to think how the whole 'Diana death' business will become, has already become, a homogenous myth, like the 'chirpy cockney in the blitz' myth along the lines of 'a nation mourns'.[1]

United in Grief: The Media and the Mourning

The 'homogenous myth' of Diana's mourning was, of course, of a nation united in tearful, adulatory grief for their People's Princess in September 1997. Such an unambiguous metanarrative of popular reactions was first, and perhaps most memorably, provided by Tony Blair on the day of the news. In an emotional tribute, widely seen as brilliantly anticipating and representing the perceived reaction that followed, he evoked an image of 'a nation united in mourning, in grief that is so deeply painful for us'. And certainly united with Blair in charting the nature of this popular opinion were the mass media during the week that followed. Across all media – television, radio, broadsheet and tabloid newspapers – the story could scarcely have been more monolithic if it had been state-imposed. For despite the thousands of pages and hours devoted to a story that quickly moved from being one about Diana's death to the unfolding reaction, a remarkably uniform picture was offered based around the unity, emotional intensity and adulation of popular opinions.

Tabloid coverage repeatedly conjured up the image of 'A Nation United in Grief' (*Mirror*, 3 September 1997).[2] Within the quality press the view was no different of how Diana's death had demonstrated her 'prized political entity', 'a rainbow coalition of diverse groups' (Moore 1998) that politicians could only dream of, embracing royalist and republican, men and women, old and young, black and white, gay and straight. 'The waiting crowd seemed as near as it is possible to get to a cross-section of the country', argued *Guardian* journalist Matthew Engel (1997) of a popular reaction from which 'only the time pressed and the hyper-sophisticated were missing'. But it was through television, the dominant medium for consuming the Diana events, that the story of popular reactions was most forcefully and memorably articulated (Kitzinger 1999b). Reporting from the Mall on the night before the funeral, BBC journalist Jill Dando told of how 'people have been coming from all over the country to really be a symbol of a United Kingdom, a kingdom it seems so already united in grief'. 'You speak for the whole nation', she told one upset woman and whether she did or not, Dando certainly spoke for almost the whole journalistic profession (5 September). 'We're all in it together', agreed ITV presenter Eamon Holmes as he told those tuning in on the day of the funeral: 'Whether you're watching at home on television, whether you're queuing up, everyone's united in grief because she was the people's princess' (GMTV, 6 September).

And the basis of such evidence was available for everyone to see. Profiles abounded of the millions who joined 'The Queue of Tears' (*Star*, 2 September) on the 'Highway of Heartache' (*Mirror*, 4 September) to offer their written or floral tributes in London or across the country. Crowds queuing up to eleven hours to sign the books of condolences told of how 'even in death, Diana's inspiration helped unite those who grieved' (*Mirror*, 3 September) as 'race, class, status, all the rest' stood 'overwhelmed in the national sense of loss' (*Mail*, 3 September). Much emphasized was the diversity and inclusivity of a reaction that saw those usually absent from royal ceremonials – the youth, blacks, Asians, gays and lesbians – all sharing the same loss. A much-used image of a distraught man with a mohican haircut laying a huge wreath offered the most striking demonstration that 'from punk to pensioner, grief knew no barrier' (*Mail*, 3 September), proof that in the people's mourning 'even the deviants cared' (Aitkenhead 1997).

As this illustrates, a second repeatedly emphasized element to the story was the intensity and emotionality of the popular reaction, as images abounded of how 'The Nation Weeps' (*Sun*, 6 September), of what seemed like an entire country breaking down in tears. Blair again set the tone when, seemingly on the verge of tears, he talked of how 'like everyone else' he was 'utterly devastated'. 'Today the people ache to their bones with grief', agreed the *Sun* on the day following the news (1 September). As famous and ordinary people alike outlined their deep personal grief, the story of how 'A Nation Weeps for its Queen of Hearts' (*Express*, 1 September) seemed graphically confirmed by the astonishing scenes across Britain. Continuous shots of mourners in tears all spoke of a people 'broken with emotion' and 'soaked with grief' (*Mail*, 3 September) by a 'sea of tears' (*Star*, 2 September). Again it was a reaction most strikingly conveyed through television, as cameras would close in on a person in tears, before panning away, giving the impression of the same collective response (Kitzinger 1999b). Such graphic evidence were confirmed in regular reports from people that 'It's like Losing my own Family' (*Sun*, 8 September) One journalist on the *Telegraph* spoke for many as he suggested:

> The difficulty of trying to write about the public grief . . . is that it is not public grief at all. It is private grief, multiplied millions of times over. Everybody I have spoken to since Sunday feels personally bereaved, as if a close relation had died. (Utley 1997)

The funeral provided the dramatic climax to such a story. Alongside striking visual pictures of the 'tears of the people', the *Sunday Times*, for example, reported, how:

> Unashamedly, thousands wept for Princess Diana in the streets of London yesterday. For long hours many had kept their feelings in check as they waited to see the cortège on its way to Westminster Abbey or followed the funeral service on a giant television screen in Hyde Park. Then the emotions took over. From different walks of life, but with one thing in common – their sense of loss – a young policewoman dabs at her eyes with a handkerchief, a sobbing woman hugs a crying girl, a sad-eyed child cuddles to her mother and a crew-cut man silently weeps. (7 September)

All this seemed proof of another related strand to the mourning myth, the apparent public adulation for a woman 'Born a Lady, Became a Princess, Died a Saint'. This verdict, from the *Daily Mirror* (1 September) captured the change in tone as a woman often vilified in life was now sanctified in death. The *Sun* hailed the 'woman of God' as 'the nearest thing we'll get to an angel on earth' (1 September). Meanwhile television coverage offered endlessly reproduced scenes from her life, often played out in slow motion, with soft music and touched with glamour, 'framing Diana in an angelic, "not of this world", light' (Kitzinger 1999b: 65). This was conveyed most notably in numerous profiles of the 'tireless work for the sick and disadvantaged' (*Sun*, 1 September) of 'a friend for life to the sick and the dying' (*Sunday Times*, 7 September). This attributed to her almost divine powers, as a latter-day inheritor of 'the royal touch' once popularly thought to hold the cure to disease. 'Di "Saved Our Lives"' (*Mirror*, 2 September) said one headline above numerous profiles of how ordinary people, from tramps to cancer victims, had been the beneficiary of the princess's magical 'Healing Hands' (*Express*, 2 September).

Again it was visually that the case for Diana's canonization was most strikingly conveyed, as pictures showed her cuddling sick children, campaigning against landmines and meeting the sick and the underprivileged. What royal critic Christopher Hitchens (1997) derided as 'an obsequious week that saw the concept of sainthood thrown around like confetti', climaxed with the death of Mother Teresa just before Diana's funeral. The two women had met on several occasions, providing a much reproduced image showing them both dressed in white, hands held together seemingly in prayer. 'The People's Princess: Mother Teresa is Dead Days After Heartfelt Tribute for Soulmate Diana', said the *Express* alongside two photos of them together (6 September). Such saintly unity in death was perhaps best conveyed by one *Sun* cartoon at the end of the week which showed them holding hands and wearing halos as they ascended into heaven (6 September).

Discussions of Diana as an icon, a term traditionally used to describe those worshipped as divine, had by this stage long since become the stuff of journalistic cliché. And there was seemingly incontrovertible evidence that her cult had achieved a popular following that the old religions could only dream about. People made what were described as 'pilgrimages' to the 'shrines' that had sprung up in London and elsewhere, leaving tributes of flowers, toys, cards, while other more unusual tokens of love included a pair of biker's boots, a headband and a road map (Bennett and Robinson 1998). Accompanying these were icons of Diana, including photographs, pictures and drawings, often based on a variant of the Queen of Hearts playing card. One carried the question: 'If Jesus was the Son of God then who was Diana?' (Evans 1997). Meanwhile newspaper 'shrines' conveyed these images to those who did not join the 'people's pilgrimage', and printed adulatory readers' letters that 'reflected the language and sentiment of many mourners' (Bennett and Rowbottom 1998: 204). Certainly the scenes highlighted, of a deeply upset people willing to queue for hours and even days to pay their respects, seemed to graphically highlight the intense strength of feelings that Diana had provoked, even without the visions of her that were being reported before the week was out.

Such extraordinary responses were presented as part of an unfolding story in which the central driving force was people power. Newspapers solicited and printed their readers' 'Moving Stories of Ordinary People Touched by the Queen of Hearts' (*Express*, 1 September) and began their own books of condolences with tributes printed daily, allowing a grieving nation to express their thoughts – providing it was within the stipulated twelve words maximum. No television programme, meanwhile, was complete without vox pops of the attitudes of 'the people'. The result was an apparent democratization and even reversal of the usual power relationship between the people and the media (Couldry 1999), as the latter responded to a popular mourning by opening their programmes or pages to 'ordinary' voices. As veteran Channel 4 reporter Jon Snow (1997) argued: 'the gathered masses waiting to pay their respects spontaneously offered their views – they did not have to be looked for, invented or requested'. The result, according to the chief executive of the BBC, Tony Hall, was that 'the people led, we followed', and in so doing offered an important lesson for 'journalists who seek to reflect and explain what's going on in the world':

> Audiences are supposed to be listening to us, not the other way round. The BBC is wedded to the notion of accurate reporting, making sense of a story through marshalling specialist knowledge; this is at the core. But last week we learnt a tough lesson. We learnt . . . that by giving voice on our airwaves to 'ordinary' individuals' thoughts and feelings, we could get at some kind of truth, which would otherwise elude us, no matter how many facts we assembled . . . We heard from all kinds of people, of all ages, ethnicities, sexual orientation and social background . . . We must make sure that this diversity of voice stays in our programming . . . this was a truly demotic week. We were following the story, not making it. (Hall 1997)

As this suggests, media coverage presented itself as speaking not to readers and viewers, but assuming the voice of 'the people' in a democratic synthesis that saw them speaking on behalf of 'us'. As Richard Madeley, one half of the couple who presented their popular 'Richard and Judy' morning television show, put it to an agreeing ITN news reader Trevor Macdonald: 'The media and the public have sort of intermingled on this one. There isn't that slight gap that there normally is. We've both learnt from each other. Everyone at every level is as one.' Macdonald had earlier been asked by a concerned Judy if he would 'be all right' anchoring the news on the day of the funeral, and he responded with this unequivocal estimate of a popular reaction that had not yet occurred:

> It's impossible not to be moved. But we are helped, the thing which helps you set the tone though is the fact that the nation feels the same in a sense and you have the job of reflecting what is so very *clearly* the will of the nation. (ITV, 5 September)

Judy's question came in a rare show of composure during a week in which she was frequently unable to stem her tears. At one point, wiping away her tears, she apologized to viewers: 'I'm sorry, I'm not behaving very professionally today' (ITV, 5 September). But in another way she was, perhaps more so than her cool, composed husband, as reporters further emphasized their affinity with 'the people' by stressing that they too were deeply upset. 'I am crying as I write this', wrote the *Daily Mirror*'s royal reporter James Whitaker in a tribute following the news (*Mirror*, 1 September). Earlier in their programme *This Morning*, Richard and Judy had sought to capture the mood on the ground by switching to a reporter there who began:

> I'm down here again outside St James's Palace with the crowd. I was down here on Wednesday and it was very moving and I thought that coming today would be easier but in fact it is just as difficult because you walk past the floral tributes and you walk past all the little messages and it really is quite breathtaking and touching. (ITV, 5 September)

Being professional now, in media terms, meant showing that you too were in mourning while at the same time doing your job. Such an approach forms part of a broader ritual in covering the deaths of celebrities which 'blurs the line between producers and receivers', as journalists, as well as the audience, 'play an active role in the ceremony . . . rather than the reactive role of objective bystander' (Kitch 2001: 173).

Faced with such an apparently monolithic popular mood, it seemed that the only institution that did not share it was the royal family. Their conflict with Diana in life, alongside their apparent indifference to her in death, provoked angry public and media demands that they return from their Scottish estate in Balmoral and, 'Show Us You Care', as the *Daily Express* put it (4 September). 'Speak to Us Ma'am, Your People are Suffering', agreed the *Mirror*'s front page, as it juxtaposed pictures of a heartless looking Queen with crying commoners (4 September). 'Where is Our Queen, Where is Our Flag?' demanded the *Sun* (4 September), referring to the fact that the royal standard outside Buckingham Palace had not, like virtually all others, been lowered as a mark of respect. Again the broadsheets were if anything more voracious in their demands. The *Independent*, a paper which had once expressed its intention to avoid royal coverage, now lamented that 'if only the royals could grieve with the people', and welcomed the idea that the Queen and Prince Charles might break down in tears and hug each other on the steps of Westminster Abbey (4 September). Not to be outdone, Simon Hoggart (1997) in the *Guardian* compared the Queen's decision to remain in Balmoral with the mythical idea of George VI fleeing to Bermuda in the Second World War.

The royals belatedly responded to such demands by returning to London to meet 'the people', the flag was lowered and the Queen issued a television tribute in what was presented as an unequivocal victory for people power. 'You Spoke, They Listened' (*Mirror*, 5 September), 'You used to tell us what to do . . . now we tell them' (*Express*, 5 September), 'Palace bows to the people's will', agreed the papers as they juxtaposed the conflict between Diana's 'adoring public' and hostile royal family (*Sunday Times*, 7 September). Meanwhile BBC news presenter Peter Sissons, with the help of long-standing royal correspondent Jennie Bond, offered this reading of the popular mood following the Queen's tribute:

> SISSONS: This was the Queen consciously placing herself in tune with the national mood. Is that a change in direction in itself?
> BOND: I think it is because I think she's been shocked to find herself so out of tune with the national mood. What she's done here is voice the emotions . . . that all of us have been suffering. She spoke of shock, disbelief, anger and concern which I think is what everyone in the nation's been suffering.
> SISSONS: And these other scenes today. The royal family reunited with the people. Was this a conscious effort to re-establish contact?
> BOND: I think so . . . She paid tribute to the nation for their mourning . . . And I think that by paying such a very personal tribute, as she said from the heart, this will go a long way to healing the wounds of what seems to have been a very nasty quarrel between the royal family and the public. (BBC 9 o'clock news, 5 September)

On what basis, aside from vox pops of the very people who congregated to meet the Queen, either journalist was equipped with the knowledge to make such generalizations was unclear. But it formed part and parcel of an image of popular opinion during Diana's mourning that was above all characterized by an 'absence of ambivalence' (Billig 1997a: 505).

This perceived response also gave rise to an almost obsessively repeated theme among the centre left, of a 'New Britain' emerging from the ashes of Thatcherism to accompany the landslide election victory months earlier of New Labour. The *Mirror* detected a 'new British spirit' in which there was 'none of that old British reserve' (4 September 2001), while the *Express* similarly hailed 'a defining moment' for 'a new sense of Britishness' in a country 'visibly renegotiating their contract with their rulers' (11 September 1997). Among the heavyweight press the view was even more emphatic. 'The Nation Unites Against Tradition' was the *Observer*'s verdict on a round-table discussion by leading centre-left intellectuals (Jacques 1997b). The views of the panel's token cynic, *Times* journalist Simon Jenkins, that 'the left always has an orgasm when it sees a crowd' were more than confirmed by the screams of pleasure around him. Will Hutton hailed a battle of 'the modern against the traditional', for Martin Jacques (see also 1997a) it was a 'floral revolution'. The response, they and numerous others argued, offered the potential for a new 'structure of feeling', a more inclusive, democratic, post-imperial, feminized, reconstruction of British identity (Moore 1997; Barnett 1997; Freedland 1997b/c; Gray 1997).

Amidst this intoxicating euphoria surrounding the popular response, the few publications that sought to question rather than fuel it were confined to the fringes. On the far left the tiny-circulation *Morning Star* largely ignored the event – just four column inches covered the story of her death – save for one passionate denunciation of 'the rotten monarchical system that continues to leech us' and a woman 'born with a canteen of silver cutlery in her mouth' (1–6 September 1997). A special edition of *Living Marxism* (1997) similarly denounced the 'Mourning Sickness' that had engulfed the country. But they were a hotbed of loyalism compared with the vitriol of the anarchist paper *Class War* (Autumn 1997) as its back-page headline celebrated: 'Dead as a Dodi: Two Less Parasites'. 'Shame it took so long and that there was only one of them,' said the text, limiting its sympathies to the chauffeur for 'a noble sacrifice and working class heroes such as this will not be forgotten'. From a somewhat more mainstream perspective, *Private Eye* lived up to its satirical tradition with a biting attack on media and public hypocrisy (19 September 1997). A front page entitled 'Media to Blame' featured bubble-quotes of mourners outside Buckingham Palace. 'The papers are a disgrace,' said one. 'Yes I couldn't get one anywhere,' agreed another. 'Borrow mine. It's got a picture of the car,' added a third. Such attacks on media and public hypocrisy seemed to prove their point as the magazine was taken off the shelves from W. H. Smith and other retail outlets, and provoked a record number of complaints from outraged readers cancelling their subscriptions. Many other readers – 90 per cent according to the magazine – wrote in support, with some puzzling how outraged readers of a satirical magazine had expected it to cover the event (McGann 1997). And as this suggests, both *Private Eye*'s coverage and that from the far left would have been far more surprising had it not occurred.

But a less predictable and rather more substantial mainstream alternative was offered, if only to Scottish readers, by the Glasgow-based national newspaper, the *Herald*. At times restricting its Diana coverage to a throw-away or keep pull-out section, it allocated 60 per cent of its news coverage to non-Diana stories and featured a range of critical articles, editorials and letters that suggested a more complex popular response, at least among its readers. Rather tamer but reaching a larger total audience, the broadsheet press featured a series of hostile letters. Less so before the funeral but increasingly in subsequent weeks and months, they were accompanied by a variety of dissenting articles that questioned the extent, depth and compassion of the people's grief (Hilton 1997; Maitland 1997; Littlejohn 1997; Lloyd 1997; Smith

1997a/b/c; Marrin 1997). On the right A. N. Wilson (1997), for instance, drew attention to 'total disparity' between public and private attitudes and attacked a media that had 'failed even to hint at the views being expressed in private . . . up and down the country'. On the left other columnists suggested that, far from being united, the country 'had not been so divided since the Falklands War' (Waterhouse 1997) in a situation where 'a substantial proportion of the population' had 'been actively discouraged from expressing any opinion that deviates from the acceptable' (Ferguson 1997). Meanwhile on Talk Radio, resident intellectual and monarchist historian David Starkey approached the subject with his 'usual combative treatment'. 'Why should you care?', he asked one mourner as he suggested: 'I can't see why we should think better of someone when they're dead than when they're alive.' Radio 4's *Call Diana Madill*, aided by journalist Anthony Howard, was also notable in seeking to encourage a diversity of views that saw one man admitting to being more upset than when his wife died but others denouncing the 'gross idolatry' taking place (Karpf 1997).

Yet these alternative approaches represented merely a drop in the ocean of mourning coverage. Television and the popular press, the two main media for consumption of the event, were massively monolithic, allowing virtually no room for dissenting voices. Nor, even in the quality press, were they exactly vocal, tucked away on the comment pages where even here they offered very little competition to the dominant tone. The profound limits to the diversity of Radio 4's coverage, much less more populist media, were illustrated clearly by the decision to postpone an edition of its audience *Feedback* programme to be broadcast the day before the funeral. A spokesman claimed that it had been delayed to allow people to reflect on coverage as a whole, but other insiders considered it had more to do with an unwelcome people-power critique which saw 98 per cent of letters complain about too much coverage. The decision, considered one senior journalist, was due to 'management paranoia' at the 'complete disaster' that could have resulted 'if they had started getting criticism after all the time and money spent, that our coverage . . . had misrepresented the public mood'. The presenter of *Feedback*, Chris Dunkley, protested in vain to his producers, arguing that 'the whole point was that Diana was monopolizing all channels and there ought to have been a forum where listeners could argue that point' (Byrne 1997). The following week, Dunkley was to provide perhaps the most powerful contemporary critique of media coverage:

> An axis rapidly developed between newsrooms and . . . those who
> placed the flowers, the soft toys and the doggerel messages outside

palace gates. It was, of course, right that the feelings and views of these numerous people should be reported by television, even though at least 51 million out of a population of 56 million or so neither laid flowers nor lined the funeral route. What was extraordinary and worrying was the way in which, in a remarkably short time, it became impermissible to express on television disagreement with, or even the mildest dissent from the keening chorus which insisted 'she was Queen of all our hearts'. Broadcasters who had previously seemed sane, adult and dependable began making assertions about how 'we' all felt and what 'everyone' thought . . . television from the very first excluded any note of scepticism or nonconformity. Nobody really knows whether the impression of public feeling conveyed actually represented the feelings of a large majority or a noisy minority. (Dunkley 1997)

From People Power to Mass Hysteria

A revised edition of *Feedback* was eventually broadcast a week later, and in the aftermath the story of the people's response increasingly took on a less positive gloss. Even 'as the tears dried', one journalist was complaining about:

the rewriting of history currently taking place over the nation's allegedly more sophisticated dinner tables. Mass hysteria, they sneer, not genuine grief: 'Of course I went along to see what all the fuss was about,' conveniently forgetting how difficult it was to hold back the tears, or the flowers they took along because somehow that seemed right. (Bond 1997)

Such rewriting, by the turn of 1997, remained in its embryonic stage in the media despite the publication of numerous dissenting articles. But one of the first to offer an extended, revised analysis was journalist Ian Jack who, in December 1997, profiled 'those who felt differently . . . the angry, puzzled and beleaguered, the people who were not quite sad enough' (1997: 17). The widespread publicity that his article attracted also brought the author hate mail, and was illustrative of the still dominant 'year the British found their voice' (Irons 1997) style verdicts that graced many newspaper reviews of 1997. One verdict in January on 'the dividend of Diana' was noting how 'the collective grief, some say mass hysteria, which drove vast numbers . . . continues, it seems, unabated', although its qualifying phrase also illustrated the emergence of alternative, less reverential views (Nicoll 1998).

But ten months after Diana's death little seemed to have changed, judging by the response to the publication of a critique of the mourning from the right-wing Social Affairs Unit. An eight-page article by Anthony O'Hear rather mildly attacked a woman who 'did quite a lot of good' but who also embodied a 'childlike self-centredness' and whose mourning illustrated a 'culture of sentimentality' (1998: 186–8). Less mildly, the tabloids responded with vitriolic assaults on the 'poisonous professor . . . a rat-faced, little loser' who should 'stew in obscurity' for his bile against a woman who 'almost single-handedly . . . launched a campaign to rid the world of landmines' (Parsons 1998). Meanwhile readers' letters denounced such 'degrading drivel' from 'a pathetic man', even if one complaint that he 'did not have the guts to publish his book while Diana was alive' somewhat missed its point (*Mirror*, 22 April 1998). Again setting the tone for such coverage, Tony Blair had earlier felt obliged to interrupt an important diplomatic tour of the Middle East to denounce critics as 'just snobs', ivory-tower 'right-wing, old fashioned' elitists out of touch, unlike him, with the popular mood (Wheen 1998).

What the politicians and the media had failed to realize, however, was that by this time the public mood was shifting and, according to BBC journalist John Humphrys, 'it turned out that they were out of touch'. At least they were according to listeners of Radio 4's *Today* programme. Humphrys interviewed O'Hear and expected a sackful of complaints from outraged listeners but they instead ran 80 per cent in O'Hear's favour (Humphrys 2000: 56). Other evidence also seemed to support this trend. 'Is the backlash here at last?', wondered one media analyst (Greenslade 1998) in April 1998 as several columnists breached the monolithic popular press tone to attack a proposed two-minute national silence for the first anniversary of Diana's death. In the *Sun*, for example, Richard Littlejohn denounced 'the latest insanity to emerge from the Lady Di industry' and warned of repeating the 'menacing mass hysteria' and 'mob rule' visible in 'a revolting orgy of emotional incontinence and exhibitionism' (Littlejohn 1998). There was surprisingly little negative reaction to such dissent. Littlejohn's postbag was 90 per cent favourable, while a *Sun* poll saw 54 per cent of readers argue, against the paper's view, that the nation had gone 'too soft over Diana' (20 April 1998).

By this time a series of other incidents had also emerged to suggest collectively a less positive impression of the mourning. Embryonic critiques of its emotional ugliness were strengthened several months later by the frenzied emotions and even physical violence stimulated by the case of Louise Woodward, the British nanny found guilty by an American court of murdering the child in her care. These, and subsequent attacks on paedophiles, seemed to show the dark side of 'people power', proof that the much-praised emotionalism of post-Diana Britain could easily degenerate into irrational mob rule and mass hysteria (Aitkenhead 1998; Waterhouse 2000). Meanwhile the danger of popular obsession with celebrities was shockingly demonstrated in 1999 by the murder of BBC journalist and Diana-clone Jill Dando, a view further reinforced by the subsequent conviction of a man with an 'unhealthy' interest in celebrities in general and Diana in particular. News that, as well as being one of the first mourners at the Mall in September 1997, he had once been found hiding in bushes in Kensington Palace carrying a rope and a knife fuelled wild press speculation that 'he tried to kill Di too' (*Sun*, 3 July 2001).

Long before this, a number of events in 1998 seemed to suggest that Diana's once bright candle in the wind was in danger of being rapidly extinguished (Turner 1998). As celebrities quickly abandoned association with a cause no longer in the headlines, a pop concert at the Spencer estate at Althorp in July 1998 turned out not to be the Live Aid II that was promised but 'a naff-fest of Cliff Richard and Chris de Burgh' (Freedland 1998). The Diana memorial fund reported a slackening of income to around £70,000 a month and falling (by 1999 it had further halved), while it did neither its nor Diana's iconic image much good when it allowed her signature to appear on tubs of margarine. As the initial predictions of £150 million in charity donations gave way to a rather more modest £12 million, it seemed, as one charity worker noted, 'as though someone got the decimal point in the wrong place' (Hobson 1997).

That these were the beginnings of a more general trend was confirmed on the first anniversary of Diana's mourning. Media hopes of a repeat of the events the previous year were sorely disappointed as 'a sudden outbreak of comparative indifference' seemed to grip the nation. In London there were rather more tourists than mourners and while 'TV crews were alert for anyone weeping . . . it was hard going' (Engel 1998b). Just 300 people, 2 per cent of those that had been expected, turned up for a Diana Remembrance Walk along the funeral route, leaving the organizers facing losses of £25,000. It was, wrote *Observer* journalist Euan Ferguson (1998), 'a shambles of buttock clenching proportions'. Ferguson, whose scepticism had been advanced with some trepidation a year earlier, was now rather more confident in denouncing a 'wacko week', safe in the knowledge that the floral revolution had long since wilted and 'nothing happened, nothing changed'. For by this time the media's monolithic coverage of the previous year was under fire for excluding 'a big, big silent minority' (Parris 1998) of non-mourners. In a Channel 4 documentary, Christopher Hitchens (1998) challenged the image of 'this supposedly United Kingdom' with interviews with a diverse variety of sceptics who together made up 'another Britain', a 'deceptively mild and understated' place that was 'always almost certainly much bigger than anybody was allowed to know'. The reason for this deception, Hitchens charged was that:

> The press and the broadcasting operators, fully conscious of its sovereign role, turned itself into a megaphone, an echo chamber, a feedback loop, a machinery for positive reinforcement, and the more coverage it supplied, the less its critical faculties were engaged. More meant worse and more meant less.

Meanwhile a fascinating documentary film of Diana's mourners, filmed without interviewers and presented with no voice-over narration in a bid 'to impose no vision, only to discover what is there' (Alexander 1998), unearthed a rather different picture from that conveyed at the time. While some in London wept, others were curious sightseers enjoying a 'just marvellous' day out and there was surprise among the crowd at how cheerful people were. One man watching the funeral in a Bristol pub captured a frequently less than reverential attitude as he laughingly considered it 'all very sad . . . but I've got me drop of Scrumpy. I don't care', while a fellow drinker, turned off by the continuous media coverage commented dejectedly: 'I came here to get away from the fucking funeral.' It was proof, as another man put it, that 'even Diana doesn't matter to everyone' (*The Princess's People* 1998).

In keeping with the more cynical mood, the left-wing publishers Verso issued a collection of largely debunking, journalistic 'irreverent elegies', framed within a mock front-cover image of Saint Diana (Merck 1998). On the right a *Spectator* magazine cover showed a disappearing princess above the line 'The Waning of Diana' (Turner 1998). 'It was cruel but not wholly wrong', wrote *Guardian*'s columnist Jonathan Freedland (1998), among the many now wondering, as they struggled to find hard examples of Britain AD (After Diana), whether the left's orgasm over Diana had turned out to be another fake. Polls showed majorities that believed that 'the British public' had overreacted the previous year (MORI 1998b), that most people thought the country was no more caring, that few were planning to commemorate the anniversary, while support for the monarchy remained high (MORI 1998a/b; ICM 1998). Meanwhile 83 per cent believed there to have been too much media coverage of Diana's death, with a massive 63 per cent saying there had been much too much, while 73 per cent thought it was time the nation 'moved on' from Diana (MORI 1998c/d).

Despite these damp squibs, this and subsequent anniversaries still provided the focus for the media to cite the appearance of flowers and tributes on the gates of Kensington Palace as 'touching evidence that a nation's love for the tragic royal remains undimmed' (*Sun*, 1 October 2001). But the potency of such images was rather undermined by the sporadic scatterings and sparse crowds which, as the anniversaries went by, offered increasingly pale shadows of the popular mood of September 1997. The *Mirror*'s protestations, three years on, that Diana's memory was 'still as sharp for millions' was at least partly contradicted by its profile, tucked away on the bottom of page 2, to the 'low key' public remembrance. Meanwhile an editorial felt obliged to denounce the 'snide professional whiners who crawl out of the woodwork in an attempt to smear and diminish her' and 'point to the small number of flowers left on this anniversary of her death compared with the countless tributes when she died' (31 August 2000). For Diana was now, in the words of the *Mirror*'s campaign for a statue to 'the people's princess', in serious danger of being 'Forgotten' (3 August 1999). The proposal of the Diana Memorial Committee for a £10 million garden at Kensington Palace, with a 300-foot statue of the princess and a 2.7-acre flower garden had been quietly dropped to little public outrage despite the *Mirror*'s best efforts. As two journalists close to Diana suggested, the Princess had been 'forgotten faster than seemed possible' by 'a seemingly ungrateful nation' (Holden 2001), that had 'swung one way then the other' as earlier adulation was now 'replaced by embarrassment at the mass outpouring of grief' (Kay 2000).

Rumours that 'Diana is dead' (Freedland 1999) were perhaps exaggerated in media terms as she initially continued to boost circulation figures as much in death as she did in life. Even in 2000 three books about her topped the best-selling lists (Hamilton 2001), although others could now be found bottoming the discount bookshops. But it was fascination, interest in her life and the still controversial circumstances of her death rather than reverence that focused interest. For the rapid sanctification of September 1997 was followed by a shift away from this process, even if the pace of Diana's decanonization should not be exaggerated, at least in public. When in October 1998 royal biographer Penny Junor (1998) published a book offering a pro-Charles version of their marriage, tabloid attacks on the author's 'Treachery and Hypocrisy' (*Mail*, 25 October 1998) were also accompanied by hate mail and even an attempted physical attack (Dodd 1998). But at the same time a Gallup poll taken on the first anniversary found that, while 41 per cent thought that Diana was 'a woman with unique qualities, a true People's Princess', the largest numbers, 44 per cent, thought that Diana should not be sanctified but remembered as 'a woman with her merits but also her faults' (*Sunday Telegraph*, 28 August 1997). It was therefore hardly surprising that a series of less reverential portraits of Diana emerged to little public protest, so that by 2001 things had changed so much that her mother was complaining, 'Why are They So Cruel to My Poor Diana?', about a 'controversial new TV documentary which claims her daughter suffered mental illness' (*Express*, 9 June 2001). In fact the programme-makers did not argue this, but it was significant that the four-part documentary provided the most balanced assessment of her life broadcast since her death (Clayton and Craig 2001).

And as the image surrounding 'the people's princess' has become somewhat sullied, so the same is also true of the tribute itself. Conservative leader William Hague had been roundly condemned in September 1997 when he accused the government of making political capital from Diana's death. But the political backlash against New Labour spin, among other things, later led others to question the sincerity of Blair's grief and portray it instead as a cynical, rehearsed, headline-grabbing soundbite dreamt up by all-powerful press secretary Alastair Campbell (Toolis 1998). The result, as one cabinet member at the time considered, is that 'people have looked back and slightly sneered' (Clayton and Craig 2001: 361). Another victim of such sneering, certainly, was the journalist Clive James. 'No', he had written repeatedly in a huge tribute in the *New Yorker* as he confessed his love 'as an obscure, besotted walk-on mesmerised by the trajectory of a burning angel'. He lamented: 'And what flowers have I to send her except my memories? They are less than a wreath, not more than a nosegay: just a *deuil blanc* table napkin wrapping a few blooms of frangipani, the blossom of broken bread' (MacArthur 1998: 84).

James had sportingly acknowledged: 'No, you don't have to tell me that I am appearing ridiculous now, but it is part of the ceremony is it not?' And his prose, extreme though it was, was hardly untypical of those being offered in the media ceremony elsewhere. But while others escaped subsequent mockery, James was not so lucky, and the subsequent derision of his 'hyperbolic lament' (Cohen 1997) was symbolic of changing popular perceptions towards the mourning. So great was the backlash that by 2001 the writer felt obliged to defend himself against a dishonest rewriting of history by 'a lot of intelligent people' who 'decided later that they had been wrong to shed tears' and were now 'saying that they never did' (Gibbons 2001). He had a point, given the marked change in tone of journalistic commentary, at least in the quality press. In early September 1997 Matthew Engel (1997) had offered some of the most insightful profiles of the queueing crowds, 'as calm as ever' in which 'moments of intense mourning have been discreet'. But his positive verdict on this 'moving' experience later gave way to less flattering, periodic asides about the 'emotional fascism' present during 'the hysteria that followed', another example of a population teetering on 'the line that divides sanity from mass hysteria' (1998a, 1999a/b).

While some journalists reflected this apparent shift in attitudes, others were left puzzling over the sudden disappearance and reversal of feelings once so dominant. The only explanation, it seemed, was a mass outbreak of collective amnesia as overwhelming as had been the rush to mourn. 'Do not deny Diana thrice', pleaded one journalist just before the third anniversary of her death as he began by insisting: 'We all cried when she died. Yes we did.' The prevailing mood, it suggested, was now:

> PRINCESS WHO? Almost two years on to the day since the accident in Paris it is fashionable to indulge in Diana denial. That outpouring of grief, the ocean of emotion that swept over us at the end of August 1997, is to be airbrushed out of individual and collective consciousness. How easily we forget what we all manifestly took a part in. Who will now admit to buying a bunch of freesias and making the pilgrimage . . . to pay their respects. You won't get anyone to own up to this anymore, but . . . it was impossible to hold back the tears.

Meanwhile a previously sanctified Diana had been swiftly relegated to 'a rather sad figure . . . a jet-setting, high-living, playboy's lover . . . who manipulated her public image and was manipulated in return, and who died in a silly and unnecessary way'. Mourners, once celebrated for their 'people power' were now viewed as 'sad folk with nothing better in their pathetic lives' (Rennell 2000).

All this suggests, in so far as generalizations can be made, a collective memory of the mourning that has become tinged with embarrassment, disdain or worse. Proud celebrations of a week of 'people power' have been inverted into a thorn-tinted memory of an outbreak of shameful mass hysteria, a term synonymous with over-emotional, excessive, unthinking, obsessive, uncontrollable, dangerous mob rule. Perhaps the clearest illustration of this increasingly negative image came in the media response to the death of the Queen Mother in late March 2002. This 'scummy sneering', as Julie Burchill (2002) noted contemptuously, saw commentators queue up to contrast 'the decent, dignified, discretion' of the contemporary reaction with 'the vulgar, bizarre, undignified, dysfunctional hysteria and unwholesomeness' of Diana's mourning. Reflecting on the winners and losers in April 2002, one *Guardian* analysis placed 'hysteria of the kind that filled the wailing crowds worshipping' after Diana's death firmly in the latter category, 'recalled in recent days as a contrast to the superior fortitude and reserve' currently visible (Bennett 2002). Similarly conservative columnist Bruce Anderson (2002) compared the 'very British, very civilised . . . thoughtful' current mood with a time when he 'once felt ashamed to be British' when London was 'full of people who seemed to have lost their wits. Faces distorted by hysteria, they were shambling about blubbing and moaning . . . like savages with their fetishes'. In the more populist media the verdict from left and right was little different. 'This wasn't a collective outbreak of hysteria as we saw when Princess Diana died', argued the *Mirror* (9 April 2002), but 'a measured, calm and thoughtful appreciation'. 'There was no hysteria' agreed the *Sun* (2 April 2002).

Yet in several ways such negative revisionism has done little to alter the popular myth of an emotional, adulatory, mass mourning. For it is less *what actually happened* in September 1997 that has been questioned, and more that the explanatory framework of *why it happened* has shifted from positive to negative. Whether seen favourably as 'people power' or derided as 'mass hysteria', the images remain as dominant as ever – indeed they are arguably strengthened rather than weakened in popular memory by the latter description.

Secondly, journalistic accounts in the grief-free aftermath routinely contrasted and polarized the subsequent indifference with a 'people's mourning' that 'convulsed the nation' and nearly brought the royal family down (for example, Holden 2001). The numerous media retrospectives frame their 'united in grief' story with an automatic focus on images of large crowds of mourners or attractive young women, usually in tears, in front of masses of flowers at London mourning sites. It offers a dramatic and memorable visual shorthand – 'flashbulb memories' (Zelizer 1992: 5) – of the response of 'the people' that has arguably entered the nation's collective memory as a symbol, for good or bad, of *the* popular response. When asked by pollsters a year later about what they most remembered about the week, 'the grief of ordinary people' was by far the most popular category, with 34 per cent choosing it, followed in second place by 'the flowers', selected by 15 per cent (ICM 1998). On another level Diana's mourning, at least in numerical terms, provides the almost perfect, gold-standard benchmark of popular feeling to be applied in judging the reaction to subsequent royal and other public mournings. This was most obvious in the contrast with the almost embarrassing levels of public indifference to the death of Princess Margaret in early February 2002, but was also evident in the very muted initial reaction to news of the Queen Mother's demise. 'Sorry Ma'am: That So Many of Us are Showing So Little Respect' apologized the *Mirror*'s front-page headline alongside a photograph of a non-existent queue to sign the book of condolences at St James's Palace that offered a massive contrast to the scenes of four and a half years earlier. On Channel 4 News (4 April 2002), a discussion between Jonathan Freedland on the left and Andrew Roberts on the right disputed the nature of the current mood, but both operated within an agreed framework in which Diana's mourning was a time when the population was truly united in grief. Meanwhile a prompt show of public grief from the royals that pre-empted a repeat of demands to 'show us you care' further illustrated what was perceived as a key lesson of Diana's death, the need for the family to be more in touch with 'the people'.

Indeed, such is its power that even those that have sought to debunk the myth have perpetuated images that simultaneously confirm it. Ian Jack's article, 'Those who felt differently' (1997), for example, was reprinted in the *Guardian Weekend* magazine. Before the piece begins, the reader's eye is drawn to a striking facing page composed solely of nine close-cropped facial shots of mourners powerfully conveying the deep, tearful grief of 'those who felt deeply' (27 September 1997). Hitchens (1998), meanwhile, provides a polarized contrast between rational dissenters and mourners, with the latter views being automatically assumed to be hysterical, emotional and adulatory. For if there is 'another Britain', 'mild and understated', there must also be a 'main' Britain, hysterical and overstated, and where there are dissenters 'that feel differently' there must be a dominant mood to dissent from. All this ensures that, for all the awareness of the 'little facts' of the week – that not everyone cared or grieved – the 'big facts' of a nation, or at least most people, deeply upset in hysterical, adulatory grief still remains the central popular image of the week.

⍦

2

Diana Studies and Mass-Observation

The previous chapter drew attention to the popular image of a nation united in mourning, and it is a verdict that has penetrated even the dark recesses of academia, judging by a predominant approach that offers qualified, and sometimes unqualified, endorsement of this story. Contemporary analyses by royal historians Ben Pimlott (1997b) and David Cannadine (1997) both, perhaps naturally, emphasized this theme. Pimlott considered that Diana was 'one of us', mourned by 'young and old, posh and common, left and right, monarchist and republican, feminist and male chauvinist'. Cannadine, meanwhile, also concentrated on explaining the 'depth and intensity' of the reaction of 'so many ordinary Britons' to news which had 'left unmoved and untouched only the hardest of hearts and the meanest of spirits'. This, he argued, was 'overwhelmingly the general verdict'.

And so it has remained as subsequent academic analyses have largely emphasized 'the unity that *was* put in place, however precariously, in the aftermath of Diana's death' (Hay 1999: 68), speculated whether it reversed 'a sense of national fragmentation' (Richards et al. 1999: 3), and stressed 'the commonality of the affect, which crossed all sorts of boundaries of class, race, gender, age and political and intellectual inclination' (New Formations 1999: 5). 'Some who did not like her were perhaps relieved', asserted one academic, 'but the majority of the people, including many who had no interest in the royal family, nevertheless felt the pity of the situation in a personal way' (Richardson 1999: 22). For Sasha Roseneil, 'the public response should be understood as a collective action . . . which expressed and distilled the *collective conscience*, the *social divine* and the *puissance* of the people' (2001: 105, 99). She, along with Douglas Davies (1999), provides the 'united in grief' story with some hefty theoretical scaffolding, invoking the writings of one of sociology's founding fathers, Emile Durkheim, to suggest the existence of a unifying sacred ritual which united the country as a moral body. They further draw on the influential work of Victor Turner to suggest the emergence of a 'liminal' bonding period of 'communitas', characterized by the temporary collapse of existing hierarchies and their replacement with a popular experience of equality, 'homogeneity and comradeship' (Turner 1969: 96).

From one angle this offers little more than new gloss to a traditional academic and populist emphasis on the way past royal events have provoked a national unity transcending class and other barriers. Durkheim's insights have been widely applied in asserting this and, on different levels of comparison, to the mourning following the death of John F. Kennedy and to media events more generally (Shils and Young 1953; Blumer et al. 1971; Verba 1965; Dayan and Katz 1992; Cardiff and Scannell 1987). In a much-quoted sociological article Shils and Young hailed the response to Queen Elizabeth's coronation in 1953 as 'an act of national communion' that was 'shared and celebrated by nearly all the people of Britain' (1953: 65, 70). Using less theory but more supporting evidence, Philip Ziegler has noted how 'a genuine sense of common interest developed, transcending temporary barriers of geography or social class' (1978: 68) during successive royal ceremonials since 1937, as have other historians of the modern British monarchy (Cannadine 1983; Colley 1992; Pimlott 1997a).

Such interpretations of popular opinion have not gone unchallenged, both in theoretical and empirical critiques, by those who point to considerable opposition and indifference towards royalty and during royal ceremonials over the last 200 years (Birnbaum 1955; Lukes 1975; Taylor 1999; Lechnowicz 1998). More recently Michael Billig (1997b) has brilliantly dissected the sheer complexity of popular attitudes to royalty, a point which Ziegler's (1978) more populist work also well illustrates. The same approach has also been applied to the Diana events, with a number of prominent journalistic analyses (see chapter 1) being at the forefront of reinterpreting a reaction that was 'far less extensive than originally supposed' (Merck 1998: 2). Meanwhile several of the above academic collections also provided alternative analyses – albeit framed as 'dissident accounts' and marginally located at the end (C. Davies 1999; Cohan 1999) – that challenged the 'myth that the Diana events represented some unproblematic expression of "the People"' (Couldry 1999: 78). Others veering towards a sociological tradition that empha-sizes conflict rather than consensus (Lukes 1975), and the media's role in constructing rather than reflecting social unity (Couldry forthcoming), have highlighted the diverse experiences of the Diana event that could not be neatly homogenized into one simple response (McGuigan 2000). More broadly Jude Davies (2001) has contextualized this within a detailed textual deconstruction of the complex media representations of Diana's life, as have others more generally within the development of a mediated monarchy (Chaney 2001; Couldry 2001).

The above studies, among others, offer important insights into the popular response, and without them this book would scarcely have been possible. But this is also true in a less flattering way, as their omissons explain why there is, despite all that has been written, more to be said about Diana's mourning. In large part this is because, for all the countless explanations of the response of 'the people', there has been little detailed, empirical exploration of a popular reaction largely assumed to be self-evidently on display in September 1997 (Couldry 1999). By the end of 1999 only one empirical study of popular attitudes had appeared, and this was a small-scale examination by two Australian academics of the responses of thirty-two Anglo-Celtic women in Queensland. It stood, the authors lamented, as a solitary 'island of data' in a sea of 'speculation and hyperbole' about the meanings of Diana to ordinary people (Black and Smith 1999: 276, 265). Since then the island has arguably become even more besieged, if not overwhelmed, by further waves of 'speculation'.

In part this is due to the way Diana Studies have been dominated by the textualist branch of cultural studies that has sought to deconstruct from above the event's meaning, but has offered less scrutiny of the mood on the ground in doing so (Kear and Steinberg 1999; New Formations 1999; Re: Public 1997; Merck 1998). This has sometimes produced a dizzying circularity in which a taken-for-granted popular response offers the cue for some highly selective analyses of the story of Diana's life to explain it. Arguments that her caring image symbolized the antithesis of right-wing Thatcherism, for example, are asserted without examining whether this was what she meant to people. Sympathetic analyses have rightly criticized the cultural elitism of intellectual accounts dismissive of an outbreak of 'mass hysteria'. But they can be no less polarized when they embrace an uncritical 'cultural populism' (McGuigan, 1992) that is sometimes more concerned with celebrating and identifying with an assumed popular response than analysing it. Diana's mourners, in some analyses, are simplistically equated with 'the people', in opposition to a non-mourning constructed as coming solely from 'marginalised intellectuals' (Johnson 1999: 35), cynical members of the chattering classes unable, unlike the authors, to empathize with the popular mood. In this rationale, Christopher Hitchens's *The Mourning After*, which despite its polemical tone, did seek out the views of 'ordinary' people, is dismissed as an 'establishment' critique (Kear and Steinberg 1999: 12), while those who 'saw disturbing signs of mass hysteria' are stereotyped as (presumably mindless) 'Sun columnists' (Watts 1999: 34).

This is not to downplay the importance of textual approaches in understanding the Diana events, and the insights they can offer are certainly profitably used in this book. Nor is it to fall victim to a naive empiricism that derides jargonistic theory as an irrelevant sideshow when it in reality forms a framework, unconscious or conscious, to the most empiricist of analyses. That said, it still remains a scarcely believable or defensible exclusion that none of the many studies of Diana's mourning have even acknowledged, much less explored, the quantitative or qualitative evidence freely available about the popular response that this book draws upon. For those who believe in the importance of empirical evidence – and especially so when talking about popular opinions – this omission can, at worst, result in influential theorists being treated as offering the key to illuminating popular reactions without even attempting to examine what people actually thought and did. Theory, used pragmatically, is clearly important in explaining popular reactions, but ideally it should complement rather than substitute for rigorous, reflexive, empirical research (Couldry 2000), and still less be treated as a superior explanatory tool that renders such a process redundant.

Linked up with some of the above weaknesses has been the highly impenetrable prose of some key Diana Studies works. This has meant that journalists have had a field day in mocking the 'practically incomprehensible . . . Dianababble' (Austin 1998) emanating from academia. This cannot simply be dismissed as traditional knee-jerk journalistic mockery of media/cultural studies given its similarity with internal critiques of analyses 'of growing opalescence and diminishing clarity' (Ferguson and Golding 1997: p. xxi). Other more traditional academics have predictably condemned, to quote the popular historian Roy Strong, the 'gibberish' of 'trash can rubbish' (Austin 1998) churned out to perpetuate an industry but for little other purpose. This does no justice to the motives behind, and insights offered, by the best of these analyses. But it is a serious concern – and a sad irony – that explorations of the response of 'the people' should be accessible to so few.

It should be stressed that this neglect of empirical research by no means extends to all journalistic and academic analyses. Perhaps the best full-length analysis is the collection edited by Tony Walter. Its aim, rather like this book, is to provide 'solid documentation' rather than 'journalistic and academic speculation' through analysis in which 'theory is used primarily to illuminate what happened when Diana died, not the other way around' (Walter 1999a: 27). But even this does not really explore how people reacted but again assumes a largely taken-for-granted popular mourning response. This means that its bid to provide 'an intelligent record of and interpretation of what happened' (D. Davies 1999: 5) is confined to a largely one-eyed history which devotes seventeen chapters to the mourning and offers just one alternative perspective on popular experiences. Such an imbalance, while understandable, remains curious given the acknowledgement that those who did not mourn were 'an important part of the picture' (Walter 1999a: 31), and as a similarly skewed analysis nevertheless suggests, 'must be included within any fair assessment of the Diana phenomenon' (Richards et al. 1999: 10).

All this suggests the need for a further examination of the popular mood, and one that descends from the ivory-tower clouds 'of meaning and textuality and theory to the something nasty down below' (Hall 1992: 278) of real, lived popular experiences (see also Ferguson and Golding 1997). To follow such an 'ethnographic' approach to the response of 'the people' down below, is not, however, to lose sight of the operation of power relations up above. For again the largely assumed nature of the popular response has meant that, within existing studies, examinations of media coverage and media power have aroused comparatively little interest. They have in fact been rendered largely redundant by a broad acceptance of the media's own definition of its coverage as the simple, passive reflector of the popular will, reporting rather than forming public opinion. Hence vox-pop interviews saw mourners rather than journalists define the nature of the story as 'the people spoke and the media reported' (Walter 1999a: 21). In fact what happened went beyond this, according to Roger Silverstone, in a popular reaction in which 'millions upon millions of ordinary folk' bypassed media representation, 'broke their own media bounds', occupied public space and put their own stamp on things (1998: 82–4).

Such an approach fits within a broader academic trend in media studies that has seen an increasing emphasis on audience resistance and active consumption, while traditional concerns about media power have become unfashionable, dismissed as patronizing, old-fashioned and naïve (Kitzinger: 1999a; Corner 2000). Indeed from this perspective Diana's mourning was counter-hegemonic empowerment *par excellence*, as audiences 'broke their own media bounds' and took their resistance to the streets in a 'floral revolution' that forced even the monarchy, as well as the media, to bow to the popular will. Hence Roseneil suggests:

> Rather than seeking to cede agency to the media, as many cultural analysts have done, the public response should be understood as a collective action . . . These performances were highly mediated . . . but to see them as produced or manufactured by the media would be to ignore . . . the way that public emotion constantly broke free of all attempts to contain, name and tame it. The media mobilised, amplified and gave voice to the collective agency of the week but people were speaking with their own voices, producing and directing their own actions in the public spaces of grief which they created. (2001: 105)

This, however, is as simplistic as the 'media manipulation' model that it polarizes itself against. To say this is not to deny that the *public* response (as distinct from the public's response) 'although choreographed by the media, sometimes exceeded its mediation' (Kitzinger 1999b: 75), or to subscribe to the view that the media caused the public mourning. Certainly there was a complex interaction between a section of the population and the media. But who was in control of the process (see Couldry 1999), and whether this apparently democratic process served to represent or distort and exclude popular attitudes as a whole remains less explored. For the vast majority of the population (at least 70 per cent) did not 'break the media bounds', did not take to the streets, did not speak, but merely watched and read. Again the basic problem with this argument is that it takes as a starting point, without the need for critical examination, 'the public response' that the media is uncritically assumed to reflect.

But this flies in the face of ample evidence suggesting that it would be distinctly naïve to see the media as an unproblematic mirror of popular attitudes in September 1997, not to mention more generally. The partiality of coverage is clear even if we restrict the analysis to the minority of the population that visited London mourning sites rather than the majority who did not. Here coverage focused extensively on an apparently hysterically upset minority of mourners, suggesting that this was the dominant response widely on display. This was contradicted by repeated, overwhelmingly unequivocal experience of numerous mourning sites that illustrated that the vast majority there were *not* in tears but were quiet, restrained, in control of their emotions, sometimes even jolly and light-hearted (Monger and Chandler 1998; Biddle and Walter 1998; McKibbin 1998; O'Hear 1998; Engel 1997; *The Princess's People* 1998; Humphrys 2000). One three-day observation during the week at the most highly charged and popular sites, Diana's home in Kensington Palace detected:

> a striking difference between the scenes we observed and those selected for presentation by the media. Newspapers and television reports had been describing scenes of mass mourning and focusing on displays of emotion from individual members of the public. Journalists still write of the 'gales of emotion awash in the streets' . . . We, on the contrary, saw few tears or emotional outbursts: the scene was one of decorum and gravity. (Monger and Chandler 1998: 104)

In a style of coverage amplified by but not confined to Diana's mourning (Walter et al. 1995), a focus on the one mourner in tears made for a better, more dramatic story than the ninety-nine that were not, not to mention the hundred who were not there at all. But it also made for a highly inaccurate one as well. More widely, even a close scrutiny of overwhelmingly mono-lithic media coverage suggests, on the basis of dissenting letters and articles, a more complex response.[1] Media coverage was therefore characterized by a double inaccuracy that not only excluded from the story 'those who felt differently' (Jack 1997), but also offered a misleading impression of the responses of 'those who didn't', the mourners themselves.

All this suggests the need for further examination of the popular mood, as well as the role and power of the media in shaping perceptions of it. Usually in any such assessment the first port of call is the polls. Yet as head of MORI Robert Worcester (1997) noted, one puzzling aspect of a week in which popular opinion was the main story was that no poll was commissioned by the media to assess it. This was a shame because those that were eventually taken offered some interesting findings. In the first poll, taken immediately after the funeral, a quarter declared themselves 'very upset', with a further 42 per cent claiming to be 'fairly upset'. As many as 26 per cent – an astonishing 10 million plus – stated that they had signed the book of condolence while one person in six said they had left a floral tribute. On the other hand just under a third were willing to admit that they were either not 'very upset' or 'not upset at all' by that stage. Meanwhile a massive 74 per cent had not signed a book of condolence and over 80 per cent had not placed a floral tribute, figures also confirmed by a later poll (MORI 1997/1998a). One poll taken on the first anniversary of Diana's death also found that 50 per cent thought that 'the British public' had overreacted in September 1997, 61 per cent thought that the media had overreacted, but only 12 per cent of people thought that they themselves had overreacted (MORI 1998b). Another found that while 46 per cent of people said that their reaction was stronger than expected, 42 per cent countered that it was about what they would have imagined (ICM 1998). And as chapter 5 explores, large majorities stated that they did not feel that they had lost a personal friend. Even aside from the way opinion polls substantially overexag-gerated mourning sentiments (see below), this further suggests a more complex picture of attitudes than was widely articulated at the time by the media.

Such a point is further strengthened by the few qualitative opinion studies that have taken place. The small study of attitudes among Anglo-Celtic Australian women revealed a diversity of attitudes to Diana's life and mourning, ranging from very positive to neutral to very negative (Black and Smith 1999). Meanwhile the one qualitative study so far published about Britain, a more specific but larger examination of responses to television coverage, also demonstrated a complex reaction. Of its 275 respondents, 50 per cent stated they were personally unaffected by the tragedy and 70 per cent played no part in the public mourning (Turnock 2000). But perhaps the most far-reaching qualitative survey of popular attitudes was undertaken by Mass-Observation (M-O), a qualitative opinion-research project based at the University of Sussex. The organization has a panel of about 500 long-term volunteers or 'observers' from across Britain, who roughly three times a year are asked to record their views, and those of other people they encounter, across a variety of social, political and personal issues. This is done through a 'directive', which despite its authoritarian overtones, is actually an open-ended series of questions and prompts to stimulate people to express their own thoughts without restricting them to the narrow confines of a questionnaire. In September 1997 the organization's director and archivist Dorothy Sheridan quickly sent out a special directive to volunteers entitled 'The Death of Diana'. It read:

> This is a special directive giving you the opportunity to respond to the tragic death of the Princess of Wales. Some of you have already written in with your immediate reactions: others of you may be expecting a special mailing from us in view of Mass-Observation's long-standing interest in national events and the significance of the monarchy. Whatever your views and feelings, whether you are a royalist or a republican, please send us your reflections, feelings, opinions, observations. Feel free to discuss whatever you think is important, including the media coverage and any other issues you feel may be relevant. If you change your opinions and feelings, please chart the change. An occasional diary might be the best way to go about it. Many of you used such a diary to good effect during the Gulf War and the last General Election. Date everything you write, and include cuttings etc if they seem to add to your account. Add your M-O number as usual, and a brief biography.

Its request for views received 249 replies, ranging from 1 to 24 pages, although the response rate of 54 per cent was, interestingly, one of the lowest in recent years. In common with the above qualitative surveys, the overriding feature of these responses (all of which have been examined) is the diversity and complexity of popular attitudes. Subsequent chapters will explore their themes, in conjunction with other evidence about popular attitudes and the media. But first something needs to be said about the history and use (or lack of it) of this key source for this book in exploring popular attitudes. Mass-Observation has an old, if somewhat disputed pedigree, reflecting the chequered history of an organization that was initially founded in 1937, wound up in the early 1950s, and relaunched in 1981, maintaining a precarious existence ever since. The original qualitative research organization or social movement

(Summerfield 1985) was founded by the anthropologist Tom Harrison, poet and journalist Charles Madge and film-maker Humphrey Jennings. It aimed, in their words, for 'an anthropology of ourselves' through a panel of volunteer participant observers composed, as Madge romantically called them, of 'ordinary hard-working folk' (Sheridan et al. 2000: 34). Their role, maintained by current 'Mass-Observers' was twofold – to describe their own opinions and experiences and to detail those of others they 'observed'.

The organization's initial focus is as relevant now as it was then, arguably uncannily so in exploring the Diana Event. For it stemmed from the need to challenge the misrepresentation of popular attitudes by a press which, as the self-appointed 'representatives of the people', found it necessary 'to pretend that its *own opinion* is public opinion' (Harrison 1940: 376–7). More particularly, M-O's very existence also owed much to the interests of its founders in popular attitudes towards royalty. The original project emerged in response to the abdication crisis and a concern to tackle the power of 'myth' in this event (Sheridan et al. 2000), its first book detailed responses to George VI's coronation and later books returned to the theme (Jennings and Madge 1937; Harris 1966). Moreover, its contemporary relaunch stemmed from a one-off survey of the 1977 Silver Jubilee (Ziegler 1978) and an interest in examining the popular significance of the 1981 royal wedding (Sheridan et al. 2000).

Whether the organization was and is capable of exploring such questions, however, is a question that has provoked dispute ever since the organization's foundation. This is not least because it relates to a broader 'fault line' (Lewis 2001: 4) dividing academia into two largely hostile camps, between those who embrace quantitative surveys as the only scientific way of exploring opinion, and others who prefer qualitatively to turn words into other words rather than numbers. Quantitative social scientists have traditionally treated M-O with a mixture of suspicion, indifference and derision. Early critiques ridiculed the organization's claims, in its first book, 'to apply the methods of science to the complexity of a modern culture' (Jennings and Madge 1937: iii). Popular dismissals that the organization's research was, to quote the *Spectator*, 'about as valuable as a chimpanzees' tea party at the zoo' were partly echoed by attacks from anthropologists on its 'unscientific' approach (Jefferys 1999; Sheridan et al. 2000). Perhaps more seriously, the simultaneous emergence of quantitative opinion polling established a rival that was increasingly viewed as rendering M-O's 'amateur' techniques redundant. In the post-war academic and commercial vogue for all things quantitative, the original project ceased operation in the face of stiff competition and what its historian described as 'something like a concerted attack' (Jefferys 1999: 48) on its research techniques from opponents. By 1947 Tom Harrison's methods were on the defensive even if he, quite characteristically, was not:

> if I have criticised what I call the 'quantitative obsession', it is not because I am unaware of the great importance of statistical work, but because I am concerned at its undue prominence at present. One or two methods should not be mistaken for the only 'scientific' ones . . . It is clear that in most sociological research we require an adequate mixture of words and numbers . . . the raw material of life with the authentic statistic of validity. We must not be afraid to explore problems not open to quantitative measurement. (Harrison 1947: 24)

For quantitative social scientists, such as leading pollster and head of rival polling organization Mark Abrams, this approach was, quite simply, 'heresy' (Stanley 1990: 37). Abrams was mercilessly to batter the final nails into M-O's coffin with a small publication in 1951 that seemed principally concerned with a blistering thirteen-page indictment of M-O's 'inchoate and uncontrolled' methods (Abrams 1951: 112). Such a conflict is not merely of historical significance, for today the same suspicions about the 'unscientific' nature of M-O's material repeatedly surface. One of the consistent complaints has remained that its self-selecting volunteers are not statistically representative of the British population, with the present panel being disproportionately female, lower middle-class, over forty and drawn from the south of England. The result, as one academic evaluation of M-O research in the early 1990s put it, was that its material 'cannot really support quantitative or graphical summaries which make any claims beyond the documentation of the characteristics of the sample' (Sheridan 1996: 1).

Rather more, however, has changed in academia since the 1950s than the above quote would suggest. Historians more comfortable with working with 'imperfect' sources have been more inclined to look positively at M-O. This has been particularly so since the 1960s, when an increasing concern with the 'common people of the past' traditionally 'hidden from history' served to develop and legitimize M-O's similar focus on the experiences of 'ordinary hard-working folk' (Sheridan et al. 2000). Meanwhile the simultaneous emergence of cultural studies as an academic discipline gave credibility to a project focused on what one of its founding fathers, Richard Hoggart, called an 'anthropological approach to the "ordinary cultures" of "everyday life"' (Stanton 1996: 349). This favourable climate should not be exaggerated. The organization may have been 'a pioneering venture' (Stanton 1996: 335) within cultural studies, but the discipline has largely ignored M-O, either as a historical predecessor or in its contemporary manifestation. Within sociology Liz Stanley was to note in 1990 that the lack of contemporary research into M-O was 'surprising perhaps only because of its completeness' (1990: 3).

Nevertheless the organization has experienced something of a gradual 'rehabilitation' (Stanley 1981: 272), as offering a valuable 'alternative tradition' of qualitative social science (Finch 1986: 96). Numerous studies have suggested that its ability to tap private as well as public opinion during the war offered 'a more satisfactory picture of popular attitudes than the rival polling organisations' through a method of data-gathering that 'encouraged an ear for the fluid, ambiguous, contradictory character of popular attitudes' (J. Hilton 1997: 268–9; see also Sheridan et al. 2000; Calder 1985; Finch 1986; Parkin 1987). Indeed the organization's 'finest hour', according to Angus Calder (1985: 180), came in its ability consistently to predict from 1942 that the Conservatives, for all the popularity of Churchill as 'the man who won the war', were about to become the party that lost the electoral peace.

M-O has certainly been extensively and profitably used by historians documenting the popular mood between 1940 and 1951 (for example, Calder 1969; Addison 1975; Fielding et al. 1995; Howkins 1998). Recent years have also seen the reprinting of various M-O original studies, along with several previously unpublished anthologies (Jennings and Madge 1937; Calder and Sheridan 1985; Richards and Sheridan 1987; Cross 1990; Sheridan 1991). But the material generated by the contemporary project remains curiously less explored or even acknowledged, an oversight perhaps most puzzling within cultural studies given its sharp 'ethnographic turn' in the 1980s to qualitative studies of audiences and its deep suspicion of quantitative surveys (Morley 1992; Lewis 1997). For such has been the discipline's preference for qualitative approaches that 'quantitative surveys of thought and opinion have been out of fashion for so long that they have, for many, been consigned to a methodological junkyard . . . seen as symbols of a jaded, more backward civilisation' (Lewis 1997: 84). Whatever the reason,[2] this illustrates that the relaunch of the project in 1981 reflected the more favourable intellectual climate (Sheridan et al. 2000) for the approach to opinion-gathering outlined by the organization's directors than Harrison's defence forty years earlier:

> If someone is asked a series of direct questions, however subtly, they can only answer 'Yes', 'No' or 'Don't Know' – they do not have the opportunity to describe themselves, their mood on that occasion, the things in life which they would have preferred to discuss. M-O, precisely because it avoids as much as possible any formal

> questionnaire, provides this sort of opportunity and it allows people to set their own context for the discussion of any matter and then to explore the pros and cons as it occurs to them, rather than those suggested to them. . . . The researcher is able to interpret the documents in a way that would not be possible from a statistical table. (Pocock and Sheridan 1985)

In many ways, as Harrison earlier noted, the conflict between quantitative and qualitative approaches is a false one. For M-O does not aim for statistical generalizations like an opinion poll but offers a qualitative complement that allows for analytical generalizations to theories rather than populations (Bryman 1988). What source is superior depends on the questions being asked, and the two are complementary rather than competitors. M-O cannot and does not seek to address precise statistical issues of 'how many' (Sheridan 1996) were upset. But through the 'telling case' studies that observers provide, both individually and collectively, it can explain the 'how', 'why' and to some extent 'who' questions which illuminate the reasons why some mourned, as well as the rather more neglected questions of why others did not or only partially did so. If one wants to find out how many people watched the funeral, then the polls are the best source (although, as noted below, they are also far from perfect). If, however, one wants to find out how, why, in what ways and with what level of emotions a variety of people watched, then M-O and other qualitative evidence provides more illumination. It offers, to quote Clifford Geertz's famous observation (1975), a 'thick description', a deeper picture of private as well as public attitudes to complement the 'thin descriptions' available to and provided by the opinion pollsters.

As this suggests, in doing so it frequently uncovers responses that are simply not open to or appropriate for quantification, a point which more directly raises the question of the competing validity of quantitative or qualitative analyses. How, for example, do you quantify the reactions of someone who was upset by the news, unmoved or hostile for most of the week, but watched the funeral with a tear in their eye? What *exactly* do the polling choices 'very upset' or 'fairly upset' really reveal about popular attitudes? Far better, surely, to turn words into other words than produce a superficially accurate statistical survey that risks manufacturing an assumed 'upset' public opinion rather than measuring it (Lewis 2001). To be aware of the limitations of quantitative evidence is certainly not to say that it should be ignored, not least because this study, like most that draw on qualitative data, ultimately tries to count, as well as explain, how people were reacting and media power impacted (Lewis 1997). Quantitative evidence, used with the same caution as should be shown to qualitative evidence, can significantly enhance an understanding of attitudes not least because, as Lewis notes, it is difficult to discuss political power and popular opinion 'without, at some point, implicating majorities' (1997: 87). That said, it is primarily words, complemented with numbers, which offer the key to illuminating popular experiences.

There are several other ways in which M-O is useful in facilitating these goals. For while volunteers do not offer a pure sample of the British population, nor are they 'seriously unrepresentative' either, being drawn from all classes, ages and areas with 'backgrounds comparable to a very high proportion of the British population at the end of the twentieth century' (Thane 2001: 219). This means that they undoubtedly 'represent the feelings of a large number of people in the UK' (Bloome et al. 1993: 17), even if it is difficult to estimate exactly how many. Certainly compared with most qualitative research that tends to be small-scale and geographically limited, M-O encompasses a more diverse and larger population sample than usual. There is an irony that, because its panel comes closer to approximating to a quantitative survey than most qualitative opinion sources, it has been criticized more for not reaching a statistical purity that it does not seek to achieve. If the sample was smaller, it is doubtful whether the criticisms would be as persistent.

While concerns about the archive's representativeness need to be taken seriously, it would equally be mistaken to abandon the challenge of making wider assertions about the popular mood. There is no perfect window to popular attitudes and, just like M-O, opinion polls do not, despite the popular impression, offer some kind of unproblematic reproduction of them and this is especially true in relation to Diana's mourning (see below). That the archive does not conform to a statistical standard does not mean it is of no use, or only of secondary use to the polls, in making broader generalizations, particularly when used cautiously and in conjunction with other quantitative and qualitative evidence. If the same phrases, the same comments, the same experiences, crop up repeatedly in this and other sources then we can reasonably assume with some certainty, if not with precise statistical accuracy, that these views are representative of wider attitudes. The challenge of reconstructing popular attitudes on the basis of imperfect evidence is one that historians face all the time – and most would be extremely envious of the massive depth and detail of the insights into popular experiences that this collection provides.

The possibilities for broader generalization are further increased by the fact that those who record views for the archive do not just aim to represent themselves. Those who write, as already noted, are asked to perform a dual function, recording their own views but also charting the attitudes of those around them. This stimulated early press attacks on 'psychoanthroposociologic Nosey Parkers', or 'peeping-toms' from a press that saw the organization as trespassing on their territory (Sheridan et al. 2000: 84). Given that this negative image persists into the present day, it is perhaps worth reproducing the organization's guidance to observers in fulfilling this task:

> It is always useful to widen your report by asking for the reactions of relatives and friends. Also you may observe a little scene or overhear a little snippet of conversation which reveals an aspect of our life in our times and is worth recording. However please do not identify people by name but do identify gender, approximate age and (if you happen to know it) occupation. *This is not an invitation to eavesdrop. There is all the difference in the world between reporting something casually overheard and deliberately listening to a private conversation.* [their emphasis]

Whether they can accurately convey what other people thought is more questionable, and clearly some caution is necessary. But certainly volunteers take this responsibility seriously and go out of their way to bring in other views. One man, for example, estimated that he came across around 300 people during the mourning and sought to summarize the main themes of the views he came across. Even when the writer is not seeking explicitly to represent others, often their authorship is not confined to their opinions as the responses of others are given space to compete with and frequently contradict the main account. For example, one woman, in the course of a passionate denunciation of the Diana events also noted how her sister had asked her to note for the record – which she quite happily did – her 'mildly sympathetic' initial feelings after hearing the news.[3]

This relates to a more radical, fundamental way in which observers seek to represent others, and which has particular importance given the way the media sought to speak for the experiences of 'ordinary people' during Diana's Mourning. Observers might not be statistically representative of the population, and indeed by their very nature they are a pretty special bunch. But one collective self-definition that they repeatedly advance is that they are 'ordinary'. This, Sheridan notes, signifies above all what they are *not*, they are on the outside rather than politicians, academics and the media, those 'people who have power to define what history is' (1996: 11). Those who write share a sense of representing ordinary people in their own words and, as they put it, 'letting the people's voice be heard' in a culture where knowledge is controlled by 'the discourse of big cheeses' among 'the media' and 'the posh'. They share a perception that 'the professional media cannot write about the lives of ordinary people because they are not ordinary themselves' (Sheridan et al. 2000: 218).

Of course these people are self-selecting and we should not automatically assume that they can accurately represent others. But they are no more self-selecting than many other sources, such as the media and politicians, that also claim to do just this. Indeed the very way the media confidently determined the national mood of 'the people' during the mourning was through vox-popping 'a blatantly self-selecting sample of Diana admirers' (Smith 1997b) (or those whose opinion was presented as such) – a process one critic described as 'about as objective as an opinion poll at a party conference' (letter to *The Times*, 13 September 1997). In a world where knowledge is hierarchical, observations about public opinion made by those in authority, be they journalists, politicians or academics, are viewed less problematically, even though they are in no sense statistically representative of others, indeed are far less so than M-O volunteers. But this suggests that it is the non-elite nature of M-O's evidence, as much as its statistically unrepresentative nature, that provokes suspicion (Shaw 1998). From this perspective the real 'representative' problem is not that its volunteers are not ordinary enough, but that they are too ordinary.

M-O has always sought to challenge this hierarchy through what its contemporary founder hailed as 'a magnificent subversion of authority' (Pocock 1987: 215) that embraces a less elitist definition of who has the expertise and legitimacy to represent the views of others and themselves (Sheridan et al. 2000). It is a challenge that has particular relevance to Diana's Mourning. For one of the ironies was that, contrary to appearances, existing hierarchies of knowledge dominated by 'the discourse of big cheeses' were overwhelmingly strengthened by the event. This is true of a media whose 'naturalised authority . . . to present social actuality', to define who 'the people' were and what they thought, was 'massively reproduced' (Couldry 1999: 79) in the course of its marathon coverage. Equally, as we have seen, the 'naturalised authority' of academia has been no less powerfully reinforced by the subsequent outpouring of analysis that has interpreted from above the popular meaning of the mourning but has sought little engagement with the attitudes of 'ordinary people' in doing so.`

The archive aims to do just this, as it positions volunteers not only as objects of research, but as active collaborators in a participatory, mutual research process, a position emphasized in the preferred description of volunteers as *correspondents* in preference to 'respondents' or 'subjects'. Encouraging people to act as participant-observers, not just of themselves but of others as well, serves to blur the boundaries between the expert and non-expert as, rather like an anthropologist, correspondents send in their report 'from the field'. It places people not just as objects for research 'on' but as active participants in research 'for and with' as well (Sheridan 1996). Such an approach, once derided, is now increasingly fashionable in anthropology (a discipline that has always had close links with M-O) and cultural studies in its concern 'to allow many voices to mingle so that the authoritative voice of the ethnographer is dislodged' (McRobbie 1997: 183; Morley 1992, 1997). Equally in its emphasis that volunteers act as participant-observers, what emerges is perhaps more deserving of being described as 'ethnographic' (albeit of an unconventional, bottom-up type) than many of the qualitative studies of everyday life in media and cultural studies that have been (mis)labelled under this heading. In this case it hopefully facilitates a suitably more collaborative (if far from democratic) 'people's history' of the mourning that profits from an awareness that knowledge flows from the bottom up as well as the top down.[4]

This is further facilitated by the nature of the archive's relationship with its volunteers, most of whom had been writing for several years before they came to outline their views in September 1997. Each writer receives the same directive, with every contribution from them being answered personally by the archive staff in a standard, regularly updated format that is topped and bottomed with handwritten comment that incorporates personal changes in their lives. Observers write under conditions of anonymity, ensured by giving them an M-O number that also allows the researcher access to basic details about them. Their replies are constructed in the privacy of their home, enabling them to take on many of the characteristics of writing a diary, despite being recorded for a public institution. This further gives them, in contrast to interviews, greater power to describe their thoughts in their own terms, to edit, think about, emphasize what they want to say. In all this, the absence of an interviewer, the conditions of privacy, the intimacy, trust and sense of mutual relationship between archive and correspondents, often built up over many years, combine to allow for particularly rich, intimate and reflective insights into the topic being discussed (Shaw 1998).

Taken together, the unique strengths of the archive facilitates, to an unusual extent, access to the 'naturalised domains' and 'naturally occurring data' (Morley 1992: 186) much sought after by 'ethnographic' media researchers. There will always be areas of the private household forbidden for the researcher to access, while the presence of an interviewer might distort 'naturally occurring' thoughts and patterns of behaviour. M-O's system cannot overcome a problem inherent in the artificiality of any research process – even the very fact of writing for a university archive might cause similar distortions – but it does minimize it as far as is possible. For given that ethnography is 'based on methods of observation that cause as little disruption as possible to a setting'

(Ruddock 2001: 130), it is difficult to perceive of any method that would cause less than M-O does.

This was particularly useful in September 1997 for several reasons. On a practical level it is unlikely that any other method of data-gathering would have enabled unplanned access to the views of such a large number of people, scattered all over Britain, at one particular moment. More methodologically, the written, private nature of responses has considerable advantages, in the context of the dominant mood of September 1997, over other quantitative and even qualitative research techniques. As chapter 9 demonstrates, there was intense conformist pressure to comment 'on the very sad news', leading to self-censorship in the face of the perceived dominant mood. Given this, there are serious questions about the ability of *public* opinion polls to chart attitudes accurately, even aside from the usual methodological critiques. In this climate, perhaps what is surprising is not that 90 per cent of a poll declared themselves to have a favourable view of Princess Diana, but that 6 per cent were willing to confess publicly to a stranger that they had negative feelings (MORI 1997a). It is also notable that the numbers who said that they *would* sign the book of condolences or place flowers were almost as large as the proportion *claiming* that they had, and both these figures should be treated with considerable caution. At least they should, given that the combined figures above proved to be 75 per cent greater than the findings of a subsequent poll in 1998 (MORI 1997b/ 1998a). And even polls such as these that were taken in 1998 were distorted by this conformist mood. The discrepancy between the 88–90 per cent of adults who told MORI (1997b/1998a) that they had watched the funeral and the authoritative (if probably still exaggerated) BARB official industry ratings estimate of 62 per cent tentatively suggests that polling estimates of mourning behaviour need to be reduced by at least a third.

Much qualitative work on media audiences has favoured individual or group interviews. But by the same token it seems likely that self-censorship in the face of the dominant, moral mood would have limited their access to the world of private opinion (Lindlof and Grodin 1990), at least judging by the following comments:

> I also feel that if I had said to anybody what I have written here, last week, I would have been made to feel callous and cruel.

> My feelings will not be popular with many people and I have not discussed them outside the family for that reason.

> When the directive for Princess Diana came out I was rather busy and didn't feel that my views were what people wanted to hear . . . My feelings, especially at first, were not what people wanted to hear.[5]

Because – as this illustrates – conformist pressures are significantly reduced when responses are written down (McIlven and Gross 1999), the archive facilitates a deeper access to popular attitudes during the mourning and unreachable through quantitative or even more usual qualitative surveys. Media researchers often prefer group interviews because of the fact that 'making meaning is a social process arising out of interaction with others' (Zoonen 1994: 138). But even here M-O can offer important insights as it encourages people to detail their own thoughts, how they change over time and alongside the interaction of these views with others. For what observers do is perform a dual or perhaps triple function, combining reports of their own thoughts and those of their immediate circle with their broader perceptions, memories, opinions of how 'others' reacted, in this case usually defined as 'the nation' or 'the people'. In this latter role they act, to quote Jennings and Madge, as subjective cameras illuminating 'not what society is like but what it looks like to them' (Sheridan et al. 2000: 34). The pictures that they offer are as valuable for their perceptions as for their 'facts' as they facilitate an examination not only of individual responses but also their broader images of the popular reaction and the role and impact of media images, as well as personal experience, in shaping such perceptions.

Some of the above comments also illustrate the sense of relationship between correspondents and the archive. It was perhaps captured best by one woman who was 'glad' of the opportunity to write after a week which had left her 'quite concerned' by her reaction that had made her feel 'quite isolated' and 'completely out of step with the majority'. For others, loyalty to the archive, their strong feelings for or against the mourning, or their determination to set the historical record straight, meant that they had already written before receiving the directive.

> 5.9.97. I may be jumping the gun a bit on this, since it is quite likely to be a subject for the next M-O project. However, the events of the past week have so appalled me that I wanted to write about it now.
>
> In view of this situation, I think it's important to record my views for M-O. To look at the papers and the broadcasts of the period, you would think that we all went around in black armbands weeping in the street. In my experience that just wasn't so.

The strength of the relationship with the archive could encourage those to write who might otherwise not have made the effort. As one woman commented at the end of an insightful reply of over fourteen pages:

> In many ways I resent spending all this time writing about her and thinking about these recent happenings. Had you not asked me to do

so and had I not felt loyalty to the archive I would not have put pen to paper! I originally meant to make my report short and snappy – about 2 sides of paper – but I felt that wasn't really fair to the Archive – so I've tried to be more objective and expansive. You do need analysis.[6]

In many ways, of course, the act of writing cannot be separated from what people wrote (Sheridan et al. 2000). For some its production was an active part of their mourning, as they supplemented their accounts with poems, decorative stamps or details of written or pictorial tributes that they had offered. One woman finished her account: 'Whoever reads this, I want you to know that I am crying for her now, but that it is one of the greatest honours I have had to be able to write for history here.' Meanwhile for sceptics, their contribution could be an active form of resisting the dominant mood. One observer prefaced her strongly negative opinions with the expressed determination 'to set the following on record so that the future doesn't think everyone in Britain was round the bloody twist'. Meanwhile another man sought to counteract the dominance of the Diana Event by setting down to compose his sceptical thoughts during a funeral that he refused to watch because it had 'nothing whatever' to do with him.[7] M-O, perhaps uniquely in September 1997, emerges as both a mourning and non-mourning site, providing a forum for the passions of both sides while also catering for those caught somewhere in the middle. It allows us to penetrate beneath the mourning veil (Thomas 2002), and to some extent at least, explore what 'ordinary' people really thought, rather than what the media said that they thought.

The question of how exactly to go about interpreting this material, even with the above comments on methodology in mind, is not an easy one. There are hundreds of thousands of words here and words, as many have noted, do not speak for themselves. There is always the danger of reporting the comments that lend the most support to the point being argued while minimizing or ignoring those that do not fit the argument (Ruddock 2001: 139). The key is to ensure that, at least to some extent, the material reflects the position of respondents rather than the preconceived assumptions of the researcher. One way to facilitate this is through a 'grounded theory' approach in which the researcher allows himself to be 'surprised' by the material he comes across, being prepared to reformulate his initial approach (Ruddock 2001: 139, 128). Here my initial broad and somewhat ill-defined aim to examine popular attitudes and media coverage developed into a structure that, while remaining inevitably selective and shaped by my interests, prejudices and intellectual limitations, seeks to reflect and explore the key themes that emerge in this and other evidence. It draws on 'multiple case-studies' (Yin 1989) (including deviant ones) to explore them from a variety of different experiences and attitudes.

This was also the intention more broadly. For it would be a foolish researcher that ignored the weaknesses and overemphasized the strengths of generalizing from any one source, however revealing and diverse. Here, as far as is possible, M-O's evidence is explored in conjunction with a variety of other opinion sources. As noted above, these include opinion polls, but also a variety of media coverage and readers' letters and other qualitative surveys, including the unpublished National Lesbian and Gay Survey (see chapter 8). Equally, Diana's Mourning is placed within a broader comparative historical and contemporary context of popular responses to royal and other relevant events. The aim, through a process of 'triangulation' (Zoonen 1994: 139), is to bring multiple sources of opinion to bear on the individual themes discussed in order to minimize the weaknesses of each source and provide a more generalizable (Silverman 2000) reconstruction of popular attitudes.

There is also another even more fundamental way that the above approach has to be set within its broader perspective for this book to make any sense. For, as suggested above and emphasized in chapter 1's approach, the aim is not just to explore popular attitudes at their most 'micro' but also set them within the broader context of the 'macro' operation of media and society. It is based on an approach that emphasizes that 'critical media research should be about more than what audiences like and what they think' (Ruddock 2001: 180). Like recent research that 'represents a merging of "reception" and "influence" agendas' (Corner 2000: 392; Eldridge et al. 1997), this book seeks to explore the complex interaction between media, society and individuals during the mourning, placing popular attitudes within an analysis of media coverage and power as well. In doing so, subsequent chapters examine how far the media myth of the mourning both reflected individual attitudes and shaped broader perceptions of the event.

ഔരു

3

The People's Princess

The starting point for many people in their accounts was obviously their attitudes to Diana. While the media offered seemingly conclusive evidence of overwhelmingly positive attitudes towards a woman 'Born a Lady, Became a Princess, Died a Saint' (*Mirror*, 1 September 1997), this chapter questions how far these sentiments were representative of attitudes in the country, or even among mourners. Instead it points to the existence of a huge complexity and diversity of opinion as feelings of admiration, praise and qualified identification competed with indifference, equivocation and hostility, sometimes among the same accounts and across a range of themes. The following comments convey something of this:

> Diana was loved by us all, nobody is indispensable but I don't think anybody can ever replace her in the way that she was.

> Without doubt she has left a superb legacy of bitterness, humanity and caring behind her. A veritable Queen of Hearts and yet fallible. She associated with the wrong people, sometimes put her foot in it with verbal gaffes, sometimes behaved illogically and yet gained wholeheartedly the love, sympathy and understanding of the public.

> A perhaps-not-over-intelligent, but rather scheming and manipulative young woman, who maximised her attractive looks with unacceptably high expenditure on clothes, hair etc.

> a rather silly woman who was extremely cunning, manipulative and inclined to be hysterical.[1]

One of Us

Of the positive themes, one of the most prominent was Diana's depiction as a woman 'who had the common touch', who was 'natural with people and not distanced from them' and 'touched our hearts with her kindness, her compassion, her mixing with just *ordinary* people in everyday life'.[2] There was often a favourable contrast here with her erstwhile family, as Diana was declared to be 'more human than the other royals', and 'more like one of us'.[3] One 35-year-old female was deeply upset on hearing the news:

> I genuinely could not take in what the reporter was saying . . . I was utterly stunned . . . There have been many tragic events over the last few years I have *never* been reduced to tears before, and I don't just mean being a little misty eyed – I really wept.

Later in the week she signed the local book of condolences in Manchester town hall and then took some flowers to the Cathedral. Inside she lit a candle for Diana and with so many others everywhere – 'a very moving sight' – she had trouble finding somewhere to place it. She was surprised by the strength of her feelings: 'I am by no means a royalist, quite the opposite – I think the whole bunch are a waste of space.' But Diana represented the 'best of them, perhaps the last hope':

> In the end Diana was a 'people' person – if protocol got in the way she just went around it. To the traditional Royals that must be like trying to stop breathing. Perhaps that is why our grief is so intense – she really was *our* princess.[4]

Such attitudes echo one of the most prominent aspects of media coverage. 'She was royal but special . . . because she was one of us', suggested the *Sun* (1 September 1997), as did numerous other commentators. She was a royal with 'the common touch', an extraordinarily ordinary figure (Segal 1998; Blackman 1999) agreed the academics. In this way she perfectly embodied what has often been argued to be the central ambiguity necessary for the popular appeal of a modern, mediated royalty, indeed arguably to all celebrities, that they appear as simultaneously ordinary and extraordinary (Billig 1997b; Couldry 2001). In the case of the royals, this perception is encouraged by the paradox that they are 'at once like us, and not like us', in an extraordinary position but in another way quite, quite ordinary. Judith Williamson suggests:

> The point about the royal family is that, unlike any other category who are rich and famous, they haven't *done* anything to be different (except be born) – they just *are* . . . No other group in the public eye, is so very ordinary . . . If they were not Royal, there would be nothing special about them at all . . . they are ourselves writ large, the ordinary held up for everyone to see. (1988: 75–6)

This means that they can, at least in theory, be identified in people's mind with the ordinary person, they *represent* or symbolize ordinary people. Williamson further suggests that royalty are felt to be on the side of ordinary people against 'them', the ruling elite. The Queen Mother's comment after Buckingham Palace was bombed during the war that they could now 'look the East End in the face' was and is perhaps the most famous image of royal solidarity with the lower classes. Even during the 1980s the Queen's alignment with the people was strengthened by authoritative newspaper reports of her 'dismay' at the damage being done by an 'uncaring' Thatcherism to a society which the prime minister had declared did not exist (Neil 1996: 196–7).

However Diana's emergence into the royal family and her subsequent battles with them at least partly undermined this image. The royal family now became negatively repositioned as 'them', an institution that did not even appear to care for their own members, much less for ordinary people, while Diana became, rather more, one of us. This was further aided by the way she symbolized modernity, in marked contrast to the archaic royals, in her personality, interests and easy, natural, intimacy with people. Diana's ordinary/extraordinary image was arguably further strengthened by the fact that before her marriage made her extraordinary, she was 'shy Di', the obscure, ordinary kindergarten-school teacher, although also one with more 'royal blood' in her than her future family. All this formed the basis for her image as a princess with the common touch who was not 'too royal' and aloof like Charles and the family or 'too ordinary' like 'Fergie' but royal *and* ordinary or 'super-ordinary' (Nairn 1988: 27). As one man put it: 'In Diana people saw her as the only member of the Royal Family who kept her dignity yet showed her true feelings (Fergie alas, had no dignity).'[5] And while apparently contradictory images, in another way they chased each other round, reinforcing each other. For the more ordinary the princess appeared, the more extraordinary she seemed, which in turn made her ordinariness all the more extraordinary.

That this was a crucial element to understanding Diana's impact is beyond doubt. Yet it should not be exaggerated or romanticized. To suggest that this was 'the overwhelming feeling' in the country (Blackman and Walkerdine 2000: 149) and that 'people didn't go round saying that this is a rich aristocrat who's died' (Brunt 1999b: 286), simplifies a distinctly double-edged opinion among really 'ordinary' people. Some months later the left-wing journalist Mark Steel (1998) suggested that sympathy for Diana needed to be kept in perspective: 'If a teacher asked a class what a victim was, they wouldn't give top marks to the kid who said "Is it someone who cruises around the Mediterranean with a millionaire, miss?" ' His comments hit upon the role of class in shaping attitudes. For despite all the rhetoric about the 'withering away' of class differences (quoted in Edgell 1993: 115), studies have clearly demonstrated its continued importance in structuring identities and attitudes in contemporary Britain. In one 1996 survey, for example, two-thirds considered that 'ordinary people do not get their fair share of the nation's wealth' (Adonis and Pollard 1998: 11). Similarly half of those in Marshall et al.'s study (1988) believed there was a dominant class possessing economic and political power and a lower class with no power. Such a class dichotomy, between 'them', the people with all the power, and 'us' the ordinary people, has been found to be a central popular image in all modern societies (Darhrendorf 1959).

While this may oversimplify the complexity of class distinctions in contemporary Britain, it remains a prominent theme in attitudes towards an institution that resides at the pinnacle of the class structure. For lurking beneath the surface has always been an undercurrent of popular class hostility to 'them' and a blunt awareness that 'they' are very far from ordinary. The Queen Mother's wartime comment about looking the East End in the face, for instance, was met not only with admiration but with cynicism that she would not have known where the East End was in order to look. Victims of the blitz articulated a well-founded suspicion that the royals still lived in unrationed luxury (Zweiniger-Bargielowska 1993) as they considered it 'all very well for them, traipsing around saying how their hearts bleed for us and they share all our sufferings, and then going home to a roaring fire in one of their six houses' (Ziegler 1978: 72). Even when the Duke of Kent was killed in a car crash, sympathy was qualified with class hostility. As one cynic said of his bereaved wife: 'She won't have to work to keep those children. *We* will' (Ziegler 1978: 74). Nor were such feelings the unique products of the sacrifices required in war. In the late 1950s Richard Hoggart noted the frequently less than reverential working-class attitudes to 'them'. People said enviously, 'They don't have to struggle with the kids when they're tired out', 'They're waited on hand and foot', while simultaneously sympathizing that 'it's a rotten job' and 'they get pushed around as much as we do' (1957: 111). As Billig's research in the late 1980s captured, there was a 'dialectic of envy and sympathy' (1997b: 127), as sympathy for the press intrusion and loss of privacy was balanced with envy for the privileges and wealth which came with their 'job' and cynicism about their 'ordinariness'.

Indeed the Achilles heel of the British monarchy has long been hostility to its cost, an attitude that has proved fertile breeding ground for opposition, be it to the Jubilees of the late nineteenth century or the cost of the Queen's wedding in 1947 (Taylor 1999; Zweiniger-Bargielowska 1993). One poll in 1966, for example, showed that two-thirds felt that the royal family should live more like ordinary people (Ziegler 1978). The 1970s saw the first contemporary public criticisms of the monarchy's state-enhanced fortune (Pimlott 1997a), and these attitudes became more vocal in the following decade, not least as they were sanctioned by increasingly undeferential newspaper coverage that shifted to a stand, as one journalist recalled, of 'whacking the Germans'. In 1988 the *Sun's* publication of a private photograph of the royals led the Palace to threaten legal action. The paper responded with an attack on 'the power of the richest families; the dominance of those born with a whole canteen of silver spoons in their mouths' (Billig 1997b: 117) – similar words, incidentally, to those of the *Morning Star* following Diana's death.

More substantially, growing criticisms of the monarchy by this time included demands – supported by 79 per cent of one poll – that the woman thought to be the world's richest should pay taxes. Nor was Diana exempt from this questioning of the 'value for money' that the royals were providing – in fact the conspicuous consumption of the younger royals was often seen as the root of the problem (Pimlott 1997a: 533–8). Her lavish expenditure was much publicized, even before her public relations battle with her husband saw his camp leak the news that the annual cost of Diana's clothes and beauty treatment totalled £161,000, over £3,000 per week (Bunting 1994). And despite her subsequent well-publicized divorce settlement of around £17 million, just three weeks before her death *Hello* magazine was speculating that Diana's 'high maintenance' expenditure of 'about £800,000 a year' might leave her 'hard up by the age of 50' (Flett 1998).

All this and more meant that, contrary to the idea that Diana's appeal and her mourning saw a collapse of class divisions, the elite position she embodied often remained present, blocking or qualifying sympathy. Indeed even the very description of Diana as 'one of us' illustrated its latent presence, for it was only because she was a member of the elite that her ordinariness was worthy of comment. To say she was ordinary was really to say she was not (Billig 1997b; Nairn 1988). For as Billig points out: 'The People's Princess is still a princess, not one of the people . . . she was ordinary for a princess. She remains a princess in the legend, otherwise there is little legend' (1997a: 506). And for some this elite position served to transcend or qualify any identification. As one man argued: 'I could not understand people who said "She was one of us". . . I do not feel I have any connection with her.' Another man's father had been on holiday in America during her death and found that people kept coming up to his party and offering their condolences. 'His response was polite but uncompromising', recalled his son. 'This woman was worth a million when she was married and twenty-one million when she died. These people's lives are too remote from us for me to really care.'[6] Meanwhile one female was attending a TUC rally in London celebrating the restoration of trade union rights at the government intelligence agency GCHQ on the Sunday morning and was unaware of the news. As she waited to board the coach she overheard one of the organizers talking about whether the event would go ahead:

> I thought perhaps a famous revolutionary had died in a civil
> disturbance somewhere like South America and I didn't like to ask
> why and where . . . It surprised me to find that trade union activists
> expressed genuine grief over the death of someone from the aristocracy
> . . . It seems absurd to call a woman brought up in wealth and privilege
> the people's princess.[7]

Nor were these sentiments merely the preserve of the political left, but were repeatedly expressed both in Britain and elsewhere (Black and Smith 1999) as the claims, including those by Diana herself, of her 'ordinariness' were scrutinized and rejected. As one woman argued:

> Nor is sensible for people to say that Diana was ordinary – she was the
> daughter of an Earl, had a privileged upbringing, married with royalty,
> was reputed to have a private fortune of about £40 million, jewellery of
> £16 million and an income of half a million per annum – nothing
> ordinary about that! Two small reports show just how out of touch
> she, of necessity, was with the way most of us live our lives.
> She complained once . . . about the problem of travelling with a small
> child (i.e. taking William to Australia, at six months) – but she had
> an entourage of about 3 dozen people to carry baby and baggage,
> change nappies etc. and arrange travel and accommodation!! She once
> remarked to Ann Clwyd that it sickened her that all rich people seemed
> to care about was getting richer!! This apparently with no hint of irony!
> Sounds like humbug to me – especially coming from someone who is
> reputed to have spent £65,000 in one year on make-up and hair-styling.
> Enough to pay a single person's pension for 20 odd years and more
> than a middle-range nurse would earn in 5–6 years! What a sense of
> values! What an obscenity![8]

As Ralph Dahrendorf argues, 'in people's mind the phenomenon of social distance is crucial for distinguishing between "them" and "us"' (1959: 287). And whatever Diana's ability to bridge this divide for some people, for others her elite position ensured that the distance remained, and positioned her as remote from ordinary life. It was a gulf cheerfully captured by one woman in a final postscript to her views written just before the end of the year: 'Over the Christmas holidays my son pointed out the cover of *Hello* magazine to me – " Our first Christmas without her" said the headline . . . I've never had Christmas with Princess Diana so I expect I will survive.'[9]

Saint Diana

In many ways the central aspect of media coverage emphasized Diana's charity work, and this agenda was widely replicated by respondents, although from a variety of different, less flattering angles. Favourable perspectives argued, to quote one, that 'she gave courage to the sick, dying, hope to the 3rd world and we must not fail her'.[10] Again it was Diana's caring, 'one of us' style, along with the way 'she espoused the less traditional charitable causes' such as Aids and landmines, that provoked favourable comparisons with the other royals: 'Princess Anne who is President of Save the Children and goes around the world fund-raising etc. but I have never seen her embrace a child. The rest of the Royals will shake hands when the call is there, but they remain aloof and remote.'[1] In media terms there was nothing but praise for such work. But there was a fundamental problem with the credibility of this hagiography, given that days and even hours earlier the same newspapers had been attacking her with as much vigour as they were now eulogizing her. The latter image fitted rather awkwardly on top of a distinctly mixed verdict on Diana's charitable efforts and her life in general. In later years Diana's attendance, in full make-up and with Sky news in tow, at an operation for open heart surgery fuelled hostile media depictions of a woman 'ghoulishly attracted to sites of pain and suffering' (Davies 2001: 163). The *Sun* issued readers with a spoof organ-donation style card to carry stating that in event of hospitalization, they would prefer not to be visited by the princess.

This image was to get worse before it got better. Reviewing press coverage of the month before her death, Catherine Flett (1998) noted that Diana's reputation was in many ways at its nadir during this time. Newspapers were denouncing 'a trash icon for our times' (Fountain 1997) and complaining that the Princess had 'slipped all too easily into the Onassis-like world of private jets, private villas, and private yachts' and was 'in danger of becoming a fast woman'. '4 hols in 40 days' said the *Sun* on 22 August 1997 as it accused Diana of 'threatening to steal Fergie's crown as the royal holiday queen'. Her new love affair with Dodi al Fayed, along with a Harrods helicopter trip to a clairvoyant, led even a once sympathetic Andrew Morton to describe her behaviour as 'stark, staring bonkers' (Flett 1998). Meanwhile a charity visit to Bosnia left most of the press cynical and questioning her motives, fuelling allegations that she 'used poor and sick people as "accessories"' to campaigns that were rather more about enhancing her own reputation (Hitchens 1997). It was hardly surprising, therefore, that some chose to reject, or at least qualify, the near-Stalinist rewriting of Diana's media image which occurred after her death and draw on the less flattering stories offered during her life:

> The impression I received through the media coverage of her visits and good works in latter years was that she seemed to be doing it as much for the benefit of her own status, as for the good of those she was ostensibly helping. I think we all got a bit jaded by her innumerable holidays and trips to the gym.[12]

Such attitudes were combined with scepticism that it was as much the shallow appeal of Diana's beauty and media manipulation as the substance of her contributions that provoked such intense coverage. As one woman put it: 'She certainly had what it takes in these days of photogenic stars, where Robin Cook can't become prime minister because his face looks like a dried apricot.'[13]

Often hostility was qualified with some praise or vice versa. One woman's verdict on Diana as 'rather silly, comparatively empty headed, vain, occasionally bad-tempered, manipulative, immature' was tempered with a recognition of 'the excellent way she acted in relation to many charities'. On the other hand one dominant sentiment was not idolization but a hostility to this process from those who 'felt appalled at the sainthood that so many people seem to be hell bent on giving her'.[14] It led one man to wonder 'Have the public gone mad?' and another to agree:

> It seemed to be a kind of quiet hysteria was developing. Everyone mentioned her beauty, her kindness and the tragedy of her marriage. Hardly any mentioned her wealth, her often childish behaviour, her obvious instability or her extremely grasping divorce settlement.[15]

Here people defined their attitudes against the media and the views they *imagined* mourners to hold – indeed it is notable that the media canonization was widely and unquestionably assumed to be reflecting popular attitudes. But despite this image there was little evidence of such sentiments as 'mourners resisted the narrative of perfection' (Geraghty 1998: 73), placing and admiring Diana as a more flawed character. As one sympathetic woman argued: 'She was not a saint, she was very human and had human failings – that was perhaps one thing that endeared her to so many.' 'Diana was not perfect – how boring if she had been saintly', agreed another.[16] Indeed the sanctification process was sometimes viewed unfavourably even by those in deep mourning. One woman who was more upset than on the death of her own father also warned of 'a danger of the Princess being turned into a saint'. Another man, similarly affected by 'the past awful week of consuming sorrow', stressed that 'she was as prone to human error, as fallible a human being as you or I or Prince Charles'.[17]

Perhaps the most sympathetic comments came from one woman who stood out in her description of Diana as 'an angel of God'. But she was not prepared to hold onto this view under critical discussion. Her mother lived in Canada and in a phone call had told her that the bishop of Toronto had stated that Diana should not be sanctified precisely because of her flaws. 'Exactly', replied her daughter; 'It is because of that we love her – she is fallible as we all are.'[18] The rhetoric of saintly perfection had been quickly abandoned in favour of the more convincing and endearing narrative of earthly imperfection. And perhaps one reason why Earl Spencer's funeral speech generated such praise was because of the belief that he 'was right to try and discourage Diana's elevation to some kind of sainthood', as he insisted that his sister should be remembered as she was, for all her flaws. Or as one woman summed it up, while also predicting the subsequent decline of Diana's reputation: 'The trouble with uncritical adulation is that it always results in a backlash. Diana the saint will become Diana the Demon. She surely deserved a more balanced send-off.'[19]

One widespread view within such assessments was that Diana's life was far from exceptional when compared with the similar work of other famous and ordinary people. One woman above had added how it was 'also supremely ironic that the real embodiment of 20th century sainthood, Mother Teresa, should die in the middle of the hullabaloo'. Her death on the Friday before the funeral found itself virtually eclipsed by the story of the week. The *Mail* (8 September 1997), for example, devoted thirty-three pages to the princess's funeral and one to that of Mother Teresa. And in any case, as one man noted, 'much of that coverage seemed to be because she had met Princess Diana'[20] in a style paraded by a *Private Eye* spoof news report headlined 'Diana's Friend Dies' (3 October 1997). But the old difficulty of keeping satire alive when reality overtakes it was brought home by the BBC's 9 o'clock news coverage on the Friday after Diana's death which opened with fifteen minutes of Diana news, and then broadcast a story allocated a quarter of this time which began:

It was the death of Diana, Princess of Wales which brought Mother Teresa out onto the balcony by her chapel on Sunday in a rare public appearance which turned out to be her last. It was a remarkable tribute emphasizing that Diana really meant something to the tiny nun, born of Albanian parents, who spent her life among the poor of Calcutta. (BBC 5 September 1997)

But while the media seemed more concerned to use the death as another peg to emphasize Diana's saintliness, it provided an obvious focus to challenge it with the contrast between a woman who '*lived* her philosophy in a much more valid way than did Diana'. One woman full of 'sorrowful admiration' for Diana was simultaneously anxious to assert: 'Above all I think she should not be made holy – by comparison with Mother Teresa, the difference is all too apparent.'[21] Others, too, noted that Diana 'wasn't even in the same league as Mother Teresa who devoted her life to the sick and dying, not just a few hours here and there'. It left one woman feeling:

> sorry that the death of a woman who was more quietly compassionate and charitable than Diana was totally overshadowed by her. I think it is telling that one woman's estate consisted of two buckets and the sari she used to wash in and the other runs into millions of pounds. I'm not denying that Diana did good works . . . but it must be easier to be charitable when it consists of going to fancy balls in dresses you'll only wear once than rescuing the poor from Calcutta's gutters.[22]

On another level, Diana's charity work hardly represented a new departure for a royal family that over the last 200 years has forged 'a popular role for itself outside politics as patron, promoter and fund-raiser for the deserving and underprivileged' (Prochaska 2001: 224). In the 1990s the royal family had well over 3,000 institutional patronages, while 25 per cent of their 3,820 official engagements carried out in 1997 were on behalf of charities. Details of these figures for the 1990s revealed Diana as no more than a moderately hard-working member of the family. In 1991, for example, she carried out 258 UK engagements, compared with 301 for Charles, 504 for Princess Anne and over 600 for the Queen (*Times*, 2 January 1992).[23] And despite much academic writing that posthumously placed a 'caring' Diana as the antithesis to the harsh right-wing extremism of Thatcherism, popular (and intellectual) attitudes at the time were rather different. One Gallup poll taken in late 1988 saw only 19 per cent rate Diana as 'caring', compared with 32 per cent ascribing the same characteristic to Charles (Billig 1997b: p. xv), whose work through his Prince's Trust perhaps associated him with a greater depth of concern for social issues. How much popular perceptions changed in subsequent years is questionable, particularly given a divorce that saw the Princess drop her involvement with a hundred charities and retain just six.

All this, along with loyalist royalism, explains why 'the impression given that Diana was the only person who did any good works' caused annoyance among those who were 'sure other members of the royal family do as much'. They sought to redress the balance and place Diana's publicity-seeking charity work alongside the frequently unsung labours of other members of the royal family:

> She has done less charity work than any member of the royal family and had cut down her charities to six, yet she gets all the credit, while they get all the blame.

> Diana has been more or less sanctified, whereas there are others who do just as much for charity and the underprivileged – Princess Anne and Prince Charles and no doubt numerous unsung people.[24]

It has long been seen as a central part of the royal 'job' that the royals are *expected* to work hard and do such work and in return are handsomely rewarded in their lifestyle. Indeed not to participate in this trade-off is to become a type of royal viewed with hostility by even the most loyal subjects, the 'hangers on' who take the money but offer nothing in return (Billig 1997b: 108). 'Well, I'd do good works if I had a settlement of 2 million', said one woman to her mother, articulating a rationale that all Diana was doing was fulfilling her part of her well-rewarded 'job' and it was, added another, 'the least that someone in that position could do'. As one woman suggested: 'Money was important to her, no worries on that score and I felt she was well paid for the job she did, but she wasn't a saint and she had a better lifestyle than many people even dream about.'[25]

Nor was it just with other famous people that Diana's efforts could be unfavourably compared, as some of the above comments touch upon. Ordinary people, it was repeatedly stressed, did much the same or rather more, and this without any publicity, recognition or financial reward for their work. Indeed, by presenting Diana as 'just like us', commentators inadvertently opened up opportunities for comparison with ordinary people (Billig 1997b: 118), and in these Diana's contributions were seen as anything but special (for similar findings see Black and Smith 1999). As one man who considered the emphasis on her to be 'deplorable' noted: 'I do not think she was exceptional', as there were 'plenty of others who exercise, or who have exercised similar regard'. Indeed, the only thing that made her exceptional was the 'other life' that she enjoyed, as Diana's influence was placed alongside 'the hard graft of the regular workers . . . who do not have the opportunity to oscillate between good works and lavish lifestyle'.[26] It was a contrast that was to be repeatedly and often unflatteringly made:

As to the good Diana did yes maybe but many, many others slog away actually working in the slums, hospitals, war zones . . . she didn't have to negotiate or painstakingly work out methods to relieve suffering. Then at the end of the day she could return to luxury, holidays and nannies etc.

We all know that she promoted good causes . . . But, let's face it, apart from being a mother – what else did she have to do. She was in the enviable position of having travel arrangements for every charity function arranged for her – so there was little juggling of family, job, hobbies and voluntary work to which some of us aspire.[27]

From these perspectives Diana's position as 'one of them' alongside a life no better in worth than the unsung and unrewarded efforts of 'us', ensured her story was dismissed or debunked, rather than celebrated, as an extraordinarily ordinary one. 'She had a privileged life', suggested one woman, 'and should anyone of us have been put in her place might we not have tried to achieve as much?'[28]

A Good or Bad Victim?

Attitudes to Diana can also be seen in terms of the sympathy – or lack of it – that she provoked as a victim, an identity that chapter 7 argues was central to her story. In his illuminating discussion of the 'other news' composed of accidents, disasters and celebrities, John Langer (1998) outlines 'the victim story', which has a long history in journalism and even deeper roots in folklore (Propp 1968). Langer identifies two main variants, the first of which is the tale of the 'good victim', which is most likely to evoke sympathy and identification and stimulate the 'reflex of tears'. It is a story of an individual trapped in adverse conditions over which they have no control, at the mercy of suffering caused by a villain or the product of bad luck. The key qualification for being a good victim is that their fate should be 'suffered not chosen' (1998: 77–83). Diana's life and death, in many ways, fitted the bill perfectly. There were evil villains, not least a royal family and husband who had taken up, exploited and deceived a young, naïve, virginal bride and even refused to honour her in death. 'Charles Weeps Bitter Tears of Guilt' was the *Daily Mail*'s (3 September 1997) remarkably informed insight into the Prince's mind as it left readers in no doubt who was to blame for the tragedy. And certainly there was considerable sympathy for a 'young and innocent' woman with 'no idea what she was letting herself' in for, who was 'treated abominably by Charles and maybe by some of the others'. As one man noted of the view in his family: 'We feel as many others do that if Prince Charles had been a loving husband instead of a philanderer, Diana would have been alive today.'[29]

One rather less principled reason for the *Daily Mail*'s efforts to pin the blame on the royals, however, was because the circumstances of her death had shifted the focus onto other villains, first and foremost a media widely blamed for literally photographing Diana to death. 'I felt so angry with the reporters on motorbikes who seemed to have caused the crash,' said one woman, articulating a wave of public hostility to the media which stimulated a lively trade in T-shirts captioned 'Fuck Off Paparazzi', and 91 per cent of one poll supported a law on privacy (MORI 1997c).[30] Very quickly, however, it emerged that the driver Henri Paul had been found over the limit and the press, mixing relief with venom, splashed with 'The Driver was Drunk' and offered character-assassinations of 'a heavy drinker with a taste for the high life'. There was little sign of hostility to the driver, although one response, sometimes instantaneous and widely shared even by those with little grief, was a suspicion that Diana had been the victim of a vaguer, even more powerful and sinister 'them' (see also the discussion of conspiracy theories in chapter 4).

Combined with such a multitude of villains, visible or otherwise, was the perception that Diana had recently moved on to a new life and love after the tragedies of the past. As one woman put it: 'What caused me so much sadness was that this was a young woman who seemed to have been treated so unfairly in life since childhood, and now has been cut down in her prime and on the verge of finding happiness.'[31] In all these senses, Diana was a 'good' victim, deserving of our sympathy. However, becoming a good victim is, as Langer notes, a precarious exercise and the inverse of the above story is 'the narrative of the foolish victim', in which sympathy is reduced by the belief that the sufferer's troubles had been at least partly self-inflicted. Here Diana's claims to victimhood were not viewed favourably by those who offered more mixed assessments of her relationship with the royals:

She . . . knew exactly what she was doing when she married Charles, not so innocent as everyone would have us believe. When things began to go wrong she used her spite to undermine our future King.

It was not the royal family who had killed her, but her own behaviour and she had behaved badly towards them.

And at least one man remained somewhat 'dubious' of 'the allegations that the in-laws drove her to this position' because, as he put it: 'You should have seen my mother-in-law and I'm quite normal!'[32] More seriously, while the royals had their fair share of defenders, there were few willing to extend this service to the media. Yet even here sympathy for the princess was tempered by awareness of her role as a far from innocent media manipulator. It was a point graphically illustrated by one man who had 'no quarrel' with anyone who called for journalists 'to be suspended by their testicles (or by other appropriate body-parts if female) from London Bridge', but also recognized that Diana used and manipulated them.[33] Certainly there was ample evidence to influence such perceptions. In 1992 Diana's secret collusion with journalist Andrew Morton to produce his sensational *Diana: Her True Story* had led the chairman of the Press Complaints Commission, Lord Macgregor, to accuse the Princess of 'invading her own privacy' (Clayton and Craig 2001: 236). It gave her a growing reputation for media manipulation that her carefully crafted 1995 *Panorama* television interview performance, when she famously attacked her husband and the royals, further confirmed.

The previous year Diana had sought to counter hostile briefings from the Charles camp to produce 'Diana Saved Man from Drowning' headlines about an incident in which the princess's lifesaving duties were confined to using her mobile phone. Among the few journalists she was unsuccessful in interesting was *Times* editor Peter Stothard (1997), who delicately recalled of their lunchtime conversation that 'some bits of her story did not fit together as well as a true story should'. Despite his scepticism his paper ended up running the story without his help. Diana may have emerged effortlessly victorious in these and other media battles with the royals, but they also meant that it was hard for people, even those sympathetic, to see her as a truly innocent victim. 'Well you could say she lived by the paparazzi and she died by the paparazzi', was the cool response from one man on hearing the news. One older female agreed:

> In a way I felt that she had brought it on herself with her manipulation of the media. It must have been awful to be followed everywhere by the paparazzi, but there must have been a better way of dealing with them than high speed chases. The driver would surely have only gone at speed if Dodi or Diana had told him to – or they could have told him to go slow. It was a very thoughtless action to go speeding and a selfish one at that.[34]

As these comments illustrate, the circumstances of her death further served to undermine a 'good victim' story. A few days after the funeral one woman came across a friend who asked her: 'What do you think of all that hype last week?' 'A bit overdone,' replied the woman. 'Overdone!', exclaimed the friend. 'There was no need for them to have left that hotel as they have a private apartment there . . . And they weren't wearing seatbelts only the bodyguard.' 'In other words', the woman argued, 'it was a tragedy that needn't have happened.' Meanwhile one man reported how his wife, 'as staunch a Royalist as could be found even in the Home Counties', kept asking during the week, 'Why wasn't Diana wearing a seat belt?'[35] In public there were few brave enough to air such views, although one exception was controversial feminist Camille Paglia who upset some *Guardian* readers by accusing Diana of playing a 'kind of S and M game . . . with pursuing paparazzi, which put everyone in danger. We were just lucky that other innocent people weren't killed and maimed by this madness' (Paglia 1997). In agreement, however, was one man who noted that Diana was being driven without the legally required seatbelt at three times the legal limit in a built-up area by a drunk driver. He noted: 'When joy riders die in these circumstances they receive their just deserts' (*Guardian*, 5 September 1997). But while media coverage emphasized the 'good victim' story, the view that her death had been caused by foolish, 'stupid' behaviour from a woman 'who chose to live in the fast lane . . . and this was what happened' was widely aired in private and diminished sympathy for her plight. As one man put it:

> I did not and do not regard it as a national tragedy since I believe she was a victim of her own lifestyle, which she chose for herself . . . Diana's lifestyle killed her. Had she not chosen to consort with the glitterati, with their dubious connections . . . she might well have been alive. She chose to dispense with official protection and drivers and she paid the tragic price. It was nobody's fault but her own.[36]

Royalists and Republicans

'Ambiguity is central to the response', argued Stuart Hall (Jacques 1997b) in one of the more measured intellectual assessments of the popular mood following Diana's mourning. The above sections have offered clear illustration of this. And another way this manifested itself was in the diverse and sometimes contradictory reactions to the Diana event from both royalists and republicans. As chapter 1 notes, one of the central aspects of the mourning was its apparent anti-establishment, even republican side as Diana reached a constituency previously untouched by royalty as blacks, gays and the homeless mingled with middle England in what centre-left commentators hailed as a radical 'floral revolution' (Jacques 1997a). When Christopher Hitchens was introduced to the Princess in 1994 he joked that 'we republicans must stick together', considering that she had done more to subvert the monarchy by accident than he had achieved on purpose (Clayton and Craig 2001: 263). And certainly this led some to admire 'a constant thorn in the side of the establishment'. As one very pro-Diana republican woman argued: 'She was as near to an anarchist as you can get in the Royal Family. I always dreamed of what would happen if a Royal became an anarchist and said "up yours" to their ways. Diana did that, almost, well, as best she could.'[37]

In agreement with such sentiments – but from a negative perspective – were some royalists, tending to the more traditional and older generation, who disapproved of Diana's behaviour and conflict with the family that had made her famous. The royal civil war over the previous decade had inevitably necessitated some taking of sides and not everyone was on Diana's, while the anti-royal edge to the mourning provoked further distancing. One royalist, 'sickened' by press hostility to the monarchy and who had formed 'a low opinion' of Diana since she went public, felt she had 'brought it on herself' with her media manipulation. Others similarly considered that her death had 'happened for the best' as 'we now have one royal family, not two' and this had prevented her from becoming 'the King's mother and the power behind the throne'.[38] One middle-aged man explained his 'mixed feelings' on hearing the news:

> Although I like everyone else had been enamoured with Diana Spencer when she married the Prince of Wales in 1981, I had become disenchanted with her in recent years, seeing her as an attention-seeking do-gooder, who wanted to smile sweetly and be the Queen of Everyone's Hearts and yet who consciously or subconsciously, wanted to cause irrevocable damage to our beloved and much needed Royal Family.

His hope that the Queen and the Queen Mother got 'suitable grief when their time comes. They certainly deserve it more than Diana . . . did' was echoed by others similarly distanced from a reaction that was 'over the top . . . as if were the Queen herself who had died, and not an ex-Royal'.[39]

Yet the extent to which the mourning disrupted traditional patterns of royalist and republican loyalty should not be overstated – and profiles of republicans breaking ranks to join royalist ceremonials have a history as old as republicanism itself (Taylor 1999: 134–5). Diana was, to say the least, an unlikely heroine of the left despite its efforts to claim her support for radical causes (Campbell 1998a) through an 'altruism, which is candy-coloured communism' (Burchill 1998: 227). While this led some to admire a 'humanitarianism on a socialist scale that transcends the monetarism of her own class',[40] for others Diana remained a central part of the problem. A letter to the *Guardian* the week after she died contained the well-known quote from a former Brazilian archbishop: 'When I give food to the poor they call me a saint. When I ask "why" they have no food, they call me a communist' (14 September 1997). Diana's 'candy-coloured communism', critics argued, was too sweet and fluffy ever to ask 'why' and in emphasizing charity over justice only served to legitimize inequalities and encourage a Victorian myth that charities could replace government intervention to alleviate poverty (Wilson 1998). And while there were good reasons for failing to see a 'radical' Diana', there were even stronger barriers to viewing her as an anti-royal figure. Her breach with royalty was blurred with ambiguity as she clung on to royal privileges, titles and homes. It took a sharp eye to spot the difference between 'HRH The Princess of Wales', her original title, and the post-divorce 'Diana, Princess of Wales' (Smith 1998: 6–7). And Diana's continued support for the principle of hereditary monarchy, as Mark Steel (1998) sarcastically pointed out, rather placed her 'on the moderate wing' of the republican movement.

Nor, despite appearances, can the mourning be equated with embryonic republicanism. Those attending the Mall were predominantly conservative, at least judging by their newspaper affiliations in which 27 per cent were *Mail* readers, 22 per cent readers of the *Sun* and 16 per cent readers of *The Times*. The centre-left *Mirror*, despite selling four times as much as *The Times*, was only read by 13 per cent (Kellner 1997). In any case even in more radical publications, critical royalism rather than republicanism was the order of the day. 'Speak to Us Ma'am: Your People are Suffering' (*Mirror*, 3 September 1997), with its deferential plea to the Queen and placement of the people as *her* subjects, was hardly the stuff of revolution. And the entire premiss of demands that the Queen lead the mourning of her ex-daughter-in-law entailed 'a casting back to the fairytale beginning' (Benton 1998: 93) to at least give the subsequent horror story a royalist end fit for a princess. This mood was further confirmed by polls at the end of the week that showed that, despite the criticism, support for the monarchy had actually risen rather than decreased (Richards et al. 1999).

This simultaneously provoked the traditional distancing from royal events from some republicans, for whom Diana's anti-establishment status was not just invisible but was replaced with the automatic assumption of the opposite perspective. As one man explained his negative feelings somewhat defensively: 'I suppose I am prejudiced being an erstwhile republican and consider Royalty an irrelevance in a modern industrial society.' Princess Diana was 'an aristocrat who voted for Thatcher', added others, a conservative figure who still symbolized an institution that was 'unarguably, indisputably, fundamentally wrong'. Or, as one royalist put it from the positive side, she was 'truly the brightest jewel our royal family had'.[41]

Again to polarize these perspectives is to risk simplifying sometimes complex attitudes. Royalists often offered an uneasy mixture of contradictory sentiments balancing praise and criticism for Diana on the one hand and the royals on the other. One, for instance, weighed admiration for 'a good person . . . doing a lot to help various sectors of society', worry at the 'danger of her being regarded as a saint', and a defence of 'perfectly correct' royal behaviour in the face of criticism 'whipped up by the wretched press'. On the other side one republican man balanced his hostility to 'a woman who spent a fortune on clothes and cosmetics' with a recognition 'on the other hand' of the 'fair measure of independence and even courage' involved in Diana's charity work for the dispossessed. While unmoved by news of her death, he was captivated by the challenge to the 'political ruling class' embodied in the crowd's applause for Earl Spencer's famous funeral speech, while more than aware of the incongruity of the source of this anti-establishment challenge. 'It was', he recalled, 'quite fun while it lasted.'[42]

The findings of this chapter are clearly at variance with those repeatedly presented in media coverage. Indeed to the extent that there is one shared theme, it is hostility to the media and perceived public canonization of Diana. Yet these conclusions show close similarities with previous studies of popular attitudes to royalty. Support for the institution has never been as monolithic or adulatory as frequently assumed, and has always been mixed with a complex range of sentiments – indifference, cynicism, mockery and hostility, but very rarely idolization (Ziegler 1978; Rose and Kavanagh 1976; Harris 1966; Hoggart 1957; Jennings and Madge 1937). Beneath the appearance of unqualified devotion – even, or especially, among royalists – were and are contradictory 'on the one hand' and 'on the other hand' sentiments, 'in which the possibility of resentment was always present, even at times of celebration' (Billig 1997b: 117), or for that matter during mourning. Further adding to the complexity, diversity and ambiguity of responses was a Diana life story that embraced many 'mutually contradictory . . . personae' (Paglia 1995: 170), which could be interpreted in many different ways (Davies 2001). That these could stimulate a range of complex and contradictory popular identifications, a point rightly much emphasized, is to tell at best half the story. For the obvious, if rather ignored, flip side were diverse, even contradictory dis-identifications or partial identifications as well. The ambiguity and diversity of an image that could signify virtually anything and everything, the source of her extraordinary breadth of appeal, was also one source of its limitations. For as one person noted, 'everything was double-edged with Diana',[43] and this was certainly true of private if not public opinion following her death.

4

The Week of Mourning

Differing responses to Diana's life and death were only part of the story offered by people. Frequently their accounts were as much about the mourning that followed. Media coverage, as we have seen, focused on two complementary stories as the emphasis on a country united in grief was accompanied by graphic illustrations of the intensity of personal bereavement people were feeling. As chapter 9 illustrates, this undoubtedly had a profound impact on popular perceptions, which were overwhelmingly in agreement in assuming that the mourning masses were in deep, intense, tearful grief. But as this and the following chapter demonstrates, this was a false perception. By briefly exploring popular reactions during the week, it outlines a lived experience of the mourning that was very different from that widely conveyed through the media, even at the traditional high points of 'grief' following the news and during the funeral.

Chapter 2 noted how in terms of the *nature* of the reaction, the media focus on those who were deeply upset ignores repeated evidence from numerous mourning sites that the overwhelming reaction of most people there was one of quiet, subdued sadness. There were as proportionately few people breaking down in tears as there were as many journalists focusing on them. Polls reported that a sizeable quarter of the nation felt 'very upset' after the news, which, even assuming its accuracy, carried the obvious implication that 75 per cent were not conforming to the widely emphasized response. Meanwhile 44 per cent of the population did not even watch the funeral, and the motives of those who did, as we shall see, were frequently less than reverential.

Initial Reactions

Initial reactions to the news varied widely. Certainly there were a number of striking examples in which people, usually women, compared their reaction to one of deep loss and personal bereavement. One 53-year-old woman on holiday in Cyprus recalled her feelings when she was told the news by a stranger. 'I felt like hitting her. I felt as though she was telling me that somebody in my family had died . . . That day and the rest of my holiday was spoilt. All I wanted to do was come home.' Others, too, made the same comparisons:

> Like a lot of people I felt that I had lost a close member of my family.

> I have felt more upset by the Princess's death than that of my father or either of my husband's parents.

> I was surprised at how I was feeling as the day went on – almost as if there had been a death in the family.[1]

Far stronger, however, within this collective response were feelings of shock, sadness but *not* personal loss, as sympathy for 'the boys' was mixed with indifference, lack of interest and occasionally worse:

> It began to dawn on me what she meant. But sitting on the stairs in my sister's house . . . at 7.35 a.m. I couldn't muster up much of a reaction beyond a kind of 'gosh, how terrible, isn't life so strange, well dear oh dear' and the like.

> It's always sad to hear of a violent, painful end to a fit young princess but my feelings for sorrow weren't for her . . . As a mother, my thoughts were for her sons. When my husband got up I told him and he said, 'What a pity – does that mean *Countryfile* has been scrapped again'. By 8 a.m. I'd heard what little news there was at that point for about the 10th time. By 10 a.m. I'd reached saturation point and was sick of the hushed tones and cliched rubbish that the 'experts' were coming out with, so I turned the sound down and had a good blast of 'Prodigy' instead. When my 17-year-old son got up about 11 a.m. and was raiding the fridge for the first meal of the day, I told him what had happened. His reaction was 'So what – where's lunch – does that mean the football's off?'

> My husband brought me a cup of tea and said 'There's been some bad news, some very, *very* bad news'. I was filled with trepidation – I don't know what I expected – possibly some awful outbreak of war with far reaching consequences – so when I discovered what he meant I was relieved.

> My first thoughts were: A drunken car crash, closely followed by 'Who cares?'[2]

Meanwhile one man was told by a friend heavily into dance music of how 'a local pirate dance station had been playing a track by Coldcut based around a sample from the Wizard of Oz, "Ding Dong the witch is dead" ', with the DJ 'shouting the odds about Diana' over the top. But a less expected source of subcultural resistance came from one retired librarian in Purley who, breaking all stereotypes, revealed, 'Whoopee! Was my first uncensored reaction'.[3] A rather more widespread sentiment after the news and during the week – more widespread than grief – was interest and fascination in conspiracy theories. One woman recalled an instinctive response: 'First I thought I'd misheard and then "poor sad girl" and then "those poor boys have lost their touch of normal life" . . . and then incredibly "Who killed her?"' One common initial sentiment was: 'Well, that solves a lot of problems for the royal family', illustrating one source of such stories.[4] Others included Diana's unconventional relationship with the Muslim son of a highly controversial figure blackballed by the establishment, a failure of the mundane circumstances of death to be proportionate to her 'importance', as well as the specific circumstances of the crash. This gave more than enough fuel, if it was necessary, to a conspiracy culture mode of understanding the world that has became increasingly popularized in recent years (Knight 2000: Birchall 1999). As one woman suggested on 4 September:

> The initial reports of the accident are quite contradictory and the way the media are concentrating on the newspaper photographers rather than the driver is strange. Also how did a man so drunk (as the driver was supposed to be) even get to be allowed to drive. People are saying that this could be Denver (i.e. Kennedy) all over again.

Less than two weeks later, as further support for this story emerged, she had no doubts: 'Personally I am sure the "accident" was caused by some British agency who did not want Diana to marry Dodi al Fayed . . . Can you imagine the mother of the King of England being a Muslim?'[5]

Media Coverage

None of this provides much support for the images of a nation united in grief, far less for one in deep collective emotion on hearing the news. As the day went on, media coverage generated some varied, sometimes polarized, reactions. One woman greeted her daughter with the words: 'Bloody cowing rotten lousy stinking bloody lousy Princess bloody cowing sodding Diana's dead and they've took everything off for the cow.'[6] Others, however, had nothing but praise for coverage which 'throughout the week was excellent' and which they found it 'very difficult to move away from'.[7] Often a complex combination of the two sentiments was visible as initial fascination – although not necessarily sadness – over the news was quickly followed by boredom with a story in which there was little more to say. One man recalled:

> I got up, put on a dressing gown, woke another friend who had stayed overnight in the guestroom with the news and went and put the kettle on. We sat around having breakfast, drinking tea and watching the story unfold on TV. Mid morning as the news sank in the pair of us discussed the tragedy, our feelings turned to the Princes – we had no strong feelings for Diana but felt sorry for them . . . we continued to watch with a morbid curiosity to find out more of what happened in Paris . . . My friend left at about 11.00 am and I switched the TV off feeling that I had heard enough and the story was just being spun out by the media. I went to my parents for a full family lunch and we discussed the shock and latest analysis . . . There was a feeling that the media were beginning to whip up the story too much.

Or as one woman, citing a newspaper letter of complaint about the 'constant updating', pointed out: 'She was dead in the morning and remained dead in the afternoon.'[8] Such sentiments sometimes extended to all shades of opinion. One man from Bristol was full of admiration for Diana's genuine charity efforts, signed the book of condolences, sent a letter to Prince Charles and would have gone to London to pay his respects on the day of the funeral had he not been away abroad on holiday. But he also praised *Private Eye* as 'one of the few publications to retain a sense of proportion in the orgy of mourning'. Quickly losing patience by noon on the day of the news, he had phoned the BBC to complain that there was 'no excuse' for dropping everything in favour of coverage that 'apart from being obvious and hagiographical, simply covered all the channels'.[9]

His complaint was given short shrift, but such was the accompanying volume from other disaffected viewers that by 3 p.m. the BBC had been forced to resume normal programmes on BBC 2 and abandon its plan to combine both channels in mourning throughout the day (Lawson 1997a). Those who were upset considered, albeit somewhat defensively, that such marathon-style coverage was fully appropriate during the day and across the week. One woman who conceded that the press went 'over the top', argued: 'I for one needed the media coverage over-load to satisfy my response to it all.'[10] Despite its earlier concession, BBC 1 reflected such sentiments as it stayed resolutely in mourning mode all night, broadcasting several Diana-tributes as well as news programmes, before its coverage ended at 12.30 p.m. But increasingly as the day turned into evening, Diana fatigue became the dominant mood in the nation. There was surprise within the industry that BBC 1's viewing figures for the evening had not been higher, with its audiences of 4.2–4.7 million – 18 per cent of those watching television – being half the number that had tuned into the channel the same Sunday the previous year. Meanwhile ITV attracted a massive 14 million – 58 per cent of the audience – when their normal entertainment coverage was resumed at 7.30 with the *Coronation Street* soap opera, followed by the drama *Heartbeat*. By this stage three times as many people were more interested in following the goings on at the 'Rovers Return' than in mourning or even watching about Diana, while even a BBC 2 repeat episode of Michael Palin's *Full Circle* travel programme drew more viewers.[11]

In the face of a media that showed little reflection of such attitudes, the level of complaints continued and intensified over the week. Some people continued to feel that the television coverage was not only suitable but functioned as a 'comforter' that linked them with the mourning crowds:

> The great shawl of grieving muffled all of the days. I tried to watch the T.V. channels showing normal programmes but it was impossible, I just had to go back to the crowds on T.V. and join with them all . . . I found a degree of comfort in that. When you live alone, there is no one to turn to and exclaim.[12]

Others, however, increasingly complained that coverage was 'totally over the top' and 'hyped up . . . out of all proportion to its significance'.[13] One woman had found the day of the 'rolling news' on the day of Diana's death to be 'pretty daft . . . intensely boring and rather pointless as there wasn't anything to report'. But:

> What was even worse was the fact that it just went on, and on, and on . . . for several days. I started to get a phobia that maybe other celebrities, royal people or famous politicians would start dying and that all we would get on British TV for two years would be 'rolling news' of their death, interrupted only by sanitised programmes such as gardening programmes or A Question of Sport repeated from 15 years ago.

Or as another woman put it: 'One dreadful thought was expressed by one contributor – now that Diana is dead the most well-known famous woman in the world is Mrs Thatcher – help!!!'[14] Perhaps the most consistent complaint was the failure of media coverage, either during the day or subsequently, to offer an alternative to those who did not want to watch or read about the event. And complaints over the volume of coverage were allied, as we have seen, to increasing hostility to its tone across all media. By the day of the funeral one man had become increasingly exasperated:

The nation has been subjected, systematically, to a continuous barrage of sanctimonious, grovelling, posthumous admiration of the late – and my view unremarkable – Princess of Wales, the like of which I have never experienced before and have no wish to experience again. It has come from all sides of the national press and not just from the tabloids, as might have been expected . . . And most of the television programmes were just as bad, devoting hour and hour to discussions, tributes and potted histories of Diana . . . It was as if there was nothing else happening in the rest of the world. If a stray asteroid had wiped Australia off the face of the Earth, it might, just, have made page 14 of the Times or Telegraph and may have got a mention at the end of a specially extended edition of the nine o'clock news.[15]

Such a response is again nothing new, judging from complaints about the cancellations of radio coverage in the aftermath of the death of George VI and the insertion of only 'suitable' programmes. As one woman complained: 'I think the BBC disgraceful – too much of it . . . all this doom and gloom . . . it's all been overdone.'[16] It is also consistent with the BFI's survey of reactions to television coverage, which found that on the day of the news 47 per cent found the coverage justified, while just over half were unhappy with it, with 20 per cent being deeply critical. In the days that followed there was a further sharp increase in dissatisfaction, with 40 per cent being deeply critical and overall 60 per cent being less than happy (Turnock 2000).

People were of course powerless to alter the dominant media and social mood of mourning. But one of the most oppositional challenges to it came in the widespread circulation of sick jokes. Christie Davies, an expert in this field, points out that they are 'truly people's humour' (1999: 254), invented in large numbers by ordinary people and circulated by word of mouth, aided in the modern era by the telephone, e-mail and internet joke sites. They begin as witticisms that occur spontaneously in conversation, which are then passed on, polished and eventually sharpened into self-standing jokes, while some are recycled from previous waves of similar humour. Such jokes owe nothing to mass media coverage that would not dare even to refer to them for fear of offence or condemnation. A full seven months after Diana's death one journalist was refusing to repeat any even in an article devoted to the subject on the grounds that that 'it would be folly . . . when journalists have received hate mail for even suggesting that maybe the People's Grief was a little over the top' (Gunnell 1998). The radical comedian Mark Thomas was to recall that the strength of this pressure during the mourning even within local public arenas produced what he considered to be unprecedented censorship of performances from above:

To talk about Diana on the week that she died was to invite physical threat. Just the mention of it would immediately divide an audience. There were comics who had censorship directly imposed on them by the club owners. There's a chain of clubs owned by Jongleurs and they phoned up the performers and said: 'We've had people . . . saying they won't come if there's going to be jokes about Diana so will you please not do it. (Hitchens 1998)

In private, however, such jokes were much more widespread. One man noted how they were circulating in his work by the Tuesday of the death and were, he was anxious to assert, 'the voices of regular, ordinary folk in Edinburgh at the time'.[17] Others too attached similar jokes that they had come across, a selection of which included:

What's the difference between a Mercedes and a Lada?
Princess Diana wouldn't be seen dead in a Lada.

Diana really died of a drugs overdose – Speed and Smack.

I'm fed up with hearing about Diana on the radio – and on the dashboard – and on the windscreen.

What did the French mortuary assistant say as he unzipped the body bag?
Zippady Dodi, Zippady Di.

Not only was the driver drunk, so was Diana. She'd got three pints of Carling inside her.

What's the difference between George Best and Dodi's chauffeur?
George Best can still take corners when he's pissed.

Why did Elton John sing at the funeral?
Because he's the only Queen who gives a fuck.

Prince Charles was out the other day walking the dog. When a passer by said 'morning', Charles said, 'No, just walking the dog'.

While 'sick' humour has an age-old pedigree, the development of contemporary jokes about disasters experienced indirectly has been a new and constant feature only in recent decades – there were no recorded jokes following the *Titanic* disaster, for example. Davies suggests that they are directly attributable to the rise of television, and provoked by the incongruity of coverage that, amid its focus on trivialities, insists on telling people how sad they must feel for someone they never knew and whose death they never witnessed. In Diana's case such jokes, far from being merely 'sick', are significant in the way their content directly counters the dominant mourning mood by mocking her lavish lifestyle, conflict with the royals, circumstances of her death and the reaction that followed. In this they 'are not really shocking at all for they indicate a sense of proportion' (C. Davies 1999: 264) and an oppositional comment against an 'over the top' reaction. One younger man who had no time for the mourning of Diana or Mother Teresa, 'another flawed saint . . . who had met Diana in a bout of mutual admiration', registered his hostility to their double-sanctification by ending his account with the following story:

> Mother Teresa dies and goes to heaven. Peter greets her as the most virtuous member of the heavenly host, and gives her a halo which he swears is the largest to be found in heaven. While walking around the place during the first week, Teresa bumps into Diana a couple of times and cannot fail to notice that Diana's halo is in fact bigger than her own. She returns to Peter and seeks an explanation. 'Oh, don't worry about that', says Peter, 'that's a steering wheel not a halo.'[18]

To emphasize this oppositional response is not to ignore the other side of reactions. One woman went to her local town hall on the Thursday after the news. When she arrived at 9.15 a.m. there were five people in the queue ahead and by the time she left there were over twenty. She wrote in her tribute, 'Diana brought a special radiance to the world. Her care and compassion for the unfortunate in our society is an example to us all', and leaving the town hall she headed straight for the parish church which she attended occasionally to say a prayer in times of deep stress. At the back an area had been set aside for people to light candles and place flowers in front of a photo of Diana and her boys. She wrote a message on a card, tears streaming down her face, to place, among many others, on a prayer board at the front.[19]

Meanwhile, despite the less than positive attitudes to media coverage, people did not as a rule switch off the television or stop buying the newspapers. Consumption of news and current affairs more than doubled during the week (BSC 1998), the funeral gained a record television audience and there was an increase in all newspaper sales during the week, which was proportionately strongest among the broadsheets (Greenslade 1997). One obvious reason was the massive interest in the news itself of a woman who, whatever she did in life, was one of the few guaranteed circulation-builders across all media. But another reason was that, while the perceived popular and media reaction alienated people, it also fascinated them. After 'a brief reaction of disbelief but not upset', one 33-year-old woman went shopping to her local supermarket in Oxford where she estimated that 'disbelief was the overriding initial emotion':

> After we got back I turned the TV on – I can be a bit of a news junkie – and found it very hard to turn it off that day and the next few days. This was not just a Diana thing. I am the same over any major event. I also watched the funeral. However, overall I found the almost continuous coverage very claustrophobic and far too much. I also thought that the mass emotional hysteria (national grief) rather over the top and a bit silly.[20]

Again in common with patterns of behaviour at previous royal events (Jennings and Madge 1937; Ziegler 1978), people found themselves drawn in despite themselves. One man who believed that 'Diana's lifestyle killed her' was subsequently 'appalled at the public's response' and the 'rankest hypocrisy' of media coverage. But he also recalled: 'As the week developed I was mesmerised by the reportage, even while it made me squirm with embarrassment. I felt compelled to watch it as a rabbit watches a snake.' The reason for this, suggested another man, was due to the 'cliff-hanging serial drama' of the week. His attitude, and that of a fellow male respondent, well captures the ambivalent as well as less than grief-stricken motivations behind news consumption:

> My information from the media was like drip feed, but I was increasingly aware of the way in which the media was revelling in the hysteria and almost feeding itself with its own emotive variations of the last hours of Diana's life . . . I became more interested in the public's response than the event and the funeral preparations – I felt no strong feelings for Diana – someone who I had never met and whom I felt I had little in common with. By Friday, hagiography ruled and I recall catching some recent images of her landmine visits being played out with some sentimentally-slushy, heartstring-pulling music. All a bit too much for me!

> I was repelled rather than impressed by the amount of press coverage devoted (an apt word, perhaps) to the death . . . My first intention was to avoid most of the television and other media coverage . . . As the days passed, however, I began to develop more curiosity about what was happening and to feel the need to learn about it although I found much of the 'expert' comment and pontificating irritating and tedious, to be avoided as far as possible.[21]

All this suggests that mourning Diana was only one element within a popular experience during the week that differed markedly from the story of how 'the people' were reacting. Indeed as Alvin Cohan (1999) notes, during the week most public spaces remained curiously ordinary for a population supposedly all feeling bereaved, with people going about their work and social lives as usual. In cafés customers were laughing and talking as normal rather than prostrate with grief. Leaving London in the early hours of Saturday morning, he was struck by the numbers of people on the streets. At first he thought they were mourners arriving early for the funeral. Then he realized that they were people leaving various clubs along the route, mildly intoxicated or high on drugs, engaged in normal routines and occupying 'fun spaces' not 'mourning spaces'. When people wanted to grieve they had to go to particular mourning spaces to do so precisely because most of the country, for most of the week, was simply not a mourning space.

Of course that does not mean that people were not interested in what was going on within these mourning spaces, but most people were outside looking on rather than inside them. Indeed, even some of those who physically occupied mourning spaces, saw themselves as emotionally outside them, as they went to see 'the public reaction' rather than join it.

The Funeral

Even when the country was most unequivocally a mourning space on the day of the funeral, the popular reaction was very far from being united in any type of grief. Again most people watched from the home, where their motives were diverse, complex and multiple. There were certainly sadness and tears:

> On the day of the funeral I couldn't wait to get it over with, almost as though she was some close relative . . . The TV went on very early and my husband and I sat there all morning . . . It was draining.

> The funeral was very personal and extremely moving. We were sniffing all the way through and when . . . Earl Spencer gave his heartfelt tribute . . . we were sobbing. I felt totally exhausted. A week of such intense emotions is very tiring.[22]

But this reaction mingled with a desire to witness a historic occasion (see also chapter 6) or watch the entertainment, with Elton John's performance and Earl Spencer's famous 'blood family' speech both generating much comment, albeit from a variety of different angles. And certainly the fascination with the event peaked during a funeral that was watched or listened to by many of those who had strongly complained about the earlier coverage or declared themselves unmoved or hostile during the week. Some of those who had been dry-eyed over the week and utterly contemptuous of the perceived public reaction managed to shed the occasional tear while still, for the most part, retaining their earlier attitude. The fine line between grief and enjoying the Hollywood-style tear-jerking melodrama of the funeral (see also Turnock 2000; Maio and Esses 2001) was captured by one woman who had little time for the public grief:

> The funeral itself was very moving. A great film director couldn't have orchestrated it better – the touches of drama such as the crying women outside Kensington Palace, the lone piper, shots of a mute crowd. Tony Blair read a passage that was well known, but in such a way that I felt I had never heard it before (though I did wonder quite what he was doing there). Elton John finished me off and I just cried through the rest of it. Why? I don't know?[23]

Similarly one woman had been very hostile to the 'sanctimonious twaddle and extemporising' during the week but found herself glued to the funeral because she 'always liked to watch events in London' and was 'impressed at the precision of the whole event, put together at such short notice. There was also another motive for her enjoyment as at the store that she worked: 'All staff employed before 9 a.m. were to turn up and prepare the store for trading, but would be able to leave at 9 a.m. and return at 11.45 – on full pay! Good on you, Di!' Similar enjoyment was reported by others – to update Byron – in the public spectacle of a celebrity gladiator 'butchered to make a Roman holiday' (*Webster's Dictionary* 1965: 773; Turnock 2000) in the media amphitheatre:

> The slow gathering of the congregation, with its mixture of royalty, the political establishment and show-business had something of the air of a Royal command performance or an even more popular entertainment event. Who was it under that wide-brimmed hat, or stuffed into an unfamiliar suit? Who was going to sit next to her? Cherie Blair defiantly hatless. Good for her!

> My mother and I watched the funeral on TV not so much due to our own mourning . . . but out of curiosity to see the public reaction and how a state funeral was done.

> The only thing that surprised me about myself was that I watched the funeral . . . and was glued to the TV all day. It was magnificently done and fascinating TV. I suppose that's why. I still feel nothing.[24]

For others even the way they watched, much less their emotional engagement was decidedly partial:

I watched the funeral service on TV, not because I had any real interest, but because there wasn't anything else worth watching, and I thought I had some small duty to witness an historical event. The commentary was inane.

Saturday September 6. We thought of fleeing to our beach chalet in Whitby for the day, but it's too chilly. All day we dip in and out of the TV coverage.

My wife took the ironing into the sitting room in order to watch the Abbey service, which I could hear from the room next door. Once Verdi's 'Libera me domine' commenced, I had to go and watch and was absolutely enthralled by Lynne Dawson's singing . . . I wandered away before the end and came back in the middle of Earl Spencer's address, in time to hear him make his very courageous and heartfelt criticism, to be followed by amazement when the congregation applauded. Had anything like this happened before? Here was something to stir-up feelings and be talked about. The next hour was tedious in the extreme and I could hear the BBC commentator from the room next door describing the cortège passing Finchley station. How trivial can one get?[25]

And while a record 32 million people watched the funeral, at least in some way or another, nearly 25 million did not do so. Given that the relentless media and social pressure and mass cancellation of all public social and media events made it almost more difficult *not* to watch, the fact that 44 per cent of the nation failed to do so is almost as striking as the record numbers that did. One man who had recently moved decided to make use of the time by phoning round friends to pass on their new number, but discovered that many people were out, with a quiet walk, some chores around the house or a long lie-in being the favoured means of escape. One woman reported on her family's day:

My husband and I went for a long walk that morning and arrived back in time for the shops opening at 2 p.m. My sister went out for the whole day, one of my sons stayed in bed all morning, one watched the funeral intermittently while doing the ironing and the other one was lucky enough to be abroad at the time.

And for all the deviants that cared, there were those who were quite proud to admit that they did not:

Another friend had been playing in a pub gig in Birmingham with his punk band the previous night. They woke up in the promoter's tower block flat on the outskirts of town and had gone in search of a lunchtime aperitif. The local off-licence, the only one on the estate, was shut for the funeral . . . They could see the staff inside, sitting watching the TV. They stood outside in their mohicans and leathers, knocking on the door and making impassioned appeals to the licensee's better nature; 'Can't you see there are thirsty punks out here?' but to no avail.[26]

On the other side we might plausibly assume that the several million who went to London to attend the funeral on the Saturday would represent the pinnacle of the national grief, the sizeable minority of the population who told the pollsters that they were indeed 'very upset'. But even this is highly questionable. Alongside some of the motivations above, the desire to be 'part of history' and a collective experience, as much as personal grief, was also a strong motive for those who wanted to visit mourning sites or attend the funeral (see chapter 6). During the week there were so many tourists present that the police created photography-only queues (McKibbin 1998), and this attraction peaked with the funeral. And while there was sadness, there was also plenty of singing and humour (Evans 1997; Engel 1997). 'If you don't have a laugh what's the point in coming', said one youngish cockney man there with two friends as he began what the media called 'the vigil' with the aid of a few cans of lager. 'Two o'clock and all is we-eel, bring out your . . .', he shouted laughingly as Big Ben struck two in the morning (*The Princess's People* 1998). There were even some complaints about fighting, as well as conflicts within the crowds between those who had camped out to get a good view and others who had tried to gatecrash later. One distressed 70-year-old woman had to be rescued by the police as she tried to get to the front and people responded by hitting her with umbrellas (*Sunday Times*, 6 September 1997). 'It was like war in there', recalled one woman in her thirties: 'all you read about is Britain coming together in grief but this was more like a media circus, it was ugly.'

More generally, others conceded that they, to quote one, 'came more for the experience'. 'I never really thought much about Diana when she was alive . . . her death didn't really upset me', one youngish man admitted. He suggested, looking around him at people laughing and chattering seemingly quite happily just before the start of the funeral: 'It seems as if they're really enjoying the occasion for what it is almost. I wouldn't really have expected them to be as cheerful as this' (*The Princess's People* 1998). Others later complained after the funeral that there were large numbers who were not watching but just taking countless pictures with their cameras. 'That's the only problem. All the arms kept going up', complained one man of his desire to capture the funeral on camera. 'Everyone wants to do the same thing. You just have to hold your camera up . . . I just clicked away', agreed his wife who now, with her aching feet, was 'looking forward to a good lager tonight' (*The Princess's People* 1998). 'It's as if they're here for a celebrity show', one person recalled as the crowds applauded and wolf-whistled the famous mourners arriving (Evans 1997). Indeed the crowds seemed keen to applaud almost everything. Cheers greeted two lorryloads of workmen as they feverishly chopped down traffic lights to open up the approach to the Abbey, to be followed by applause for the Westminster council workman who, cigarette dangling from his lips, hoovered up the mess left (*Sunday Times*, 6 September 1997). A policewoman's horse that urinated on the Mall was greeted with much hilarity as the crowds struggled to avoid the oncoming stream of liquid (*The Princess's People* 1998). This at times light-hearted atmosphere should not be a cause for much surprise, based on past royal experiences. Ziegler found that the mood of the crowd following George VI's funeral was 'curiously similar' (1978: 94) to that during the royal wedding a few years earlier, with similar passionate preoccupations with what might pass the time and the arrival of the dustmen during the funeral causing much merriment.

All this suggests a popular reaction that defies easy generalization, but certainly showed little correlation to how the media were saying people reacted. It would be wrong to overlook the sadness that was also certainly felt by some during the week (although it would be equally wrong to overstate its extent). People joined the queues, attended or watched the funeral for different and often plural reasons. To be a tourist, seeker of a historical experience or even a voyeur one minute does not automatically rule out being a mourner the next (Walter 1999a). But whether this can actually be equated with a mass reaction of grief is highly questionable. Walter argues that it can, suggesting that, while most people were 'not left with an empty bed, with nobody to hold them, with one less at the dinner table, or with nobody to bring in the bread, but that doesn't mean that for a few days they did not grieve' (Walter 1999a: 34). One small-scale study also found significant psychological distress among its sample, although whether this constituted grief or merely shock or dismay, and precisely what stimulated it, was not clear (Shevlin et al. 1999). Turnock also found that 40 per cent of the BFI audience registered feelings of shock, disbelief and distress, responses that he suggests should be taken seriously but may not have been 'specifically grief but another kind of emotional or psychological response' (2000: 35). For as some of the comments above illustrate, to feel shock and surprise are very different emotions from feeling grief as popularly defined in contemporary Britain, and the vast majority of the population – even the vast majority of mourners – simply did not see themselves as grief-stricken in the way that was continually emphasized. The following chapter explores this point further, and demonstrates how the population was quite literally divided over issues of grief and mourning.

ജാജ

5

Divided in Grief

This chapter explores several ways in which Diana's death produced a population deeply divided across cultures of grief. It first examines how Diana provoked feelings of loss in a minority of the population who saw her as a friend, or almost a friend, but also demonstrates how a large majority were alienated and puzzled by the intense 'public grief' for a stranger. Secondly, it demonstrates how her death provided dramatic focus for a sharp clash in precisely how people publicly grieve in contemporary Britain between 'stiff upper-lippers' and touchy-feely expressivists. Thirdly, it illustrates how the re-emergence of a highly authoritarian communal mourning that demanded that everyone should grieve clashed with the dominant, liberal tradition of grief which states that life goes on for all but those personally affected. Taken together they combined to leave a population largely united against the idea of grief for a stranger, while even if people did feel what they defined as grief, the type of reaction widely on display was often not something with which they could unproblematically identify.

A Grieving Matter?

As we saw in the previous chapter, for some Diana's death did stimulate an emotional reaction of deep distress which on occasion they compared with the pain of personal bereavement. Obviously the identifications some people made with Diana's life help explain these feelings, as did the shock of her death or feelings of their own mortality. Even for those with no admiration, the news sometimes triggered past grief. One 47-year-old woman, who was largely distanced from the 'false' sorrow on display, the media hagiography and the 'nauseating' press attacks on the royals, recalled the impact of the news:

Time may heal but it doesn't erase the memories and at the very word 'crash' I am catapulted thirty years back. I am talking to my boyfriend's sister and she is telling me that a lorry pulled out in front of her car on a stormy night and there was nothing he could do. I need to go to church this morning, in part to pray for the victims of today's terrible accident, partly to be somewhere quiet to reflect on the shadows rising from the memories of long ago.

Underlying much of the reaction of sadness, however, was a feeling of personal loss. As one woman noted: 'What you hear again and again, both on the media and first-hand is how people felt that they knew Princess Diana – "she was my friend".'[1] Such feelings can be traced to the way the contemporary mass media has shrunk the world into a global village, producing what media theorists describe as a new form of social 'relationship', in which people achieve 'intimacy at a distance' with famous people. This process, long since identified by psychologists as parasocial interaction (Giles 2002; Myers 2000), can affect people in similar ways to normal friendships and the relationship can develop as people get to know more about their celebrity 'friends'. This is heightened by the way, as Richard Dyer (1986) notes in his pioneering analysis, that the whole media construction of stars encourages us to think in terms of what they are 'really' like'. Celebrities have both public and private personae and increasingly the two are blurred if not obliterated, as the private lives of stars stimulate as much if not more interest from a media and public anxious to uncover the real person behind the image. Even the very mode of coverage of celebrities offers a taken-for-granted, first name, even nickname familiarity with Di, Charles, Camilla, Dodi and the rest that encourages viewing through this lens of intimacy. Diana's life and death offered the supreme embodiment of this process, as her public stardom increased in direct proportion to knowledge of her private persona (Lumby 1999: 91–2).

Certainly the reaction to Diana's death illustrated that some people did see her as just a friend, or almost like a friend. In a poll in March 1998, 28 per cent of people agreed with the statement, 'on hearing of Diana's death, I felt I had lost a close personal friend'. Similarly in September 1998, 14 per cent 'strongly agreed' with this statement, while 12 per cent 'tended to agree' (MORI 1998a/b). Even taking into account polling exaggerations, this suggests a sizeable minority of perhaps around 10–20 per cent felt at least some sense of personal bereavement. Partly this relates to Diana's ordinary/extraordinary appeal (see chapter 1), partly to the way people, especially women (see chapter 7), not only liked Diana but could identify, in a variety of different ways, with her life and/or death. Thirdly, the strength of a parasocial relationship is likely to increase the more we come to know a person. In Diana's case, we knew more about her life than about most of our friends, much less our neighbours. For seventeen years, information about what 'the first lady of the global village' (Appleyard 1997) was 'really' like had been relentlessly conveyed across all media, so that by 1997 it would have been virtually impossible for someone living in Britain not to know anything about Diana's life. The absurdity of this point illustrates the ubiquitous nature of knowledge about her, which meant that there was no M-O respondent unwilling to attribute personal characteristics to her. Only one man stood out memorably when he sought to explain that as he did not know the princess, he had no right to use her first name without qualification. Another man noted this process:

> It's a strange world but in this world of instant media coverage, it's like you are living things more as they happen . . . I'm not for a moment saying that there was not a real and great sense of loss. I felt that myself but I think that the reason why so many people that I have spoken to feel that was again to do with the media. They made Diana, the images that we all saw. We saw her image so often in so many forms and mediums that it's like we knew her personally and that's why our sense of loss was so great.

Another woman illustrated the point inversely when she contrasted her deep sadness over the death of Diana with her inability to mourn the death of Dodi. 'I never knew him or his qualities', she explained.[2] This intimate sense of personal knowledge is further helped by the way the story of Diana and the royals functioned as a long-running soap opera, and on another, perhaps deeper level, how the royal family are seen to represent the family (see chapter 7). Yet to compare Diana's life with that of a soap opera is hardly to do justice to the level of intimacy she could stimulate. For this was real life and death, not fiction, and popular experience of Diana, while primarily mediated, was not fully. All but a couple of respondents had never met her, but there was always the possibility of this – while others had seen or met members of her erstwhile family. And much of Diana's publicity in life, and even more in death, featured her contact, 'friendships' and down-to-earth common touch with ordinary people. All this encouraged the idea of Diana as a friend and provoked some of the feelings of sadness that were visible on her death.

But the bottom line was that, in the end, Diana remained a stranger, not a friend in a reciprocal relationship. 'It's like we knew her person-ally', said one man above, rather than 'we knew her personally'. One of the above polls also found that 70 per cent of people disagreed with the proposition that they felt they had lost a personal friend. The other found that 37 per cent 'strongly opposed' this proposition, over two and a half times the number who had 'strongly agreed' with it, while another 30 per cent 'tended to oppose', again over three times the number who 'tended to support' (MORI 1998a/b). This reflects a common sense view that, if our friendships with stars are not real, then neither is our grief. As one of the above writers added: 'It's odd. They have never met her.' This point was regularly made by mourners as they puzzled over their grief 'for a stranger' – 'There's no logic in it. I didn't know Diana', noted one – as well as more contemptuously by others who thought they should 'get a life'.[3]

More specifically, such comments illustrated the deviance of mourners from a cultural assumption that grief, for it to be genuine, has to be personally experienced. In twentieth-century Britain grief and mourning behaviour had been privatized. Older traditions of socially required mourning where everyone is expected to grieve regardless of closeness to the bereaved have gradually been replaced by a situation in which the real grievers are those personally affected. As Greg Myers (2000) notes in an insightful article, when someone dies there is a sliding scale of how upset people are *entitled* to be, based on if, or how well, they knew them. So if Person A dies, conventions of grief dictate that their friend B is entitled to be upset. But Person C, who is a friend of B but hardly knows A, is not allowed to be grief-stricken and their role is a secondary one, confined to supporting those really bereaved like B.

This rationale formed the basis of sceptical analyses that this mass grief for Diana, whom few mourners had even met, much less 'knew', was not real grief but 'grief with the pain removed, grief-lite', which produced an enjoyable 'warm glow' instead of the 'searing stomach-twisting agony' associated with bereavement (Jack 1997; Aitkenhead 1997). Similar criticism of 'virtual grief', an inauthentic, tear-drenched celebrity-obsessed voyeurism had also been made of the public mourning which followed John F. Kennedy's death (Kitch 2001). Support for this has also been found in empirical research which suggested that those most upset after Diana's death were those who actively sought out and embraced emotional experiences more generally, finding them satisfying and enjoyable, rather than feelings to be avoided (Maio and Esses 2001). On another level it also relates to the argument that we have entered a post-emotional era (Mestrovic 1997), in which mass-produced, McDonaldized emotions rather than real ones are routinely stimulated by the culture industry around death and suffering, a culture that has massively expanded in recent years (Berridge 2001).

The week after, *Guardian* cartoonist Steve Bell mocked mourners in a strip featuring a family of penguins trying to calm down one of their distraught members after she had tried to leave some fish at a mourning site but had been sent away by a policeman:

> Prudence – come down. This keening on top of the wardrobe has got to stop! . . . We know you feel bad – but remember – this isn't real – this is phantom grief . . . You didn't know her. She didn't know you. She was too tall to be a penguin and too rich to live in Peckham. (*Guardian* 11 September 1997)

His satire hits precisely on the common-sense view that people felt was central to explaining their disengaged reaction. As one man suggested about the non-mourning views he came across:

> The underlying basis of 'the alternative view' is that while naturally, it is very sad when a young woman is killed, the more so if she leaves young children . . . Di was not a personal friend and it would be hypocritical to pretend to be personally affected by her death more than by that of any other celebrity known only through the media.

Others agreed, whether they felt sympathy and sadness or not, that not knowing Diana was a fundamental barrier to mourning her. As one young woman put it: 'I at least couldn't really mourn for someone I didn't know. It would have been a challenge to the nature of mourning and grief.'[4] And while Diana's death acted as a 'trigger' for some who grieved past personal losses, among others there was a strong resentment at the equation of the two very different experiences. Letters and newspaper profiles following the funeral featured recently bereaved individuals angry at the equation of personal, *real* grief with the false grief for Diana (Knowsley 1997). Elizabeth Stern, a London student, had lost her parents in a car crash in Florida months earlier. It took two and a half weeks (not six hours as was the case with Diana) for their bodies to be flown back. She angrily denounced the mourners as 'vastly deluded' if they believed themselves to be grieving as much as they would for members of their own family, in feelings that were echoed more widely. As two men put it:

> I resented being told, over and over, that I was in mourning. My mother and a close friend have died in the last couple of years. I know what mourning is. As for Diana, I never knew the silly woman.

> Diana . . . died a week or two after my wife – an event which taught me how acute the pains of grief are. That is the pain of losing somebody close whose departure leaves one – or has left me – intensely sad, more so than ever before experienced. There seems little point in going on, nights are disturbed and the sight of some article brings vividly to

mind a memory and a rekindled sense of utter loneliness . . . Can it be, I now ask, that the national – even international grief – brought about by the death of Diana be anything comparable to the personal grief felt by most of us sooner or later? . . . a mass outpouring of grief for some person that 99% of the population never saw is to be deplored for it is not true grief, a strictly personal matter best eased in private helped by a few proven friends.[5]

The extension of this rationale determined that the public were simply not entitled to be upset in the way those personally affected were.

The most moving part [of the funeral] was the eulogy by Earl Spencer – I felt it was more meaningful to me because he had a right to be bitter and angry and mourn the loss of his sister. That was a genuine grief to me, not the outpourings of Betty from Bradford who had been poring over tittle-tattle the week before.

I have found this [the public reaction] quite bizarre and rather uncomfortable. It seemed to be totally inappropriate to grieve so ostentatiously for someone they had never met briefly or not at all. In addition, I felt it was disrespectful to the Princes and other family to try and equate their grief with public's feelings. How can loss of a public figure compare with death of one's mother at the age of 12 and 15? I know that children of a friend of mine whose father died when they were 12 or 14 found this aspect disturbing.[6]

Far from expecting the royals to conform to the public requirements it was 'after all . . . for *us* to give them sympathy not the other way about'. The criticism left some outraged at 'cruel, spiteful and totally unjustified' behaviour from a public that 'could not recognise genuine stunned shock, disbelief and grief displayed by the royal family but had to have their own melodramatic demonstrations of extreme mourning for a woman they had never known personally'.[7] And even some of those out of sympathy (Pearce 1997) with royalty joined traditionalists in defending their decision to remain with 'the boys', those really bereaved, in Balmoral where they had peace and privacy.

More broadly in terms of the public response, 'the display of uncontrollable weeping and grovelling', as it was perceived, was simply not culturally legitimate as it was 'barely commensurate with the extent of the loss suffered' and even symptomatic of 'a more fundamental emotional imbalance' (letters to the *Guardian*, 3 September 1997). Indeed those who spoke publicly about Diana were well aware of this and actively sought to justify their feelings for a stranger – they had met Diana or 'attended' her wedding, their lives had grown up with her

(Myers 2000). People often couched their feelings in the rhetoric 'I feel just like everyone else', indicating a certain defensive need to assert that their personal feelings were not abnormal. But the fact that Diana was a stranger, coupled with the media impression that most were deeply upset, left them open to the charge that their level of grief was 'excessive', 'over the top', 'and certainly not worth the grief of millions who *did not know her*'.[8] Such a 'truly unnatural . . . ridiculous' reaction left people 'horrified that so many millions of people should have shown such totally exaggerated expressions of grief at her demise'.[9]

This feeling of entitlement was also evident in the distinction sometimes made by observers that they 'could see that people who had actually met her or who had been helped by her would have been deeply upset'. But equally they 'couldn't understand the "ownership" that people seemed to feel for her' who had no connection. The apparently irrational behaviour of people towards someone they never met frequently left many feeling that there was no explanation apart from a mass outbreak of media-induced collective madness. One man reported how his daughter, who worked at a London hospital, told him that the staff there 'joked about the population having "caught a virus", namely mass hysteria'.[10] Others agreed that the event had 'thoroughly unbalanced a section of the population', and that 'the visible public response appeared to verge on psychosis'. Or as one woman argued:

> I found it impossible to comprehend the scale of the emotions which Diana's death seems to have caused. Having suffered three bereavements this year and having a close friend with cancer who is unlikely to survive another 12 months, I find it totally unrealistic to feel that degree of grief for a person I didn't know. I do honestly believe that what happened *was* a case of mass hysteria which was ably fanned by the media.[11]

This attitude more broadly also forms part and parcel of a broader popular common sense ultimately contemptuous of the perceived abnormal, unhealthy or superficial feelings stimulated by our connection with media stars. As one woman argued:

> I mourn for a life ended too soon and so violently. But I cannot get hysterical over it. I did not know the woman. Like the majority of all people, all my information was fed to me by the media and therefore to be taken with a pinch of salt . . . I do feel that we are in danger of losing our sense of proportion, if indeed we haven't already done so. The reaction of many people seems way over the top, bordering on hysteria. This is fuelled by the media, certainly, but it shows a worrying picture of

the way many people now view the world they live in. The majority of these 'mourners' never knew Diana . . . Why are people grieving more for the death of someone they didn't know than for the death of their own family? . . . Is this natural behaviour, or behaviour based on too much Eastenders/ Emmerdale type soap operas, where everything constantly has to happen at such high emotional levels?[12]

Most of us interact with media figures, saying hello to a newsreader or getting embarrassed when a soap star does something stupid. But we simultaneously consider that the feelings stimulated by the media are not real and taken too far are at best symptomatic of social inadequates and, at worst, pathological obsessives. Fan is after all an abbreviation of the word fanatic, and there is a fine line between the two. Popular culture is full of such negative stereotypes (Jensen 1992), and there have been more than enough real-life instances to fuel them, which have seen celebrities stalked, even attacked or killed, by obsessive fans (see also chapter 1).

Such negative characterizations were visible even among those upset in September 1997. One woman, for instance, wrote in an internet tribute that 'as a happy well-adjusted woman, I was stunned by the emotions I felt and of the tears that flowed' – the obvious implication being that it would only be sad, badly adjusted people who could be this upset over the death of a stranger (Giles and Naylor 2000). Others, left 'extremely angry and unutterably depressed by the public reaction', considered that 'so much attention onto one person cannot be anything but extremely unhealthy' and was symptomatic of a 'people who are unable to live their own lives with content'. This verdict was further strengthened as it could quite plausibly be argued that it was precisely the public obsession visible in the mourning that had been responsible for Diana's death:

To my mind it seems that it was exactly the unhealthy obsession with her, almost a 'personality cult', which led to her being hounded by the press in the first place. The more I think about it the more unhealthy it seems.

I think a lot of the country's 'grief' is a little self-indulgent and hypocritical. Surely those masses that left flowers and signed books all bought the tabloid newspapers?[13]

As hinted at above, it would be wrong to attribute such feelings just to those who had no time for the mourning. For what is perhaps most interesting about the responses is that even those who were upset and at times in tears – people who might objectively be described as mourners –

had little time and often much contempt for the excessive mass grief that they perceived to be occurring around them. At the time media coverage ignored the fundamental cultural difference between the levels of grief people were entitled to show to strangers as compared with friends. As one journalist subsequently wrote: 'It was deemed "inappropriate" to ask why so many people were grieving for Diana as if she was a mother, a sister or a wife. Or to wonder why the grief was so disproportionate' (Christy 1997). But beneath the surface some coverage seemed to suggest that there were sensible mourners grieving appropriately and others whose reaction was plain excessive. In the *Guardian* Simon Hoggart (1997) devoted most of an article to welcoming the belated departure of the royals from their 'cold stoicism' to 'join with the rest of us' in grief. But at the same time he could not identify 'with those strange, emotionally deprived people who queued for 11 hours to sign a book of condolence which will never be read by a woman they have never met'. Similarly Nigella Lawson (1997a), while outlining 'why the nation is right to share the family's grief', also believed that 'to snivel too loudly and too publicly . . . would be inappropriate'.

Such distinctions between appropriate and excessive feelings were also found among those who clearly did feel something, but were not prepared to equate their reaction with the levels of grief they imagined mourners to hold – or indeed with the very definition of grief. People talked about sadness and distress but saw this as an emotional reaction distinct and less intense than grief as they defined it. The term was in fact largely notable for its absence in this and other surveys (Turnock 2000), and, in conjunction with the above polling evidence, suggests a population that was largely united *against* the idea of grief for a stranger. It meant that even those who had been 'immensely distressed' on Diana's death, as one woman reported, also 'felt uncomfortable with what was almost hysteria'. As another woman argued:

> Although I too, like so many others feel shock and utter disbelief, I can't understand the weeping and wailing, the emotional outpouring and near hysteria that has issued forth from my fellow countrymen for someone they didn't know . . . I can't believe that my feelings about Diana's death amount to grief. You only feel grief for someone you knew and had strong feelings for. But I do feel terribly sad that such a young life was wasted.[14]

This suggests a subtle but clear operation of appropriate and inappropriate emotions in which the excessive grief of the 'mourning masses' were viewed negatively, even by those whose views were probably not that different. So one woman wrote a tribute to 'a beautiful woman who will always be in our thoughts', but nevertheless considered that 'the whole thing smacked of mass hysteria'. A 35-year-old man was initially unmoved, sad enough after all the media coverage by the Monday to compile a special tribute to Diana, but was then strongly alienated from the public reaction:

> I guess she was one such person who we all felt we knew, we all owned a small piece of her . . . So yes, I did feel sad on Monday. And then on Tuesday. But not after that. After all, I didn't really know her. She was neither friend nor family . . . So the sadness one can feel for someone who is ultimately a stranger is finite. Yet the public grief was astonishing. As the days passed it became worrying . . . I saw some of the testimonies of people and thought 'get a life!' . . . I suspect many of those who got involved were those whose lives were coloured by sadness and loneliness.

Similarly one 45-year-old woman returned from abroad just after the crash to what she called 'a nation in deep mourning', a sentiment she shared – but only to some extent as she recalled: 'I didn't feel sick and distraught like when my sister-in-law died last year, but I did feel a sense of personal bereavement'. But there were limits to her feelings, which in any case she recognized as abnormal. 'If I felt strangely moved by the death of a stranger – she was the most famous person in the world but after all I didn't know her personally – what about the hysteria of so many?' Notwithstanding this she found the funeral 'unbearably moving', and was relieved to go out for a long walk after. But a few days later Steve Bell's cartoon (mentioned above) caused her much amusement. 'It does sum up the ridiculous state some people have got into. One man is quoted as saying he was more upset than when his wife died! There must be something wrong there.'[15]

Stiff Upper Lips and Wobbly Bottom Ones

'Grief should be personal', said the recently bereaved man above, and it was also 'best eased in private'. This, and some of the references to 'public hysteria' and oversentimentality, also touches on the way the mourning gave dramatic focus to an underlying cultural conflict in how people grieve in contemporary Britain. The dominant norm in mourning behaviour in Britain is a private, stiff-upper-lip style of grief. Under this we grieve behind closed doors, but hold ourselves together in public, while giving subtle hints that privately we are grieving deeply. In many circles it is still seen as unacceptable for people to grieve openly and emotionally in public, even during funerals. Challenging this idea in recent years has been the cultural advance of expressive grief, the idea imported from America, much promoted by the caring professions and found mostly among the young and women, that it is good to cry and we should let it all out, even in public (Biddle and Walter 1998; Walter 1999b).

Diana was of course a prominent symbol of the latter philosophy and her expressive approach to both her own problems and those of others was all the more notable for its contrast with traditional royal reserve. This 'queen of hearts' philosophy appeared triumphant during a mourning in which the wobbly bottom lip was widely legitimized by Tony Blair and the media as the only acceptable response from the royals down. Some who shared this criticism of the 'emotionally inarticulate' royals viewed this apparent shift with some enthusiasm. 'People from all walks of life are now actually verbalising their feelings more fully. How wonderful', noted one woman. There was much talk about how the new emotionalism somehow signalled a new, more caring, modern Britain which Diana and the recently elected New Labour government embodied, a perspective shared by one man:

> I could not think of a family I would least like to be comforted by than the Windors. Their stiff upper lips freshly starched, they showed the world the British way to be the face of grief. Not to portray the slightest hint of emotion, let their guard drop for a split second. But what was happening on the street spoke volumes. The royals didn't represent the nation anymore. WE were crying in the streets, we were hugging, comforting and consoling each other, men and women showed and shared reactions like never before. Was this new Britain that had eased out of the mould along with New Labour? Blair was there as he should be, the elected head of the country expressing joint collective grief, a tear in his eyes, a tear for us all.[16]

Yet, as we have seen, while it was this expressive grief which *appeared* dominant, in reality most mourners were largely concurring with notions of 'private', restrained grief, based on the assumption that people should grieve in private but hold themselves together in public. Even media coverage, while legitimizing and disproportionately emphasizing expressive grief, reflected the clash in these two traditions. So while 'the people' were commended for casting off their 'emotional straightjacket', Princes William and Harry, not to forget Elton John, were awarded the status of brave 'men' for not breaking down in tears in public. This, as Walter and Biddle (1998) point out, represents a classic performance of private grief, grieving deeply internally but publicly retaining composure while giving clear hints of inner feelings. One woman captured this contradiction, while defending the stiff-upper-lip mentality against the feared consequences that such Americanized emotionalism might produce:

The Royal Family could not win whatever they did. Harry and William were praised for keeping a 'stiff upper lip'; the rest of the family criticised for not weeping in public. It's the way we English are. It may not be right to bottle up emotion, but we do. Looking at the USA and Clinton with his carrying on, better a stiff, some would say old-fashioned Royal Family than a President who has zipper problems.[17]

Those, republicans as well as royalists, who believed that grief should be personal and privately expressed were again united in defending the royal family from unkind attacks because 'people grieving need at least a few days to do so in private'. In one sense, however, the earlier criticisms of the royals stemmed less from their failure of expressive grief and more from their apparent failure to show any grief at all. The problem was not so much that they didn't break down in tears in public, but that they didn't appear to be shedding any in private, indeed the popular suspicion was that they were secretly rejoicing at being rid of such a damaging influence. As one man put it:

> The Teletext proclaimed 'Prince Charles is going to undertake the saddest journey of his life, going to Paris to escort her body back to Britain'. Really he was going to make absolutely sure she was dead. My brother in law went as far as to suggest he would take a holy stake and a mallet.[18]

And the way the bitter conflict with Diana in life even extended into her mourning – the failure to issue a tribute, return to London, fly the flag at half mast, or even mention her name in the royal church service on the Sunday morning – all seemed to confirm this impression. A local library assistant was in conversation with two customers:

> 'She's treating it just like you'd treat the funeral of a neighbour – you don't know them that well so you don't put yourself out. I think it's disgraceful.'
> 'And what about that flag at Buckingham Palace. Why can't they fly a flag? It's just lack of respect. They've always had it in for Diana, but surely now it wouldn't harm to have a flag flying.'[19]

Meanwhile, whatever the reality in which private traditions of grief still remained strong, those who conformed to this were profoundly alienated by the expressiveness on display. One man noted how his 84-year-old father had learnt the news from a 65-year-old fellow churchgoer who threw his arms around him and wept openly: 'For my father', he added, 'this was nearly as terrible an event as the death itself' (*Guardian,*

5 September 1997). It was all 'undignified contrived' public wallowing in grief, complained one 75-year-old man, which he compared unfavourably with an older British wartime tradition where 'we mourned our friends in school prayer and then went about our business'.[20] He speculated, rightly, that it was after the Hillsborough disaster (see p. 92) that this new style of mourning behaviour had first emerged, which led others to complain at the time that oversentimental Liverpudlians were wallowing in grief (Walter 1991).

Diana's mourning provoked similar complaints on a much larger scale. Feelings of revulsion against mass emotions that 'seemed somehow tasteless and smacked of cheap sentiment' were reinforced by one particularly prominent observation that 'the millions of pounds spent on flowers that were left to rot would have been more valuable if the money had been put into a charity'.[21] One woman recalled seeing the flowers in her home town of Aldershot with the messages that 'everyone says are so touching' and feeling 'a kind of revulsion. I can't explain why – it just seems "tacky", clichéd – I don't know what'. Meanwhile the more dramatic scenes in London stimulated even greater hostility from one middle-aged male who worked virtually opposite Kensington Palace and who returned to work from a holiday the week after the funeral:

> I felt compelled to cross to the scene on the day after my return – there were still hundreds, if not thousands of bouquets on the grass, along the railways, across the pathways and I just couldn't comprehend it. The word that kept going through my mind was obscene – and yet why should I think this? Although I wouldn't personally send flowers in memory of someone I had never met, it surely wasn't for me to object to other people doing it – and yet I found the whole sight (and the feeling behind it and the gushing sentimentalities of many of the cards) truly distasteful. Is it because I am middle-aged and was brought up in the years following the Second World War, when there was obviously so much grief and unhappiness experienced by the loss of loved ones, but we weren't expected to wallow in it as people obviously did over the death of Diana?[22]

'Life Goes On' versus Communal 'Respect'

Linked in with the above conflicts of mourning traditions was an equally divisive cultural disagreement over how Diana should be mourned. In twentieth-century Europe and America grief and mourning became privatized and death was seen as a personal, private tragedy in which the individual's loss should not prevent other people's lives from proceeding as usual. Life goes on for all but the personally bereaved (Walter 1999b;

Cannadine 1981). Occasionally, however, and usually following a communal disaster, tragedy or high-profile death, older and conflicting traditions of communal mourning quickly and spontaneously re-emerge. In other words, death temporarily becomes renationalized and everyone is expected to mourn regardless of whether they feel personal loss. The years before Diana's death saw a marked intensification of this de-privatization of death, beginning with the Hillsborough football disaster in 1989 when ninety-five Liverpool football fans were crushed to death. The aftermath saw a rediscovery and publicization of large-scale communal mourning which in some ways anticipated that of Diana. Flowers and scarves were left at Anfield, Liverpool's football ground, and over a million people – twice the entire population of Liverpool – visited Anfield to pay their respects, sometimes waiting up to six hours to do so, while a minute's silence for the victims was held at football grounds across Britain (Walter 1991). Similar conventions of mourning behaviour had been firmly reconfirmed after subsequent tragedies, so much so that according to Peter Ghosh:

> The mourning seems almost overdetermined: it would have been extraordinary if it had not happened . . . anyone who watched the coverage of the death of the murdered black teenager Stephen Lawrence, or the Liverpool toddler James Bulger, or of the Scottish children massacred in Dunblane, knew exactly what the conventions were regarding cellophane and messages. (1998: 43)

Yet this temporary renationalization of death was almost bound to clash with the more normal, privatized tradition. For while one says life goes on for those who are personally unaffected, the other says that, as a matter of respect, life must come to a halt. One woman from Kent captured the clash in these two very different types of mourning from the latter perspective.

> That weekend was the town's Hop Festival and despite what happened the Festival went on. It seemed inappropriate to hear jolly music for Morris dancing through the open window and when we walked into the town centre I began to feel that the event should not go on. My husband, more forthright than me, spoke to a couple of those responsible for its organisation and expressed his shock and dismay that it had not been cancelled; he was quite upset that their answer was 'Life's got to go on'.[23]

In many ways her desired approach quickly predominated. Normal politics, including the campaigning over devolution in Scotland and

Wales, was suspended while all public and even private events were cancelled on funeral day. The Somerfield supermarket chain, which had wanted to stay open on the day of the funeral and donate all their profits to charity, was forced to join the rest of the retail community in the mass shutdown on the day of the funeral (Hitchens 1998). Indeed, perhaps the most graphic illustration of how the omnipotent demands of communal mourning had penetrated even the darkest recesses of the private realm were the window signs on the sex shops in Soho announcing that they were closing on funeral day in a rare 'mark of respect'. Few social events continued unchanged in the face of this mood. BBC journalist John Humphrys recalled one such 'ridiculous' occasion:

> I went to a concert in the Albert Hall the night before the funeral and the programme was changed, the Fauré Requiem replacing the symphony we had expected to hear. The conductor warned the audience beforehand not to applaud at the end of it, as a mark of respect . . . How could applauding a group of fine musicians be disrespectful to anyone? (2000: 55)

Television banned all programmes considered 'inappropriate', purging them of any sign of violence, humour or even Paris. The same story was true of radio, as Robbie Williams's *Angel* and John Lennon's *Imagine* offered occasional interruptions to Elton John's lyrical hegemony. Even the week after the funeral the BBC, paralysed by fear of being 'disrespectful', announced that it had given Radio 1's irreverent pop double act 'Mark and Lard' another week off as it was 'too early to bring back the gags' (*Mirror*, 8 September 1997). The world of pop has historically generated more than its fair share of anti-establishment protests, but on this occasion there was not a peep of dissent as they united in grief behind Elton John, to the considerable disgust of some fans and critics (*New Musical Express*, 20 September 1997). The band Del Amitri shelved a single because it contained a fleeting mention of a 'wreckage', while Kylie Minogue took the costly step of recalling and renaming her album because it was entitled 'Impossible Princess'. Perhaps most surprisingly, the self-styled bad boys of pop, Prodigy, who were happily promoting an album with a sleeve boasting the Nazi war cry of Joseph Goebbels, 'Do you want butter or guns?', halted the release of their most controversial single, 'Smack my bitch up'. This was not due to any offence the lyrics or the accompanying soft-porn video might cause, but because of a cover photograph of a car smashed into a lamp-post. When the single was later released the song and video remained unaltered but the cover had been changed (Barber 1997). It was a level of ludicrous and atypical oversensitivity to the perceived requirements of communal mourning that led one journalist to later wonder whether the words 'Diana' and 'Wales' were now in some way tactless or emotionally illegal (Moran 1997).

Yet as we have seen, in other ways beneath the directives of communal mourning, life carried on uneasily much as before, as politics was cancelled but *Richard and Judy* kept broadcasting, *EastEnders* continued to entertain the nation and government ministers still attended an arms fair at Farnborough. This veneer of mourning was well illustrated when the National Lottery draw continued on the Wednesday after Diana's death but the BBC did not televise it. Millions were still trying to win the jackpot and life was *really* going on, but there remained a media and social pretence that it was not. Such facts may have intensified the conflict, visible across Britain, between these two traditions of grief. The small Shropshire town of Wem had held an annual charity fair for the previous eighteen years on the first weekend in September. Their decision to buck the national trend and go ahead with it on the day of the funeral had bitterly divided the town. Hastily written tributes placed on the front of carnival floats to 'Diana Queen of Hearts' were not enough to appease half of the town's traders, whose shops remained unequivocally closed, and decorated by the pictures of the princess looking accusingly out at revellers. Others also stayed away, convinced that the dancing and marching was not appropriate for the day of a funeral. The organizers, however, were told by others that 'they just couldn't stand it any more and they needed to get back to normality', a sentiment shared by the forty dance and marching bands, drawn from across the Midlands and North, none of whom pulled out of the carnival. As one pro-carnival shopkeeper put it: 'The carnival is all we have, and it's usually a joyous day – even a bit of a drunken day. The organisers have spent a lot of money already, and life has to go on' (Wolffe 1997).

This conflict was also to be found more widely. For some the mass shutdown was no less than what was required. The woman complainer above from Kent was satisfied by the end of the week 'that people were responding in an appropriate way after the fiasco of the Hop Festival'. Others similarly found it 'very moving to think that people will do this', and were 'pleased to see that many shops will be closed on Saturday. They don't close for much these days.'[24] But not everyone agreed that this was 'appropriate'. One woman wrote to a volunteer friend who was abroad for the funeral complaining about how a horticultural show she was due to attend had been 'cancelled due to the untimely demise of Saint Diana, Princess of the Dispossessed'. 'It was', she mockingly added, 'not thought appropriate to hold such festivities on such a solemn day.'[25] Indeed the traditional norm of grief formed the underlying basis of the *Herald*'s alternative coverage as it argued that life, and with it politics and sport, should go on and denounced the 'commissars of grief', directed by Blair 'the messiah of Middle England', for their authoritarian efforts to dictate otherwise (1–6 September 1997). Meanwhile right-wing journalist Richard Littlejohn found some unusual allies on the left (Ferguson 1997; Waterhouse 1997; J. Smith 1997b; Lloyd 1997) in his complaints:

> What is really disturbing is that it appears not to be enough that people grieve and are seen to be grieving in public but that everyone must grieve – whether they want to or not. This enforcement of mourning is being pursued with a fundamentalist zeal. Life must not go on. To suggest otherwise is heresy. (1997)

'People should have a choice' about whether to mourn or not, agreed one woman, and it was 'not right to impose this austerity on people who do not want it'.[26] Despite the revival in communal mourning, the basis of privatized sentiments has also been recently further strengthened by a decline in the social policing of how people should grieve in favour of the more tolerant attitude that it is up to each individual how they mourn (Walter 1999b). The fact that the inverse views now prevailed – derided by one man as 'Sorry sir/madam, we're having a funeral. England is closed until 2 o'clock' – was seen as 'over the top'[27] and as offering worrying signs of dictatorship. Walter dismisses the latter argument, suggesting that 'this is merely what happens after any death' (1999a: 31).

But it clearly was not. Reading the news during the week BBC reporter Anna Ford offered a 'quote to Di for' (*Observer*, 30 August 1998) as she added: 'and let's not forget the other people who died this week, like Dodi al Fayed whose death has rather taken a back seat'. Unfortunate as her choice of words were, they hit upon a common source of complaint or comment, even among Diana's mourners – the profoundly atypical levels of respect now being shown which bore no relation to the way death was normally treated. People noted the lack of attention given to Dodi al Fayed or the driver – except to demonize him – or complained that tragedies like this 'happened all the time' to ordinary or quite extraordinary people without life coming to a halt or any respect being shown. As one mourner, so upset that she had to sit down, also noted, 'thousands are killed on the road every day'. One of the above women noted the contrast: 'Where my husband works (a food production factory) they are closing from 10 a.m.–2 a.m., yet if someone wants four hours off one day to attend their best friend's funeral they will not be allowed it (a problem which regularly arises and causes a lot of ill feeling).'[28] Others, like the woman below, angrily focused on the changes to television coverage:

The fact that so much programming on radio and television was changed was rather an insult to everyone's intelligence. Films with car crashes were taken off, hospital dramas were removed, a BBC short story was replaced because it recounted how a woman's life was changed when she took hold of a disadvantaged baby. An item on travelling by the Orient Express to Paris was taken off a holiday programme I had particularly wanted to see. WHY WHY WHY? Will Paris be ever synonymous with the death of the Princess of Wales and for nothing else. For heaven's sake! I could not believe the amount of replacement programmes, and this was all before the day of the funeral. Why? We were all shocked, yes. But if we are not expected to be able to cope with the usual trash that is served up as entertainment – a diet full of death by car crashes, death in hospital dramas (by boredom?) and depression in soap operas – in our real lives, while each and every one of us copes with bereavement, injuries and ill health how insulting to be 'nannied' by a programme diet of 'pap' – nature films and a three times repeat of Michael Palin's 'Full Circle' and all because a modern day icon has been killed.

But what 'really annoyed' her and was 'possibly the worst thing in the whole saga' was a subsequent government advertising campaign to get motorists to reduce their speed by featuring children who had been subsequently killed by speeding cars. The government revealed that they had thought of delaying the campaign because it might be 'inappropriate', a puzzling judgement given that Diana's death in a car being driven too fast made its message all too appropriate (Lawson 1997b).

This campaign has been planned for some time but when it was realised it was to be launched so soon after Diana's death the organisers sought special permission from the Palace to continue with it as they did not want to upset the family!!! Never mind the families of all the other people killed on the roads (especially children) who would identify with it much more easily. This senseless deference really annoys me. There is no way that the Royal Family should have their feelings taken more account of than those of other people is there?![29]

Similar complaints to an earlier M-O directive on disasters (No. 28) of 'the different value put on death' by a society which 'overdoes the pomp and circumstance of the death of a notable person' suggested that such views were hardly new.[30] But Diana's position at the pinnacle of this media and social hierarchy of death undoubtedly intensified them. It led people to draw attention to those who had not been given the same respect as Diana, be they other notable individuals who died during the week, the thousands killed on the road every year or simply those known personally to them who deserved grief more than Diana. It was a point demonstrated movingly by one female nurse who ended her account with a tribute, not to Diana, but to a woman dying of cancer whom she had treated when first diagnosed with the disease:

> I saw her for about eight weeks, at the end of the 'chemo', it was taking 4 to 5 days to get over one treatment, then the next was due, she got up to get her husband to work, and children to school, before collapsing on the bed to rest, but she is a fighter and before her last treatment, although very tired, still fighting back, for the husband, who still had to work and her children, who needed a real mother (no boarding school here). When all this fuss over Diana's death was going on . . . Jane's face kept coming back to me, how was she, how were her children? In November of this year, in the office I heard her name, community nurse to visit Jane, her cancer has returned, in her bones, her spine has crumbled, pain terrible . . . she can no longer walk, toilet is upstairs, has to have commode downstairs, she knows she is dying and is worried for her children, the eldest seems to be getting an eating disorder (15 years old) and is very quiet and withdrawn, the little one is now aggressive and angry. Jane still wears all her make up, her hair has returned, she's still a pretty young woman but dying slowly, the strain on her family is tremendous, her mother, a widow about 55–60 is helping the family, but has to work herself (her husband committed suicide about 15 years ago). Jane is so worried not about dying but about her children's future, she has been and can go anytime to a hospice for rest and care, but usually discharges herself to get back to the family. She has surrounded herself with family photos, her courage in all this is enormous, she's still fighting, but only a miracle can save her life, she is worth 1000 Diana's, and I probably will weep when Jane dies.[31]

These views stemmed from the sharp contrast between communal, media-saturated mourning for the few and the private, uncelebrated privatized deaths of the equally worthy many. But others complained that the level of respect demanded was disproportionate compared with other recent, and perhaps more 'worthy', examples of communal mourning, where in fact less respect had been shown. 'As one boy was reported saying to his mother, "They didn't do all this for Dunblane, did they?"'[32] – or, others noted, after Lockerbie, Piper Alpha or Hillsborough. The Scottish Football Association had initially planned to hold a minute's silence before their international football match, timed to kick off three hours after the funeral, and which would have also seen all players wearing black armbands. This was now ferociously condemned as a shameful gesture of disrespect (see chapter 9), and left critics puzzling how a response that was fully appropriate for all prior communal mourning, including that of Winston Churchill's, had somehow become the reverse. Meanwhile several older respondents bitterly noted the difference between Diana's communal mourning and the lack of respect shown in honouring the heroes of the Second World War:

> What will happen on November 11th – will all shops shut, will all the traffic stop – will people write in books of condolences – will hundreds of thousands of people attend funerals at war memorials? I doubt it – after all November 11th is only for the memory of thousands upon thousands who gave their lives in two world wars so that we can enjoy the freedom that they fought for.[33]

Far from Diana's death and mourning contributing to the 'communitas' and unity of the occasion by functioning as 'the great leveller' (Turnock 2000: 74), this chapter suggests it had precisely the opposite effect. Ultimately Diana's mourning as it was presented and perceived was so deviant from the dominant British cultures of grief that it was bound to provoke such conflicting, diverse and complex responses and leave a population deeply divided rather than united in grief.

8003

6

England's Rose – or Argentina's?

Closely linked with the subject of grief was another theme that divided popular opinion during the week – nationalism. Nationalism is the Siamese twin of modern monarchies for without it they cannot exist. There might be nations without monarchs but you cannot be a proper king or queen without being, or claiming to be, the head of a nation (Billig 1997b). It has been widely argued, if much disputed, that the paradox of nationalism is that it is actually a product of the modern age but rests on myths about the antiquity of nations (Smith 1991; Gellner 1983; Anderson 1991). And a central pillar of the British national identity that emerged from the eighteenth century has been the monarchy and the way it has been presented as symbolic of the nation in both its ancient and present form (Colley 1992; Cannadine 1983; Nairn 1988; Kuhn 1999; Billig 1997b).

In an important article David Cannadine (1983) noted how between 1820 and 1877 the monarchy was the head of society but not the nation, and was widely unpopular and vilified in the press. The monarchy presided over ineptly managed, inaccessible elite ceremonials that had little mass significance within a largely provincial, localized, pre-industrial society. From the 1870s a whole series of modern royal traditions were 'invented' – cynics would say faked – to emphasize the monarchy's link to a long British past as the monarch was now seen not just as the head of society but as 'the head of the nation as well' (1983: 133). Crucial to this success was the way ceremonials were conveyed to a mass public via a now obsequious mass media, initially through the popular press, radio and newsreels, and latterly through the powerful way television made them 'accessible in a vivid and immediate manner' (1983: 158). The investiture of the Prince of Wales in 1969, for example, was a new ritual dressed up as a very old one. Lord Snowdon gave a further touch of antiquity to proceedings only first invented in 1911 so that at the most dramatic moment Charles 'would utter archaic mumbo-jumbo about becoming "liege man of life"'. The incomprehensible words carried the easily understood message, 'We are ancient, we are your past' (Billig 1997b: 26).

Just as monarchy plays a central role in the imagining of the nation's glorious past, so it is seen as symbolizing the nation in its present form. To support the royal family is automatically to be associated with national pride. To oppose them is to run the risk of being accused of being unpatriotic, of being disloyal to the nation. Repeated research has demonstrated that the monarchy was seen to provide a unique dimension to the country. Take it away and you remove the very thing that makes Britain/England itself. As one man put it, 'If you've not got the royal family there, then, you'll not have the British Isles as we know it, we'll perhaps be another state of America or something' (Billig 1997b: 34). Royalty is a classic example of 'banal nationalism' (Billig 1995), that, as distinct from the hot nationalism of movements that seeks to establish new nations, provides people with daily reminders, in barely conscious ways, that they are members of a particular nation state. So the British monarchy, as Tom Nairn points out, 'doesn't appear to be nationalist. It defines itself, necessarily, as being above that sort of thing' (1988: 127). But it is, of course, precisely that sort of thing.

Little has been said about the operation of national identity during Diana's mourning. In so far it has been discussed, it has been seen in terms of either the 'New Britain' that it signified (see chapter 1) and/or a manifestation of an international reaction in which traditional loyalties had little relevance. 'Unlike previous royal ceremonies it was one in which British national identities played little part', asserted Ben Pimlott in his updated biography of the Queen (2002: 651). The global mourning that Diana stimulated was one obvious manifestation of this, while others have suggested that her international charity campaigning, celebrity and even choice of lover provoked an appeal that 'blocked nationalism and fuelled internationalism' (Johnson 1999: 27), or 'supra-nationalism' as journalist Susan Moore (1997c) called it.

'Proud to be British'

While not denying the global dimension, this chapter suggests that nationalism was in fact central to both the media coverage and the lived popular experience of the week in Britain. In terms of the latter, it argues that national identities drew people into the mourning but also alienated them in ways that combined some marked continuities with some very different responses. Ultimately, it suggests that far from serving as a basis for a new British identity, Diana's mourning marked a serious and largely unwelcome challenge to the popular imagining of the British national character.

In the first place the force of 'banal nationalism' was a dominant, automatically assumed theme of how the mourning was covered. Coverage (as we saw in chapter 1) repeatedly conjured up an 'imagined community' (Anderson 1991) of British mourners united in adulatory, tearful grief. 'Diana: The Nation's Vigil' said the BBC news strapline the night before the funeral (5 September 1997). We were a nation or a country united in mourning 'England's Rose' rather than a society in mourning (Billig 1997b). 'The people' were the British people. Individuals similarly conjured this very same 'imagined community' of British mourners in their responses as they littered their accounts with generalizations about 'the nation's mood', 'the national response', the country's behaviour. One older woman was 'shattered by the tragic news' and, with a little help from the media, imagined others shared her reaction. 'It seems ENGLAND has become DIANA LAND. Every town, village and hamlet appears to be providing books of remembrance and places to lay flowers in her memory'.[1] As we have seen, the 'imagined community' of mourners was frequently not one with which people could identify. But while it was sometimes viewed with contempt, derision or puzzlement it was still a *nation* in tearful, adulatory grief that was widely imagined.

As we saw in chapter 1, much was made at the time of the way the perceived popular reaction symbolized a 'New Britain', a new 'structure of feeling' for a more inclusive, modern, compassionate, feminine, identity. Subsequent chapters below more directly question the extent of this feeling even among the women and gays that were supposed to be in the vanguard of the 'floral revolution' (Jacques 1997a). What such concentrations also ignore is the extent to which it was this very 'glamour of backwardness' (Nairn 1988), albeit mixed with a generous spice of the modern, that was so appealing in national terms about the week. The funeral in particular seemed to stimulate national pride of a type hardly distinguishable from the responses to past ceremonies in a country unique and special, 'the envy of the world' – and even the Americans (Jennings and Madge 1937; Ziegler 1978; Billig 1997b). As one man observed: 'There is no doubt that when it comes to unprecedented events like this, Britain organises them brilliantly and with exactly the correct amount of solemnity.' Another man, very much a sceptic over the course of the week, described his plans for the day:

> I had a load of paper sorting to do which I had every intention of doing in front of the TV. I know the world would be watching and I felt quite proud that 'we British would do it properly' and that the public in London would play their parts in this amazing show . . . I was proud to see that Britain could do it well.[2]

It 'makes you proud to be British' (Ziegler 1978: 113) commented one woman; 'the only country where you could have a ceremony like this without someone throwing a bomb', agreed another (Jennings and Madge 1937: 285). These last comments, taken from the 1953 and 1937 coronations, demonstrate the way the response was, as Paul Gilroy (1997) suggested, 'entirely congruent with the patriotic spectacle and ritual' of the past in an event which looked backwards to the eighteenth century rather than forward to the twenty-first.

Implicit or explicit in this were international comparisons of the type often stimulated by royal events, a feeling that Britain was once again proving itself to the world. 'They've all got their answer today', said one man about the 1937 coronation (Jennings and Madge 1937: 58), while by 1953 'the note of national self-approval, that in some ways we were scoring off other nations, was perceptively more strident'. Other countries were considered envious. Despite having all the money and world power 'the Yanks have nothing like this' argued one middle-aged woman (Ziegler 1978: 100, 113). By the 1970s and 1980s such national self-approval became ever more strident, as Britain's decline as a great power became ever more evident. The 1977 Silver Jubilee, for example, provoked pride that 'here at last was something we could still do better than the rest of the world' (Ziegler 1978: 178). And the *Mirror*'s suggestion that 'we can still show the world a clean pair of heels when it comes to a ceremonial' (Cannadine 1983: 160), was echoed twenty years later by one man who contrasted the 'great difference' between the 'well nigh perfect' organization in London and the 'organised chaos' in Calcutta for the funeral of Mother Teresa.[3]

This backward-looking theme was also to be found coexisting somewhat uneasily within the media emphasis on the emerging 'New Britain'. For coverage almost subconsciously placed the 'united in grief' story as the latest, modernized version of the 'myth of the blitz' (Calder 1991), drawing on or playing out the popular memory of a glorious past when the country stood united together against Nazi tyranny. A people's war became a people's mourning, characterized by a rediscovery of caring community spirit, camaraderie, popular mobilization, resilience and bonding among strangers. The *Mail* (6 September 1997) detected in London 'the same powerful spirit of bonding which cemented the city against the wartime Blitz'. The *Express* (4 September 1997), attacking the royal failure to respond to the country's mood, claimed Diana's death had 'brought together the nation in a way not seen since we came under attack from Hitler's armies . . . for the first time since the second world war we all know the same grief and sadness'. Profiles of the queuing crowds repeatedly told the story of a population sharing their life stories and their flasks of tea as they joined the mourning queues as strangers and left as friends (*Mirror*, 3 September 1997; Freedland 1997a). Such an experience was more directly conveyed in television vox-pops, of which the following from the Friday evening, is entirely typical:

> REPORTER: Here outside Westminster Abbey people have been camped out for over 24 hours and here with me I've got three guests who've been here perhaps the longest . . . It's extraordinary isn't it, the whole scene here?
> WOMAN 1: There's a great sense of camaraderie, everyone's pulling together and it's quite awesome really.
> REPORTER: And it's not exactly been pleasant weather has it?
> WOMAN 1: No, it's been raining, it's been very, very cold last night. Lots of people didn't bring enough to wear so there was lots of helping hands, everyone tried to help each other . . .
> REPORTER: Because a lot of people didn't know each other at all and yet now there's lots of people making friends here, and there's been people handing out chocolates and all sorts of things.
> WOMAN 2: . . . Yes I think everybody's been very good with each other.
> (BBC, 5 September 1997)

While largely ignored, it was perhaps nationalism (as well as a demand for respect) rather more than radicalism which motivated the demands of those who questioned why the royal family was not in London 'sharing this with the people', as a woman from Cardiff put it.[4] Indeed it is no coincidence that the debate over the royals' behaviour became centred on another symbol of nationhood, the flag. More broadly, this criticism stemmed from the perception that they were failing adequately to represent the nation in their grief and were now, unlike in the past, reflecting a far from 'enchanted glass' (Nairn 1988) of national identity onto the country. Again the demand, at least in the media, was for a recreation of a backward-looking story which saw the royals function as the national figureheads that popular memory attributed to their role during the war. As the *Express* editorial above went on:

> During wartime, King George VI and Queen Elizabeth [the Queen Mother] were accepted by the nation as a symbol of a common determination to see off Hitler. Now the nation has been brought together by a common tragedy once again. And yet – so far at least – the Royal Family has been unable to respond and unify the nation and express its suffering in the way that they have in the past. (4 September 1997)

Given all we have seen about media selectivity, there are good grounds to be cautious about how far this was reflecting the public mood. But certainly one prominent sentiment, a widely used phrase by those inter- viewed in public, was a desire to participate in a 'historic event'. People were queuing, Decca Aitkenhead (1997) suggested, not because they wanted to express grief but to take part in a memorable 'collective historic experience . . . a desire to locate themselves in the spot where history will for once reach out to them'. The queuing, the bonding, the friendships were not the touching, accidental by-products of the collective gathering – they were the reason for it. Take them away, allow people to sign the book in six minutes rather than six hours, and you take away the point. In the context of our modern atomized lives when we knew all about Diana but didn't speak to our neighbours, it offered a rare opportunity for recreating a 'quintessentially old-fashioned British moment . . . not a modern, Americanised Britain'.

This undoubtedly oversimplifies motives. People joined the queues, attended or watched the funeral for different and often plural reasons. To be a tourist or seeker of a historical experience one minute does not automatically rule out being a mourner the next (Walter 1999b). Indeed, being deeply upset could reinforce the sense of the occasion, as the attitude of one woman whose views have already been noted demonstrates:

> [Friday] I have spoken to my daughter by telephone and persuaded her that tomorrow is possibly one of the most famous days in History and suggested that she come and join me and other friends to watch the ceremony on television. [Saturday] . . . Up washed and early as my daughter was coming to breakfast. A new eight hour videotape was started at 8.30 a.m. for BBC 1 and the television set was also switched on to BBC 1. A nice hot cup of tea was the next thing on the menu but with a cold breakfast as I did not want to be distracted from the television screen, history in the making.[5]

Others who were far from upset, however, were attracted to watching or going to the funeral for much the same motives:

> I thought I might get a flavour of it but I was sucked into the general sense of needing to participate in a major event – one of those significant moments in history when people will later ask: 'Were you there? What did you do during the great funeral Mummy?'

> I cancel my hairdresser's appointment for the Saturday . . . not so much out of a need to show sympathy but of a desperate longing to see the funeral. I thought it a shocking moment of history and like anything that smacks of Pageant in any case.

'I don't know if I'd have gone to London or not – if I had it would only to have been part of a world shattering event, not for any feelings I had for Diana', speculated another woman who was abroad during the funeral.[6] And certainly this was a motive among those who did attend. After the funeral a middle-aged couple who had been among the crowds lining the route were sitting drinking in a pub, showing every sign of considerable elation and very little of grief. The man considered:

> It's been marvellous, that's all I can say. It's been *absolutely* marvellous. You'll never, *ever* see anything like this in the history of mankind I don't think . . . It's been worth every single penny. If I had the opportunity I would pay twice as much to come and do the same weekend bearing in mind what the history I've got, I've got it all on tape. I've got history on tape. There you are [shows video]. This is the hearse as it moves past. (*The Princess's People* 1998)

Again this shows little difference from the same history and collective solidarity that people flocked to London to experience in past royal events. Here discomfort was an essential, even actively enjoyable part of the ritual, as were the bonding and friendships with strangers that provoked frequent comparisons with the collective solidarity of the past. How wonderful, as one 28-year-old woman remarked in 1953, it was 'to feel the old wartime camaraderie and friendliness' (Ziegler 1978: 108). In doing so Diana's funeral provided another royal event to add to what Billig calls 'the heritage of the future' (1997b: 202), collective memories of a memorable British experience which, alongside the photographs, video-recordings and newspaper clippings and commemorative records, were to be stored and returned to in the future. As one woman put it: 'I have many newspapers with coverage of the funeral and magazines featuring Princess Diana in happier times – I just can't part with them. It was living through a historical moment, which I and many people will always remember.'[7]

To look at Diana's mourning in nationalistic terms seems to ignore, as already noted, its global dimension. Certainly one element alongside the Britain 'united in grief' media story was the emphasis on how 'The World Weeps' (*Sun*, 2 September 1997). But far from blocking nationalism, paradoxically this international response fuelled British pride even further. In September 1997 the story was first and foremost a national one, of a country united in grief while the world looked on and mourned with us, rather than an internationalist one, of a world united in grief of which Britain was merely part. Diana may have been a 'people's princess' of all people, but she was ultimately a British princess. This sense of national superiority, embracing the allegedly admiring gaze of the rest of the world but keeping them in their place, was illustrated by this discussion on the popular *Richard and Judy* television chat-show about the Queen's speech. Royal commentator Christopher Wilson was arguing:

> I think that most of the population are going to be happy with that but I think it's going to look different to the outside world. I think that internationally and in America in particular where . . . they're as involved as we are in what's going on, I think they're going to be analysing the Queen's words and looking to see what hidden messages are there and . . .
> RICHARD (interrupting): You know it's funny. I don't really care about that now. I think –
> JUDY: Well it's us isn't it?
> RICHARD: It's *our* royal family and its *our* funeral tomorrow, and it's *our* time of grieving and of course we hope and pray that the world grieves with us. But actually it's now moved back to us. Yesterday it seemed appropriate to talk of what other countries were saying. Now I couldn't give a fig. It's family now. It's *us*. (ITV, 5 September 1997)

But the fact that the rest of the world was watching and grieving with us for our princess was important. As some of the above comments suggest, one key element within the nationalism stimulated by royalty has always been pride as we imagine foreigners also looking into 'the enchanted glass' of Britishness (Nairn 1988), seeing and envying us as unique and joining with us on these occasions (Billig 1997b). So the fact that the world was watching, admiring and grieving with our nation, was a source of national pride and illustrated our national importance. As Tony Blair declared in his first public speech after the funeral: 'I want to begin by saying how proud I was to be British on Saturday when the whole world could see our country united in grief' (quoted in Hume 1997: 4). The subtle but unmistakable feelings of additional pride stimulated by what one man called 'the world's reaction to what was an English girl (i.e. belonging to our nation)' was also well illustrated by one woman whose feelings have already been noted:

> I would imagine that if visitors to this country would have the chance they would all try to be in London to witness this sad occasion and find out what makes us British tick at such a time but will they also understand that this is history at first hand and that they will also be very privileged to witness such an event and to be able to go home equipped to tell everyone that they shared it with us.[8]

England's Rose, Not Britain's Rose

One of the themes of media coverage, both nationally and locally, was its focus on the unity of the national response across a *United* Kingdom. News items would span from London to Scotland to Northern Ireland to Wales to emphasize 'some of the images of how a kingdom united remembered Diana', as the BBC put it on the day of the funeral (5 September 1997). Unequivocal verdicts on the popular mood for Wales competed with similar estimates for Scotland, while Diana's mourning had even apparently succeeded where so many others had failed in uniting Ireland's warring community in peace:

> The whole of Wales is remembering its much loved and much admired Princess. Perhaps it's really in this principality that the community will feel the severe loss hardest . . . No-one can really believe what they're seeing all around the country but particularly in Wales where they hold her in such great esteem in their hearts.

> Here in Northern Ireland the death of Diana has united in grief an often divided community. Unionists and Nationalists have come together to place flowers in her memory . . . But it is not just in Northern Ireland that the Princess is being mourned. People in the Republic of Ireland have also been deeply moved by her death . . . In marking the passing of a Princess, if in little else, the people of Ireland will be united.

> The sadness reaches every corner of Scotland. (BBC, 5/6 September 1997)

History, not to mention common sense, would rather doubt the plausibility of such stories given that the Celtic fringe has historically always shown greater opposition to an English monarchy whose identity was 'stretched' to encompass the multinational nature of Britain (Nairn 1988; Worcester 1997; Taylor 1999). That this extension might also mean dilution (Nairn 1994) was captured by one man from Glasgow in 1997 who noted cynically: 'As a Scot I should note that "an overwhelming sense of national unity" usually means that large numbers of people are waving plastic Union jacks somewhere in a city about an hour and a half away from me by air.'[9]

Post-war royal events have always generated lower levels of interest in Scotland, and to a lesser extent in Wales, while opinion polls have also shown lower levels of support in these countries. In Wales the expected vast crowds for Prince Charles's investiture in Caernarfon failed to materialize, perhaps because, as he put it, 'you can't expect people to be overzealous about the fact of having a so-called English

Prince come amongst them' (Nairn 1988: 107). More outright opposition to an English monarchy has always come from Scotland, with its more developed national identity. In 1977 the spirit of devolution was one factor that ensured that the Jubilee was met with 'an indifference far more widespread than in England, a feeling that the monarch is . . . something alien . . . that Elizabeth is, in fact, Elizabeth II, Queen of England, rather than of Scotland' (Ziegler 1978: 192). Twenty years later, as another devolution campaign approached, a television poll in early 1997 reported a majority in favour of abolishing the monarchy and confirmed Scotland's status as the most anti-royal of the British nations (Nairn 1998). Such attitudes were arguably further heightened during the mourning by the concurrent devolution campaigns, not to mention the Southern-English-centred nature of the mourning, that demanded that the royals come home to be with 'the people'. For not everyone in the regions was, like the woman above from Cardiff, prepared to equate London with the home of the British people. As one woman from Glasgow complained: 'Are not the Scots their subjects too? You would have thought they were abroad or something.' She, among others, considered that the mourning was lower key in her country as 'she was after all England's rose not Britain's rose'. Another woman who knew of only one person who signed the book of condolence in Glasgow similarly stressed that she 'would not say the Scots tore their hair out like the English',[10] a judgement supported by the Scottish home of both the main dissenting newspaper, the *Herald*, and public institutions (see chapter 9).

While Wales was typically more quiescent than Scotland, the available evidence points to a more low-key response there, as the pull of the Princess of Wales competed with the push of England's Rose. As one woman suggested: 'I disapprove of her "Wales" sobriquet, as I do that of her former husband, for being an artificial royalist imposition on the Welsh.'[11] When a publisher putting together a book of memories of the Princess appealed for responses across England and Wales, they got 3,000 replies from England but just three from Wales (Sterio 1997). And four years on there had been no memorial set up to commemorate the Princess, despite numerous plans at the time. One suspects, too, that there were regional variations. Peter Ghosh suggested that 'the way the emotional temperature dropped as one moved outside a 100-mile radius from London was palpable' (Ghosh 1998: 46). Others considered that the response in their regions was rather more low-key. One woman from Southampton stressed:

The mass-hysteria, of flowers etc. in London quite staggered me – nothing like that here. Two books for people to write in were provided in the foyer of the public library and I went there on 3 different days. At no time was there more than a queue of 12 people waiting (six per book). A couple of shops had wreaths on their door, but I saw no other flowers.[12]

The evidence is not available for a more conclusive assessment, and how much the comments above were illustrations of actual national/regional differences, or how much they were assertions of such identities remains difficult to establish. Arguably it was 'London' that, as the forum for public mourning, inevitably offered the most atypical if most emphasized popular reaction. Certainly Diana's mourning replicated earlier patterns in which the excesses of the metropolitan celebrations were not echoed and even sometimes derided in the regions (Ziegler 1978). M-O reports from the small town of Havant in Hampshire following the death of George VI, for example, found that 'the shops had not gone into any sort of mourning'. 'Nothing's been done here', admitted one owner of a grocery store rather guiltily.

Ashamed to be British

All this shows continuity rather than change. But a sharp break with the past was also visible in the way the force of nationalism drew people away from the event in ways which were unprecedented. Writing soon after the mourning Paul Gilroy (1997) was to speculate: 'The mythical togetherness of the Blitz and the Battle of Britain are likely to be displaced by a new folk memory of communal mourning. Where did you stand to watch the coffin pass? Where did you place your poem, teddy bear or posy?' But there was a big problem for people in seeing Diana Week positively in terms of Britishness/Englishness. Partly, as we have seen, this was because Diana's conflict with the royals meant that some traditionalists could not equate her with the nation or felt able to join in. What the mourning gained from more radical participation (and its extent is questionable), it may have lost by the absence, or equivocation of traditional royalists (see chapter 3). And while for republicans their 'deviance' was normal, for royalists such a development was a rather unsettling experience, as the following account from one older man illustrates:

It became quickly evident that the nation was to be media-led into self-indulgent wallowings of emotional displays. An anguish previously unheard of even at the height of the blitz. Suddenly being British meant it was all right to shed tears in public over a young woman who few had met, and less of ever having had the remotest chance of getting to know personally. What I found most disturbing to those of us who managed to remain dry-eyed, was being made to feel callously unfeeling, if not downright unpatriotic. To my mind, at first, the only lead of any dignified restraint came from the Queen, who in the end had to give way to media hysteria and herself appear on television to prove that she was suffering with 'the people'.

Similarly a female royalist who considered that Diana had 'damaged the monarchy' recalled, 'As the hours and days passed I gradually felt like an alien in my own country'.[13] Such comments also hit on a more important general way in which the popular images of the mourning marked a serious challenge, and not just for conservatives, to the 'imagining' of the British character. This, in death as well as in life, is popularly associated with restraint, reserve, moderation and stability (Paxman 1999). This is true more specifically for the royal family, which since the Glorious Revolution of 1688 and 'purged of its earlier extremism . . . became a cherished symbol of that moderation and give-and-take' of English identity, characterized by 'muddling through' and 'not too much' (Nairn 1988: 147, 160). Supporters of the monarchy regularly and almost instinctively see it as a bulwark against extremism and dictatorship that abolition would allegedly provoke. All this represents the polar opposite of 'inferior' countries abroad with their dictators, mob rule, revolutions and unstable emotionalism (Paxman 1999; Billig 1997b). But in many ways this was what appeared to be happening in Britain in September 1997, so much so that the mourning marked a serious challenge, even an apparent negation, of Britishness. Indeed the collapse of these certainties of national identity that the popular images of the week provoked could be extremely disconcerting as people declared themselves 'ashamed to be British', as one man told an observer, a sentiment which most would have found inconceivable to express in past royal ceremonies. Others were similarly 'horrified and ashamed at the mass hysteria which took over the country' or admitted to 'a feeling of relief when the mourning was over and the country got back to normal'.[14] 'I felt like I was living in a foreign country' recalled one man. 'It was as if the whole country had lost leave of its senses'. 'I was not able to identify with the rest of my countrymen at all', noted another.[15]

There were several interlinked reasons why this was the case. First, as we have seen, there was a reaction against the high level of emotionalism on display. An earlier M-O survey on the subject of 'death' had seen people contrasting an English habit 'to make less of a death than in other countries' with the way people in continental and Arab countries would 'keep up the weeping for several days'.[16] But in many ways this was exactly what appeared to be happening in Britain in the course of what an aghast Boris Johnson (1997) described as 'a Latin American carnival of grief'. 'Where is this', he wondered, 'Argentina?' Observers agreed, convinced that the 'Evitification' of the country suggested what one older man described as a 'prolonged emotional spasm suffered by the national psyche'.[17] 'We' were now forced to see ourselves as no longer unique, special and different from foreigners but just like them. One older woman was 'uncomfortable and embarrassed' by 'the sights and sounds of the wailing crowds with their tearful faces, seemingly wallowing in grief'. It forced her, and a fellow observer, to see a country that was, quite simply, no longer Britain:

> Whatever will the foreign nations be thinking of us now? The stoic, unemotional 'stiff-upper-lip' British have been seen in a new light – watching the scenes of public mourning in London . . . I could imagine it was France, Spain or one of the Latin American countries where uninhibited emotional outbursts are more common.

> I found it truly hard to understand the public reaction. Someone remarked that it was like the scenes in Argentina on the death of Eva Peron. An English family watching the scenes on French television thought they were looking at scenes in a foreign country. It was hard to believe this was happening in Britain.[18]

Meanwhile the man above who expressed his distance on the basis of his Scottish identity also felt distanced as a British person as he wondered: 'Could this really be happening in late 20th Century Britain. Iran yes, with the death of the Ayatollah Khomeini, but Britain? Surely not?'[19]

As chapter 5 notes, fitting within such perceptions was a broader cultural clash between traditional stiff-upper-lip British grief and the American-imported expressivism. But it also suggests that the 'problem' in terms of sharing the apparent popular response was not just to do with a reaction against emotionalism in itself, but was fundamentally based on the perception that it was irrational and even pathological to mourn a stranger in this way. Meanwhile, revulsion against such irrational foreign-style emotionalism combined with hostility to an equally alien authoritarianism, mob rule and extreme intolerance of alternative views (see also chapter 9) that was seen as a worrying threat to traditional British liberties. A centrally imposed mourning more reminiscent of the state funerals of communist dictatorships was one negative comparison. 'I remember the pictures in Red Square when Stalin died', noted one female who found the 'hysteria' 'a little worrying'.[20] But a more common form of negative comparison was with the antithesis of all things traditionally British, Nazi Germany. Angus Calder (1991), in his history of wartime Britain, made a list of opposites to show how the English saw themselves and the Germans. England stood, among other things, for freedom, tolerance, calm, Germany for tyranny and frenzy. And the dis-identification provoked by the mourning led some people to see the traditionally calm British identity falling victim to a 'mass hysteria stirred up that has outdone the Nuremberg rallies that the Germans put on for Hitler', as one man argued. Others agreed:

> On Wednesday last I watched the BBC programme about the rise of Hitler. I do not wish to be disrespectful, but I could not help thinking of Diana as I saw the enthusiasm for Hitler on the streets of Germany. I was shocked by the comparison but the display of *mass emotion* in both cases caused me a great deal of discomfort.

> The public was drawn into the fascination and I cannot help but wonder at the mentality of people dragging little children to queue for hours and throwing piles of flowers all over the place. There was something very un-English about the whole thing . . . I would suggest that the world has not seen this sort of mass hysteria since Hitler.[21]

Again we should not assume two neatly opposing sentiments played out over the week. Sometimes those who derided the 'hysteria' were pulled in by national pride during the 'dignified' funeral. One woman was so sick of the media coverage during the week that she stopped buying the papers and watching television. But she was back on board by the Saturday: 'I watched the funeral on the TV . . . and I am glad I did. I always love ceremonies and I was so proud of the way it had all been arranged in such a short time.' Another was so detached from the perceived mood that she wondered whether she was 'the only person in the country not suffering from the mass hysteria' and found it 'impossible to comprehend the scale of the emotions' stimulated. By the time of the funeral she had gone for a holiday in America, which she watched with friends 'whose attitude was similar to mine thank goodness'. Despite such scepticism, she considered that 'it was extremely well done, dignified and impressive as these events always are in this country'.[22] On the other side even those who had been 'immensely distressed' during the week were by no means free from a nationalistic counter-pull as they 'felt uncomfortable with what was almost hysteria. It didn't seem "British" '. One man whose national pride is highlighted above also noted: 'I suspect there was an element of mass hysteria involved, common in Arab and eastern countries but quite rare to be observed in English people.' Meanwhile one woman declared that she would 'love to see the flowers' in London – and the day after the funeral she did just that. But she had mixed feelings:

I am not sure if I agree with it at all. If ever there's an accident or tragedy of any sort nowadays, people always leave flowers. I think in some ways the old English thing of bearing up and keeping a stiff upper lip was preferable. This seems so emotional, far more Mediterranean than British.[23]

The way national identity could both push people towards the mourning and also potentially alienate them was even found in some accounts of the funeral. One man's pride in the way 'the English did it right as usual, a perfect service at Westminster Abbey, adroitly handled as one expects' was countered momentarily by distaste at the 'very peculiar, very unBritish' clapping and throwing of flowers as the hearse made its way to Althorp. 'Is it a foreign custom?', he wondered. Others agreed, as they balanced an 'impressive and dignified' event, 'moving at times, but strangely alien' and 'much too extravagant' in parts.[24] Here the dignified British ceremony and chilling silence of the crowds that media coverage, for once, accurately captured (as it was live it was difficult not to), was combined with distaste at the isolated wailing heard from a couple of women as the funeral cortège left Kensington Palace:

The sound that I found shocking was as the gun carriage bearing Diana's body came through the gates of her home, Kensington Palace, a woman standing close by started crying and wailing, calling out Diana repeatedly. That was very disturbing and so unlike the way we do things here. Even this incredible outpouring of love and grief for Diana is still in its way restrained, compared to other countries where we see scenes of people prostrate in the streets and tearing themselves apart with grief.[25]

Other mourners were similarly dismayed at this intrusion into the British way of mourning, attributing it to a reaction which 'must be from foreigners as it is not commonly a British tradition at such a time'. As one man put it:

My heart sank at the thought that this middle Eastern idea would continue all the way to the Abbey and that such audible displays of grief would find their way into the British way of life, but fortunately it was an isolated case. A colleague at work has since told me that she was in the crowd at this place and that the wailers were two African women.[26]

For the most part, the 'unBritish' excesses of the funeral only momentarily disrupted the national pride that it stimulated. A MORI poll in the aftermath found a third of people felt more proud to be British, although the evidence above suggests it was as much of a highly traditional type as signifying a 'New Britain'. But the week as a whole was seen as something different and more negatively. By the following March, the proportion of those saying that the funeral had made them more proud to be British had dropped to 19 per cent. As chapter 1 notes, by September 1998 50 per cent considered that 'the British public' had overreacted the previous year, an unfavourable verdict which was all the more notable for its divergence with the small numbers who said that they personally had overreacted (MORI 1997c/1998a/b). This illustrated a clear gulf between people's perceptions of their own behaviour and that of the country in general. Hopes that the mourning could serve as a model for a new type of Britishness were fundamentally flawed for various reasons, aside from the lack of clarity of what this entailed and Diana's position as a divisive rather than unifying figurehead. Anthony Smith points out that national identity, at its deepest level, is all about the nation's 'peculiar genius, its own way of thinking, acting and communicating' (1991: 73–9). This 'peculiar genius' of Britishness – moderate, liberal, unemotional, rational – seemed under such fundamental challenge by the perceived reaction – above all synonymous with irrational excess – that it was hardly likely to serve as the lasting basis for a new 'structure of feeling'.

Secondly, identity also means *sameness*, the sense of a common national life that members share with each other but not with others. 'The point is not what the nation means but that you belong to it' (Baxendale 1999: 301). During the mourning the constant message from media, society and politicians was 'we all feel the same way, the nation is all mourning Diana'. By defining the nation and 'the people' as those in mourning, the experience was profoundly exclusionary for the vast majority who did not see themselves in this way (see also chapter 9). As one man noted:

> The situation after her death reminded me intensely of what happened during the wars in the Falklands and the Gulf. Very suddenly, one opinion was being pumped at you from every segment of the media. 'We all feel this way . . . we must all believe . . . we must all hope'. If you dissent from this view, it is a very strange feeling. In this case, it was a matter of relative indifference to me, rather than one of outright opposition to this official line, but it was still enough to give a sense of alienation.[27]

The rhetoric about an inclusive, 'people-power' transformation of subjects into citizens ignored the many who felt effectively disenfranchised, who 'were literally "excommunicated"' (Merrin: 1999: 52) as members of the nation. As broadcaster John Humphrys argued: 'To invoke a national mood is to create an almost threatening notion of belonging. There are echoes of totalitarianism if you do not share that mood. In the midst of the Diana funeral hysteria there were those who said that the experience made them feel that they no longer belonged' (2000: 211–12). Hailing the reaction as proof of the existence of 'one of the world's most liberal countries', as Oxford Professor John Gray (1997) did, ignored the blunt fact that those who disagreed with such a verdict felt unable or afraid to express their views.

The inevitable result, once the period of mourning was over, was a negative backlash against the 'mass hysteria'. This was particularly as so very few people – even mourners – were actually reacting in the emotional way that was being hailed as characteristic of this new 'structure of feeling'. If we define a myth as 'a widely held view of the past which has helped to explain the present' (M. Smith 2000: 2), it is clear that the popular memory of Diana's mourning as 'mass hysteria' serves as a largely negative narrative of national identity. Just as the wartime experience functioned as 'a landmark for who and what the British people are' (Hill 1999: 324) so the myth of mass hysteria serves as a mirror image, of what we should not be. For 'in the story we tell ourselves about ourselves' (Geertz 1975: 448) this is the only explanation for how a deviant, foreign, irrational dose of mob rule managed temporarily to 'take over the country' before, as one man put it, 'the nation got back to normal'.

7

A Women's Mourning

Chapter 3 noted how Diana's mourning cut across traditional boundaries of popular behaviour at royal events as monarchists and republicans found themselves united with each other on both mourning and non-mourning sides, or else not quite sure on which 'side' to respond. But a more traditional difference in attitudes came along gender lines. Media coverage, in line with its rhetoric of inclusivity, was concerned to emphasize the presence of the 'men in suits' who went to work with flowers in their hands and tears streaming down their faces. But overwhelming evidence demonstrates that this was a women's mourning for a women's princess rather more than a people's mourning for a people's princess. One examination of books of condolences in Reading, for example, found that 72 per cent of messages were written by women, with just 16 per cent by men and the rest joint or unclear (Jones 1999: 204). Meanwhile an ICM survey of 400 mourners leaving St James's Palace discovered that women, largely conservative women of middle Britain, outnumbered men by four to one (Kellner 1997). One psychological analysis also concluded that British women were 'significantly' more affected by Diana's death than men (Shevlin et al. 1999). Meanwhile instances of suicides, while remaining numerically tiny (the total increase was only forty), showed a 17 per cent increase in the month after, and were up by over a third among females and by 45 per cent among those aged 25–44 (Hawton et al. 2000). More generally, critical letters featured in the quality press were overwhelmingly from male readers, a gendered scepticism that did not pass without comment and condemnation from female mourners. A year later one commentator was noting how it was women rather more than men who were making the journey to the 'Diana museum' at Althorp. As one 45-year-old woman there with a female friend noted: 'My husband's not bothered one way or another. He thinks I'm silly coming here – he went fishing on the day of the funeral' (Bradberry 1998).

A number of polls also provided evidence of gender differences in reactions. A MORI poll (1998a) in March 1998 saw 29 per cent of women, as against 18 per cent of men, state they had signed the books of condolences, while 17 per cent of females claimed they had placed flowers, as against 10 per cent of males. Similar differences were found in the proportions stating that they were still upset, and claiming that they felt they had lost a friend. Meanwhile 20 per cent of men, two and a half times the figure for women, later took the most hostile option in a Gallup poll in agreeing that Diana was 'a privileged woman with an exaggerated public image' (*Sunday Telegraph*, 28 August 1998). And asked on the first anniversary a question that undoubtedly demanded a socially acceptable response, 'do you still feel sorry over the death of Princess Diana?', 77 per cent of women and 56 per cent of men said that they did, with 22 and 41 per cent respectively replying negatively (ICM 1998). Women also seemed more interested, with BARB television ratings figures suggesting that female viewing figures for the funeral were 30 per cent higher than that of men.

It was not only in Britain that such differences were reported. In America a number of commentators suggested, as one headline put it, that 'Men just don't get it but women relate to Diana's plight' (Griffin 1999: 245–6). In Australia a major Sydney hotel called in counsellors to help their female staff deal with their strong emotions. Men appeared less moved, with one comparing the news to 'coming home to find the couch gone – a shock but not devastating' (Durez and Johnson 1999: 149–50). The same pattern was replicated in cyberspace, with 44 per cent of one sample of internet books of condolences being clearly written by women, 24 per cent by men, with the rest joint or unclear (Jones 1999: 204). The polarities were visible in the online magazine *Salon*, which featured an article from a female contributor explaining 'Why Part of Me Died with Diana', while one male reader countered with 'I Don't Give a Rat's [Arse] about the Death of Diana' (Williams 1997).

This pattern also extended to analyses of the reaction. Women journalists and academics have dominated writing on the subject, despite the male-dominated nature of these professions (Walter 1999a: 28). There has also been a noticeable gendered difference in approaches, with women more likely to adopt pro-mourning perspectives while male contributions (including this one) have been overwhelmingly skewed towards the more critical side. It was a point illustrated dramatically by American academic Janice H. Rushing as, 'red-faced and bleary-eyed', she rejected the 'proper critical distance' demanded by male colleagues who would 'trash this event' and her 'overly emotional' reaction. Instead she called for a 'more empathic criticism', a 'female gaze' of 'reverence, awe and love' to temper the masculine aggression of 'academic *paparazzi* . . . profane hunters, chasing a textual prey into a corner and, when the bloodlust is especially high, ripping it apart' (1998: 154–66).

Such reactions were also clearly replicated in M-O's survey. Women were keener to voice their opinions – 56 per cent of women as against 49 per cent of males replied – while women also had more to say, they tended to write more. Women were collectively and also individually far more upset, if rather more divided in opinion than men, who remained largely unmoved or hostile. And it was women, not men, who could be found signing the book of condolences or placing flowers. In a postscript to her account a year after the funeral one 36-year-old female added: 'When I talk to other people about her, I find generally speaking that men of my generation have little time for her but women, even those who are anti-monarchy, will admit to being upset and a secret liking for her.'[1] Such a gender divide did not go unnoticed at the time by those who saw 'men by and large bemused by the strength of feeling expressed', or 'sorry but not as upset as the women'.[2] On the day of the news one sympathetic woman reported:

> Friends came to lunch and invariably the first thing we talked about was Diana's death; the wife was very sad and very critical of the Royal Family, saying that they had used Diana and discarded her when she had produced an heir and another son. The husband (I remembered he had previously been critical of the Princess) was very unbothered by her death and metaphorically shrugged his shoulders and said 'Well she's dead now'.[3]

These differences continued and sometimes intensified over the week. One recalled: 'my husband went to a (church) meeting, mostly men, who thought "it was all O.T.T.". I did not agree with them.' Similarly, a 44-year-old female teacher, herself something of a cynic, reported that her 'two male colleagues were the most disparaging of all, an unintelligent manipulative woman dies and the whole country proves that Hitler could have happened here.'[4] On the day of the funeral a middle-aged woman went with her husband to watch the cortège proceed down the motorway. Afterwards they were interviewed by local reporters who asked them, in the classic question of the week, how they felt. The woman replied that she was glad she had come to see Diana go by, but her husband said nothing: 'He wouldn't have been there but for me', she recalled. Rather less tolerant of such behaviour by this time was one older man who, his wife recalled, had 'had enough' of her bursting into tears every time she turned on the television. As a compromise she suggested a quiet walk to avoid a conflict over the funeral, which she taped and watched later when her husband had gone to bed.[5] Meanwhile a rather more ambitious effort to bridge the gender divide was gleefully recorded by another woman:

A married couple differed (50s age). She was devastated. Desperate to sign books of condolence – he, arch sceptic, what good did she *ever* do (Diana). Wife decides to buy (original) Andrew Morton book to talk him into being a Dianaphile. I'd love to have seen his face when his wife gave it to him.[6]

In all but two cases (unfortunately only briefly mentioned) there was no reverse gender divide, of mourning men and sceptical women, recorded. Moreover, the archive provides striking testimony of the intense nature of the engagement some women clearly made with Diana's life. One woman, a female teacher who was around the same age as the princess, wrote:

like most of the country I wanted to know her, felt I did know her because of her ability to inspire you, to touch you, to empathise with you. She reached millions of people, including me, in millions of ways and I think each person felt it personally to them, however she reached them. I had problems with self worth, so did she, I wanted to be loved, so did she, I was Di, so was she. I admired her for what she did – her charities, her compassion, her wearing her heart on her sleeve, her difficult role as a mother and wife. But I also wanted to be like her – I wanted her hairstyle, her figure, her poise, her ease with people, her assurance – things I don't have. To both ends I was fascinated – I admired and wanted to be like her.

Such personal feelings were also behind the reaction of a middle-aged female who was driving to her local swimming pool when she heard the news. She broke down in tears but carried on with her routine despite her instincts to go back:

So many thoughts were going through my head. A lot of the time I was crying as I swam, a lot of the time I hated men on her behalf. Not just the Paparazzi who it seemed had caused the accident which had killed her and caused much of her lifetime's misery, but the unkind husband who had loved someone else better and not seemed to try and help with the hurt he'd caused. I decided that a fitting tribute would be the banning of all land mines, another male invention.

Her 'aching feeling' of loss peaked on the day of the funeral. She walked alone to the local town hall and waited, along with about thirty others, in complete silence, to sign the book of condolences. She had thought every day over the previous week what she would say but recalled: 'In the end I was overwhelmed by reasons for my feelings, her beauty, her compassion, her suffering, her vulnerability, her stubbornness, her femininity . . . her generous heart'.[7] This intense level of identification was, however, far less visible among even the small number of sympathetic male accounts. Even when men were upset, Diana did not *mean* as much to them personally as she clearly did to some women.

Before we proceed further, however, one very important qualifying point must be emphasized. *To say that Diana's mourners were mostly women is certainly not to say that most women were Diana mourners.* As the polls above illustrate, at least 70 per cent of women did not sign a book of condolence, over 80 per cent did not place flowers, even if the vast majority of those who actually did so were female. We should be dubious about making generalizations that assume a monolithic and unique response among all women, or implying that women's (and men's) responses were determined solely or even mainly by their gender. Many women remained hostile, unmoved or ambivalent, while some men were upset, for the general reasons, shared by both sexes, outlined elsewhere in this book.

A 'Feminist' Story

Yet the striking gendered pattern of behaviour undoubtedly necessitates further exploration of this theme. There are a number of general explanations for this. Studies have consistently shown a greater level of women's interest in the royal family and a clear, underlying assumption that the subject was 'a woman's realm' from which men were largely absent (Billig 1997b). A MORI poll in October 1987, for instance, found that 25 per cent of women described themselves as 'very interested' in the royal family, more than double the 11 per cent of men, with over half of males declaring themselves uninterested (Billig 1997b: 173). In 1997 89 per cent of readers of the British royal magazine *Majesty* were women (Williams 1998). One reason for this is because 'the family on the throne' in Bagehot's famous phrase, symbolizes just that, the world of the private and domestic, often seen as a 'woman's world', a private sphere which is associated with the body, intimate relations and emotions. This is contrasted with a public sphere, a male world associated with reasoned debate, rationality and work. Among families interviewed in the late 1980s, people regarded royalty, and its association with gossip, weddings, fashion and glamour, to be so obviously of interest to women rather than men that it hardly needed stating (Billig 1997b).

Interest in royalty has long since formed a staple diet of women's popular culture. As far back as 1950 *Women's Own* serialized, over eighteen issues, Marion Crawford's *The Little Princesses*, the account by the former governess to the present queen, of life behind the scenes at the palace (Nairn 1988). Such an interest reached epidemic proportions by the 1980s, not least because Diana became the star pin-up of women's magazines across the world, whose every appearance on the front page was guaranteed to increase sales. On another level the royal story has some close similarities with the format of soap opera, in which women have always shown higher levels of interest. With strong female characters, 'feminine' themes of marriage, divorces, children and depression, and in privileging emotions, empathy and talk, soap operas can offer particular, if far from exclusive, appeal to women (Geraghty 1991; Gauntlett and Hill 1999). Long before Diana there were references to 'the royal soap opera' (Muggeridge 1955), but it was from the 1980s that this comparison was to be endlessly, if often disdainfully, made about the long-running saga of 'the royals' (Coward 1984). More particularly, the twists and turns of Diana's dramatic life and even more dramatic death 'made the soap format an irresistible framework for understanding her life' (Geraghty 1998: 71; Aron and Livingstone 1997).

So given that women showed more interest than men in Diana's life, it should hardly be surprising that this was repeated on her death. We might also expect Diana's mourning to replicate patterns in which men apparently grieve with less intensity than women (Walter 1999b), and also experience 'compassion fatigue', switching off from suffering more quickly than women and holding sufferers responsible for ills that afflict them (Tester 2001). More specifically and certainly, Diana's life as played out since 1981 had more relevance, and was likely to generate more sympathy, among women. They obviously had more affinity with her marital difficulties, while her depression, eating disorder and attempted suicide were all problems far more common among women than men (James 1997). All these sentiments were visible on her death. One younger woman, for example, wrote: 'In spite of her beauty and fame she abused herself and really suffered. She was open about it and I admired that. She cared about suffering people, about people like me with an eating disorder.'[8] She, as noted in chapter 3, had considered Diana 'as near to an anarchist as you can get in the Royal Family'. And likewise embracing the mantra of second-wave feminism that 'the personal is political', a number of high-profile accounts have hailed a Diana transformation from feminine to feminist role model. This was implicit in Andrew Morton's Diana-assisted biography *Her True Story* (1992) which presented her story as one of victimization, recovery and then empowerment. Issued in 1992 after being serialized – to massive controversy – in the *Sunday Times*, it sold four and a half million copies by the end of 1993 to make it, and two successive volumes (1995, 1997), undoubtedly the most influential story of Diana's life (Davies 2001: 91–2). But it was above all Diana's famous *Panorama* interview in 1995 that led feminist critics to embrace her. Journalist Susan Moore (1993) had initially been far from sympathetic to Diana's rebellion while hanging on to her privileges 'between colonic irrigations, *Vogue* covers and holding hands with lepers'. 'So I wouldn't cry too hard for her now that she has woken up to find herself "a prisoner in a gilded cage". At least her cage is gilded, unlike most,' she argued. Within two years (1995) she had turned Diana partisan as she hailed the 'I Will Survive' philosophy of a woman who, in prioritizing female emotions and wanting a modern marriage, had 'seen the light'.

But it was only in the aftermath of her death that this interpretation became dominant as feminist academics and journalists queued up to place their written tributes. American academic Elaine Showalter (1997a) hailed 'a courageous activist' who 'had achieved independence against enormous odds' while similar eulogies even replaced the normally arid prose of academic journal editorials (Purvis 1997). Most popularly both Julie Burchill (1997, 1998) and Beatrix Campbell (1997, 1998), in very different but similar stories, told how Diana, the self-described 'Prisoner of Wales', freed herself, beat the establishment and 'got a life' which embodied 'radical' causes. And certainly this approach reflected the changing attitudes of some women on the ground. The 36-year-old woman mentioned above noted how her position had shifted from initial antipathy to increasing, if still surprising, sympathy by the time of her death:

> My friend called from Dublin and we couldn't believe how upset we were. I mean, to us, Diana had been a bit of a joke, a sloane into big yucky gold jewellery, perhaps a bit dim. We were left-wing, radical, into feminist politics, and yet, and yet. During the past couple of years I had grown increasingly sympathetic towards her. Her intelligence may not have been academic, but boy! Did she know about media manipulation . . . and revenge (against the Royals). What she had was a fearsome intelligence of sorts. I also enjoyed seeing her, just as something beautiful to look at.

And by the end of her life this story of 'the bunny that hit back' certainly served as an inspiration to some. 'I can understand why she fought. Those faceless grey suited men who rule our lives make me fight', wrote one.[9] For one woman such gendered identifications cut across her royalist loyalties:

> She entered a family of rich bullies, who were used to getting their own way and whilst her actions irritated me at times because I felt it was adding to people's disrespect for the Royal Family, I can only admire her for the times she found strength to stand up for herself.

Less equivocal was another woman who attached a 'brilliant' Julie Burchill (1997) article she clearly agreed with:

> It is as a woman and as a feminist that I most deeply admire what Diana achieved. She fought for the truth despite a terrible betrayal which would fell most people. She was unafraid to speak of her bulimia. She was unafraid to utilise psychotherapy (when mental illness has such stigma). She was unafraid to speak out. She was a role model for women all over the world. We shall not see her like again.[10]

A 'Conservative' Story

Nevertheless these sentiments were confined to a minority and far more prominent in this collective response, in common with the one other empirical study to explore this theme (Black and Smith 1999), were more conservative identifications. Alongside the appeal of Diana's glamour and fashion and feminine qualities of compassion, the tragedy of a love story gone wrong with Charles and/or just about to go right with Dodi generated much comment among women but little among men:

> I loved her for her looks. I loved her for her compassion and I loved her for her showing the world how much she loved her children. If only Charles had loved her, what a wonderful Queen she would have been.

> I have a daughter the same age as Princess Diana, just like Princess Diana her marriage collapsed in similar circumstances, my daughter also has two children and has not remarried and I can understand the sadness of women in Princess Diana's situation. Prince Charles and the Royal Family should have looked after Princess Diana a bit better than they did. I feel Princess Diana became what she was because she was looking for love and I am glad she found love with Dodi, it is so sad that their lives ended as they did. This is what makes me cry.

As this demonstrates, others mourned a belated fairytale end to the Diana love story. It led one woman to assert: 'I do think she had found a good and loving man in Dodi . . . They did not look like new lovers to me.'[11] Before she died Diana's links with her 'playboy millionaire' had been the source of much critical commentary. But now the press stopped sneering and started romancing, posthumously elevating Dodi to the role of Prince Charming long since vacated by Charles. Among the public such a story was found in the large number of mourning cards, around a fifth of sites Walter (1999a) visited and many more at Harrods, that were addressed to the couple. 'Diana and Dodi RIP . . . May you have as much fun in Heaven as you did in St Tropez', said one of the sweetest (Monger and Chandler 1998: 105). The way this story tapped into 'a long Western tradition of doomed love' (Wilson 1998: 116) partly explains the attention given to a weeks-long relationship which some insiders considered was little more than a summer fling for her (Clayton and Craig 2001). It led some to view the accident as almost a happy ending. As one woman put it: 'I also felt then – and now – that perhaps this death was the best thing that could have happened to her. She'd found someone who she seemed to love.' Another who had initially heard that Diana was injured while Dodi was dead was 'in a way pleased that they had gone together and she had been happy and would not be unhappy again but always remembered as a very beautiful woman, ageless'.[12]

But the most central form of identification which women made was also the most obvious. If there is one collective emotional reaction that distinguishes male and female replies, it is Diana's role as a mother. Throughout her life this 'defined her more powerfully than any other identity; it was the role she felt most deeply; and it also constituted Diana as her most ordinary' (Davies 2001: 33). Even when Diana was claimed as at her most publicly assertive in her *Panorama* interview, at least half of her 'strength' was defined by her maternity as she stated, in the one clip shown before the opening credits: 'She won't go quietly, that's the problem. I'll fight to the end, because I believe I have a role to fulfil, and I've got two children to bring up' (Davies 2001: 115). And her maternal role was strikingly reproduced in an almost instinctive, repeated identification made by women – but much less so from men – with 'the boys' following the news, in sentiments which often transcended sympathy for Diana.

> My first thoughts, as most people's, were for William and Harry. Poor kids, they've been through so much in their young lives.

> My first reaction was sadness at the tragedy of it all to be followed by realisation that Prince William and Harry who were obviously devoted to her and had already been through the trauma of the divorce were now without their mother at the ages of 15 and 12.

> My first thought was for the young Princes William and Harry cruelly losing their mother who adored them and was adored in return.[13]

Mothers often explicitly made the link with their own children:

> My first thought was for the princes . . . having two sons myself I thought of the devastating impact this would have on them.

> I felt for her sons too. Her eldest boy is only slightly younger than mine. They looked like each other when he was young. Say what you

liked about Diana the woman, Diana the media manipulator (if so), Diana the abused, Diana the user etc.; she was there for her children and they loved *her* whatever she was and that in itself is important.

At no time did I want to cry and disintegrate. I was shocked by the suddenness and horror of the manner of death and the awful loss of her two boys – one of whom is much the same age as my son.[14]

Over the twentieth century one central level of popular identification with the monarchy was through its symbolic position as 'the family of families' (Schama 1986; Williamson 1988; Billig 1997b). Such a cult of the model 'family on the throne' was particularly strong in the 1940s and 1950s, so much so that to avoid tarnishing such an image Princess Margaret was prevented from marrying the divorcee Group Captain Peter Townsend. By the later 1970s, the image of a 'model family' was already breaking down and the Charles–Diana marital disaster was only the most damaging of a series of crises which saw the 'model family' image now spectacularly implode to leave one more reminiscent of a royal family from hell. Yet despite her close involvement in this negative rebranding, Diana emerged as the institution's most normal – or perhaps least abnormal – warm embodiment of family life.

Morton's accounts (1992, 1995, 1997) were highly influential in shaping such perceptions, offering almost caricatured contrasts between a good Diana, oozing feminine emotion and warmth, and a bad Charles, crippled by masculine coldness (Davies 2001). In death the contrast was further heightened. The emotionally stunted response from the Royals – Charles's failure to hug his boys for all to see – was compared with the expressivity of 'the people', as a 'good' almost proxy expression of Diana's mothering. Images of Diana with her sons abounded, laughing and soaking wet on a water-ride at the Alton Towers theme park, winning the mother's race at the school sports. Most repeated of all (and apparently her favourite photograph) was a 1991 picture of her exuding warmth from every pore as she greeted the arrival of her boys on board the royal yacht *Britannia* in Canada (the photographs of Charles hugging them seconds later were quite literally absent from the story). It was, indeed, difficult not to be moved by such images. As one of the above women added: 'Seeing pictures of Diana having fun with her boys was heartbreaking and I kept thinking of them.'[15]

Such emphasis on Diana as a mother peaked on the day of her funeral, which saw Earl Spencer's passionate tribute which emphasized the importance of her children and was defined above all by one heartbreaking image, the card to 'Mummy' placed on top of her coffin (Davies 2001). And again this contrast was widely reproduced, even among those who wanted little to do with the 'mass hysteria' but who still 'felt really sorry for the two princes because their mother had seemed to really care about them and to have put a bit more warmth into their duty bound lives'. As these comments illustrate, Diana's appeal as 'one of us' was a particularly feminine, maternal one:

> I felt sorry for the boys William and Harry, not only had they lost their mum but they'd lost the one person who let them live a life a bit more like normal boys their ages unlike that which they experienced with their dad's side of the family.
>
> I mourned the fact that there would no longer be any 'normality' in their lives. Who was going to take the boys to McDonalds, the pictures, the fairgrounds or get them togged up in normal clothes. I had a horror of seeing them dragged into Balmoral and tightly buttoned in tweed jackets and bleeding kilts.
>
> I could feel tears springing to my eyes and I felt sick and numb. With two young sons myself, all I could think about was how this would affect Prince William and Prince Harry. Who would be there to give them the unconditional love that mums do and who would now do all the fun things that normal children take for granted . . . Like a lot of people, I felt that I had lost a close member of my family.[16]

Such attitudes were notable largely for their absence among men. This difference was also illustrated by a 1998 poll in which 20 per cent of women stated that their main memory of the previous year was of the sorrow of the two boys, two and a half times the 8 per cent of men who remembered this (ICM 1998). And taking the comments of the last woman further, it is significant that it was almost always women who commented that it was as if a member of their family had died, a gendered intimacy towards royalty also shown to be visible in life (Billig 1997b). In this sense it is arguable that Diana functioned as what sociologists call a 'condensed social symbol' (D. Davies, 1999) for the existence of normal family life and her death struck at the heart of fears of its disruption among some women.

Again, however, given that most women did not feel grief-stricken – 68 per cent of one poll (MORI 1998) stated that they did not feel they had lost a personal friend – we should be careful in exaggerating the extent or depth of even these identifications. And some indeed specifically rejected Diana on gendered grounds. Some saw Diana as a bad victim (see chapter 3) in conventional feminine terms or rejected her image as the mother of the nation.

> She had been driving in a car at top speed whilst wearing no safety belt. Why at this point was she not thinking of her children? (Spent

years trying to be careful feeling I had to remain alive for the benefit of my *children*). What had she been thinking of?

We had this pumped into us morning, noon and night that what a good mother she was. Yet in the month prior to her death (school holidays to boot) she hadn't seen her sons. She was cavorting round the Mediterranean with an Arab.[17]

Another woman resented the repeated images of a perfect woman looking beautiful and doing something caring. 'It was as if the media were saying, look at all you other women, this is how you should be and it bugged me.' She was tempted to ring in to disrupt a radio eulogy and mention Diana's alleged role in the break-up of Will Carling's marriage, but her husband, perhaps wisely, cautioned that they should 'lay low'. More radical class-based gender was among the reasons for the angry hostility of one woman:

I DO NOT think she was a wonderful, loving mother, nor an inspiration to single mothers everywhere (what an insult to single mothers!) She was a rich woman who had her kids looked after by a nanny and packed them off to boarding school to be bullied by strangers at the age of seven, when any loving working-class mother would still be protecting and cuddling her sons. She never had any of the work or struggle involved in being a mother. She and her children were kept at the expense of the taxpayers.[18]

Such evidence illustrates how, on a positive level, Diana stimulated both 'radical' and 'conservative' identifications and sometimes even a combination of the two. But the predominance of feminine rather than feminist identifications tend to reinforce alternative arguments from the latter camp that Diana's life reinforced an almost caricatured combination of reactionary images of women (Macdonald 1995) fusing glamour, sexuality and beauty with victimhood, caring and mother-love (Holt 1998; Smith 1998; Gerrard 1997). For the predominant story, as told by the media and seen by 'the people', seemed to place Diana, when viewed positively, as a caring, beautiful woman who loved her children, was betrayed in marriage and whose life ended in the fairytale romance that her husband failed to provide.

In particular the above comments illustrate two linked problems with the feminist story of victim turned empowered survivor. What is notable about the Dodi link, not to mention the importance of her ex-husband during the mourning, is the comparative lack of availability of the story of Diana as a strong, single, independent woman. Diana's story was told in romance and maternal rather than feminist terms, and Charles 'whatever love means' Windsor was the great villain in a bad romance story, not the embodiment of deeper patriarchal domination of society. In this story Diana is placed as a victim rather than a survivor, whose chief complaint was that she was denied her rightful role in the fairy-tale romance. This was exactly the negative trait – her habit of playing the victim card – which some feminist writers criticized her for almost wallowing in during her life (Holt 1998). Even in Morton's account, for example, the 'story of her transformation from victim to victor' (1992: 3) is undermined by the repeated emphasis on her descent into horror-story victim (Smith 1998; Davies 2001). The same, even more so, could be said for the image of Diana's *Panorama* interview which firmly established her life story as the 'Princess of Wails', as Joan Smith described it in an essay written just before Diana's death:

> The princess looked and sounded drained, like a crime victim who had been persuaded by the police to meet the press and talk about her ordeal . . . This was someone . . . to whom terrible things had been done and whose statement 'I am strong' was contradicted at every turn by language and visual cues which insisted 'I am a victim'.

This may have made Diana the leading star of a growing contemporary culture of victimhood (Furedi 1998). But far from having constructed 'a new life', Smith suggested, Diana was recycling her old one in taking up the traditional role of 'the archetypal wronged woman' who 'all wind up young, beautiful and dead'. 'Her public likes her this way, no question', Smith concluded eerily, 'but is it a role she is prepared to die for?' (1998: 8–17) And, to put it most bluntly, ending up dead was not exactly the most empowering end to an at best embryonic 'new life', but naturally positioned her, and identifications with her, largely as a victim.

A Woman's World

This suggests a life that certainly offered scope for progressive identifications, but still remained largely seen through conservative lenses. In many ways the same could be said for her mourning, an event that inspired some feminists as much, if not more than Diana's life. A revolt against 'a patriarchy gone dry-eyed and stiff' (Showalter 1997a) saw a sudden and overwhelming irruption of the 'popular feminine' into a masculinized public sphere, 'a temporary undisputed triumph of all that is so frequently deemed by official culture to be embarrassing, excessive or trivial' (Barcan

1997: 37–9). Issues and emotions once seen as part of the private, personal, female world now became the basis of public debate – indeed outside this 'there was very little space in which to speak' (Geraghty 1998: 72). The popular mourning was proof that emotions could be political and offered the opportunity for a more feminine, caring reconstruction of British identity and politics (see also chapter 1).

Chapter 3 questioned the 'radicalness' of the event and so the same could be said about its 'feminist' nature. Some of the more celebratory feminist Diana analyses have parallels with work within feminist media studies, where much has been written on the pleasures and validation of experience that women gained from soap operas, women's magazines and romance novels. They have profitably explored the complex, diverse and sometimes subversive ways that people can interpret media texts, even apparently reactionary genres like romance-novels (see Zoonen 1994 for a summary). But they have also been criticized for an exaggerated and misplaced equation of pleasure with resistance and gendered empowerment (for example, McGuigan 1992; Seaman 1992). The same could be also said for her mourning. For it was not easy to determine quite what this new Diana-friendly feminism actually stood for apart from a 'good' emotionalism. Indeed its vacuous content, as the personal washed concern for political change clean away, led other feminists to lament the ultimate degeneration of an ideology so that it no longer meant 'believing in equality but believing in Diana' (Gerrard 1997; see also Holt 1998). Celebrating emotions and feelings now became seen as the goal in itself, as a substitute rather than a prelude to political change and the active pursuit of equality, as if a good cry could automatically bring the patriarchal structure toppling down.

Most certainly, women's voices and emotions predominated in public to an unusual degree during the week, while men were for once pushed into the background – although they still, in the end remained 'in control', both of the event and their emotions. Yet far from being sudden, this simply involved a temporary, marked expansion of a 'cultural public sphere' (McGuigan 2000), an area distinct and down-graded from 'normal', male-dominated public life, which provides a focus for discussion of issues normally associated with the private world. Soap operas and popular talk shows, which explore a diversity of personal and public issues from a personal, emotional standpoint, are the most obvious examples of this. And as their predominantly female participants and audiences illustrate, this standpoint frequently comes from the perspective of the 'women's world'.

This approach has also increasingly taken place within the main-stream media. The way the story of the week became a story of emotion fitted into broader shifts in news and entertainment values towards softer, more emotional, celebratory, 'feminine' and less macho styles (Hartley 1998). Over recent years reporting the facts has become less important than emoting them, as veteran BBC journalist Kate Adie found out when she faced internal criticism for her 'cold' reports on the Dunblane massacre in 1996. Diana's coverage, she argued, symbolized this shift to a 'new type of news' that was 'a great deal more senti-mental'. An increased emphasis on the 'personal, private and con-fessional' meant that, far from being 'told off for wearing their hearts on their sleeves', reporters were called on to 'show that you care as a journalist rather than just report in the traditional way' (BBC News 1998).

One rather more long-established manifestation of this 'cultural public sphere' is a royal family whose unique role is the way it functions as a rare public symbol of the private realm of the family. As Billig notes: 'It is that part of public life that is the presentation of the private. Therefore, it is, potentially at least, a feminised area of public life' (1997b: 173). Even before Diana's arrival it had served as a focus for the public discussion of 'women's issues', of marriage, children, glamour and relationships. Diana's impact, in both the content and style of what she said, certainly symbolized this broader shift in popular culture. Yet in many ways this emergence of 'the feminine world' during Diana's mourning was strikingly traditional, little different from the past patterns of behaviour concerning royalty. For just as Diana's mourning had produced a massive eruption of the feminine into a masculinized public sphere, so the same was true for her wedding – which no one had of course suggested could be claimed for a feminist movement whose slogan was 'Don't Do It Di' (Simmonds 1984: Billig 1999). Both, it might be argued, produced a Bakhtinian 'carnival' (Shepherd 1993), as 'a world turned upside down' by a temporary invasion of feminine values during a far from ordinary week only confirmed a masculinized normality when turned back again. It was a point well illustrated by one woman mourner who, after going to Hyde Park for the funeral noted: 'After all the outpouring of emotion I felt it was time to get on with ordinary life.'[19]

In many ways all this did, in terms of the popular reaction, was to reproduce the above gendered division of popular culture and more particularly, a taken-for-granted assumption from both sexes that royalty was 'a woman's realm' from which men were largely aloof. During the royal wedding, some men, even royalist men, sometimes remained absent, doing manly things like mowing the lawn or working in the shed, while women, even republicans, sometimes watched (Billig 1997b). Similarly in 1997 this gendered pattern of behaviour could transcend common feelings in attitudes to Diana. One woman, alarmed by an intolerant and 'over the top' public and media reaction, nevertheless watched and enjoyed the funeral with her daughter but recorded: 'Neither my husband nor son were interested.' Another female who shared much of her husband's hostility recorded in her diary for funeral day:

> My forty-seventh birthday and one that will be hard to forget. As the main part of the day is being taken up with watching Diana's funeral on television, my husband has arranged to go out. Rather ironically, he's volunteered to go and help with the school's Duke of Edinburgh scheme! . . . Soon after nine I kiss my husband goodbye and warn him to look out for goblins . . . He says that if the goblins do get him, I can be sure they're royalist. I wave him off and sit down in front of the television with my daughter.

One male sceptic, with an apparently equally sceptical wife, explicitly made the link with the past:

> My wife wanted to watch the coverage (on most channels) as a historical event, but I refused to participate in this spectacle, even on this level, even for a minute. I was reminded of Diana's wedding, when my sister had watched the event on TV for similar reasons and I'd retired to my bedroom with a copy of NME for the duration.[20]

None of the above people saw this pattern as requiring any explanation, this was just how it was. There were no instances of men settling down with their sons to watch the proceedings while their wives and daughters declined, declaring their lack of interest. Of course not all couples divided in this way, many watched or went to mourning sites together. One woman who watched with her partner and another couple noted that 'both husbands were amazed at the number of men in the crowds',[21] while there were frequent expressions of surprise made in media coverage at the number of 'men in suits' deeply upset. But on a deeper level even these very comments illustrated the naturalized dominance of a female world. These assumptions made the 20 per cent of men at mourning sites visible and noteworthy – especially those shedding feminine tears – while the remaining 80 per cent of women who dominated remained invisible, their interest and emotions taken for granted.

In such ways Diana's life and death may have reproduced traditional enactments of masculinity and femininity found in past royal events. For while women expressed their interest and emotions in relation to 'women's things' concerning the family, emotion and 'the boys', men, by contrast, were largely absent from the debate and even the home, deriding the over-emotional females and concerning themselves with rather more serious, rational matters. This is particularly true given that, as gender historians have argued, women's experiences must be seen 'not in isolation but in a persistent system of gender relationships', within which 'the actual nature of the social activity is not as critical as the cultural perception of its relative value' (Higonnet and Higonnet 1987: 34).

A Gendered Backlash

In the first place 'the cultural perception' of the 'relative value' of the Diana Event has been the source of division among women in general and feminists in particular over whether it, and she, was 'a good thing'. Such conflict was demonstrated dramatically in the immediate aftermath of Diana's death when Beatrix Campbell (1997) denounced Joan Smith's 'raggy and rageful . . . lazy leftist pout' against Diana in a vitriolic review that asked if the publishers had wondered 'whether they should pulp this book?' Secondly, in the emphasis on women's responses there is a tendency to overlook the other side of the equation – how the mourning impacted on both men and masculinity, and its relationship to this 'overwhelming eruption of "the popular feminine" '. We have seen how women were divided in mourning, not only between conservative and radical identifications, but also between those who mourned and those who saw little to identify with at all. The same is perhaps less true of men. During the week, according to the polls above, a quarter of the population signed the book of condolence, three-quarters of whom were women. The non-participation of more than 80 per cent of men in Diana's mourning, alongside the limited involvement of a large majority of women, tentatively suggest that men were more united against or distanced from the mourning, than women were drawn towards it.

Certainly male hostility has been evident in the media, where male journalists have been scathing both of the mourning in general and 'the feminist canonisation . . . of a modern Marie-Antoinette' (Steel 1998; Cohen 1998) in particular. Singled out for particular ridicule was Campbell's assertion that in telling her story on *Panorama*: 'Diana joined the "constituency of the rejected" – the survivors of harm and horror, from the Holocaust, from world wars and pogroms, from Vietnam and the civil wars of South America and South Africa, from torture and child abuse' (1998a: 203). 'This stuff is easy to piddle on', noted the BBC's political editor Andrew Marr (1998) and although he refrained, fellow male journalists joined the post-September non-mourning queues to soak the whole area with their personal acid. *Observer* columnist Nick

Cohen remarked scathingly: 'Let me see if I can get this right. Marrying into the admittedly unpleasant Windsor family is the equivalent of being napalmed in Vietnam . . . Diana and a survivor of a Nazi death camp are comparable' (Cohen 1998). The remedy to Campbell's lack of proportion, added Mark Steel (1998), might be found by offering a Vietnam veteran the advice: 'You think you had it rough, I know someone who was on *Panorama.*'

Such mockery did not amuse, however, but provoked bitter counter-attacks on a 'sexist socialism . . . uncontaminated by the people' (Campbell 1998b), from 'mute monarchists' guilty not only of 'sneering elitist condescension' but collaboration with 'those frozen sticks of fossilised shit that are the Court' (Grant 1997b). But the intolerance of pro-Diana feminists to dissenting views only added to the derision from male sceptics who accused them of 'chanting from the Ayatollah Khomeni's mosque' in prose that hysterically 'slipped the constraints of reason' (Cohen 1997, 1998). Such gender conflict was replicated on the ground, as the following extracts, from before and just after the funeral, further illustrate:

> Today (FRIDAY) I was in the library . . . and overheard a brief exchange between an elderly man and this time a young (25 yrs) female library assistant. The man obviously couldn't see what all the fuss was about . . . The young woman was obviously trying to keep her temper with the man and said tersely. 'Well everyone's entitled to their own opinion' and excused herself.

> One older bachelor I know who is quite friendly approached me outside our local supermarket . . . he could not wait to get onto the subject of Princess Diana and proceeded to insult the attention, love and emotion ignited by her passing. He made me very angry and when he spoke of the 'moronic masses' I did not take to it kindly and told him so. I thought to myself, 'I can imagine his ilk being a Nazi'.[22]

Another woman mourner was 'upset' by 'all those . . . snide remarks by left-wing males' she knew, while there were also disputes within relationships. One 37-year-old female was upset on hearing the news but her partner 'wouldn't stay in the room and retreated to the shed for a smoke' and later in the week 'started sounding off about how everybody was going overboard at saying how wonderful she was'. The division peaked on the day of the funeral, which she watched with her two younger sons, the eldest comforting her when she burst into tears. Her husband, meanwhile, remained in the kitchen before announcing at 11 o'clock that he was going out to buy a paper in what his wife angrily viewed as 'a deliberate act of disrespect'. Meanwhile the contempt of men for the reactions of predominantly female mourners is well conveyed in the following account:

> Friday, September 19, D a friend rings for a chat – mid 40s, male, UK sales manager for a tin and jar lid maker. He's West Yorkshire to the last vowel and blunt with it . . . and he tells me, 'J & G (wife and friend's wife) watched the funeral in floods of tears. Box of tissues each. Stupid.' . . . Anyway, continues D, had I seen all the dipsticks standing on the hard shoulder of the M1 as the hearse went by. He found it incredible.[23]

This attitude should not only also be combined with the scepticism among some women, like the narrator above, but also their defensiveness, even embarrassment in their interest and feelings towards the mourning. Numerous studies have found marked gender differences in male and female media preferences (Gauntlett and Hill 1999: 213–17). And although women found their favoured world, of fictional shows and romantic drama, a pleasurable one, it was a guilty pleasure, not only derided by males, but one they were embarrassed or apologetic about for their own supposedly inferior interests. While 'seen as interesting and relevant to them', it was 'also seen as secondary in rank to the "real" or masculine world' (Hobson 1980: 111) associated with politics and current affairs.

Similar findings have been reported in relation to royalty, interest in which was downgraded, by women as well as men, as inferior to the 'proper' rational world. It was, to quote two females, 'just gossip', the 'stupid things that women think of' (Billig: 1997b: 176, 186). There are hints of the same downgrading of such 'stupid' interests and emotions over Diana, a process given added weight by the cultural deviance of expressing such feelings for a stranger. One woman mourner captured some of this as she pointed out that her husband's motives for watching, in implicit contrast to hers, were 'more historical than hysterical'. Another woman noted afterwards that she had saved certain news-papers, 'much to the family's amusement'. And it may have been past experience of such mockery that led one woman to record: 'Thankfully my partner was not at home to see my watery eyes and make cutting comments during the funeral service. Most of my friends watched while alone and were glad of the privacy to do so.' And the comment, a year later, that women would admit to a 'secret liking' for the princess further suggests a certain embarrassment, even increasing shame, in 'coming out' as a Diana mourner.[24]

These above comments link up with a final point. 'One of the most potentially far-reaching consequences of Diana's death', suggested one contemporary analysis, 'is a rupture in the long-held association between emotional expressiveness and a hystericised popular femininity' (Barcan 1997: 37). But with the considerable benefit of hindsight, it is clear that the reverse is true. Suspicion of emotion in itself has often been seen as a highly gendered attitude, much more prominent among men. This was illustrated by one poll of the London population in August 2002 in which 57 per cent of men, compared with 37 per cent of women, dismissed the 'Diana grief' as 'hysterical' rather than 'heartfelt' (YouGov 2002). This pattern was explicit in the following comment:

> What I find nauseating is the frequency with which one hears 'We all loved her'. This is not only untrue, it is also deeply insulting to those unaffected by the mass hysteria. It is on a par with the reaction of the attitude of the females (I'm not being sexist, it's the females who do it) who stop to watch a wedding procession with the bride robed in virgin white and utter 'Aah! Isn't she lovely'.

In one sense it might be accurate to talk of a masculine backlash, which has successfully associated the mourning in general and in particular 'all those women over-reacting'[25] with the concept of 'mass hysteria', an age-old, reactionary stereotype of feminine irrationality (Showalter 1997b). But if this was a masculine counter-revolution, it was one which women, as well as men, were central in shaping, with the negative attitude to the 'mass hysteria' being a highly prominent feature of private female attitudes as well as being found in most male accounts. For it was not just suspicion of emotion in itself that the mourning stimulated, but suspicion of excessive feelings that were perceived as illegitimate to show towards a stranger. Far from being positive and emancipatory, this only strengthened profoundly reactionary stereotypes 'in which men have a monopoly of reason while women are creatures of emotion' (Holt 1998: 191). For arguably the most striking feature of popular attitudes is not the emergence of a 'feminine' emotionalism increasingly shared by men as well as women, but precisely the reverse – a 'masculine' attitude among both sexes that such an irrational, mindless, even dangerous emotionalism should have no place in rational public life.

8

A Fairy Story

Queen of Hearts?

The myth of mourning, of a British nation united in grief, was of course composed of numerous sub-myths that contributed to the broader picture of popular reactions. Media coverage conjured up a series of 'imagined communities' (Anderson 1991) of local, regional, ethnic, sexual and international mourners, united alongside and within the overall story of the British 'people's mourning'. Chapter 6 illustrated how reactions in the constituent UK nations were frequently presented in this way. And another less conventional but prominently emphasized 'imagined community' was what Earl Spencer called Diana's 'constituency of the rejected', groups that supplied the unusually rich and diverse colours of Diana's 'rainbow coalition' (Moore 1998: 33). Tributes from traditional royalists mixed with those from criminals, the homeless and many others not normally associated with royal events to 'a princess for women, for children, for blacks, for gays' (*Mirror*, 5 September 1997). The leading black newspaper *The Voice* hailed a 'Queen of all hearts' alongside pictures of black mourners (8 September 1997), while also much emphasized was a 'fairy story', which told of a considerable lesbian and gay mourning for a woman who was 'obviously a big gay icon' (Moore 1998: 33). News reports repeatedly 'dwelled on the same-sex couples who comforted each other in their moments of grief' (*Pink Paper*, 12 September 1997). One American journalist in London was among the many commentators to express himself 'shocked at the number of blacks, Asians and gays who were there laying flowers', seeing this as testimony to a Diana appeal which 'was able to transcend differences of race, sexuality and social background' (Cassidy 1997). Such a pattern also seemed visible globally as gay and lesbian communities in America and Australia responded with mourning tributes and fund-raising appeals.

Numerous commentaries stressed how Diana's Aids campaigning gave her a particular appeal to the gay community, a point visualized in an oft-repeated image during the week of the princess holding the hand of an HIV-positive patient in 1987. Through such efforts, the *Sun* considered that Diana had 'helped dispel the fear and ignorance which surrounded the disease' (1 September 1997), even if this conveniently forgot its own extensive efforts in promoting both. The *Mail*, similarly, profiled 'the compassion that overcame prejudice' and made the princess 'an icon for men and women suffering from Aids' (1 September 1997)'.[1] Strong support for this fairy story was offered by both leading and 'ordinary' gays and lesbians who, from Elton John downwards, found their views highlighted as they emerged out of the closet to head the mourning queues. Symbolic of a Diana appeal that had apparently transcended political and sexual barriers was the response of radical activist Peter Tatchell who hailed 'the de-facto patron saint of people with Aids'. His view was shared by, among others, Nick Partridge, chief executive of the Aids charity the Terrence Higgins Trust, who argued that Diana had 'taken away the stigma' from Aids (*Guardian*, 1 September 1997).

Such positive verdicts were replicated not just in the mainstream media, but in the gay and lesbian press in Britain and elsewhere. *Gay Times* (1997) dedicated their October issue to 'a good friend, someone who supported us and cared deeply about our suffering'. In Britain the *Pink Paper* considered that her 1987 gesture was 'the single most important action from a member of the Royal Family in 200 years' as it reported at length how 'The Gay World Mourns Diana'. A series of editions eulogized 'a queer icon' whose healing touch was 'said to have had the power to temporarily ward off death itself' as it said 'Goodbye Diana. You will always be the Queen of our Hearts'. 'Really devastated' gay and lesbian mourners profiled spoke of 'a deep spiritual identification' for a woman who had 'bluntly, changed their lives' (5–12 September 1997). Meanwhile the National Lesbian and Gay Switchboard was flooded with calls from those feeling personally bereaved after the news (Teeman 1997).

The paper responded to such sentiments by organizing, in conjunction with the National Aids Trust, a Red Ribbon mourning area on the day of the funeral to allow readers to 'come together to show how much we loved her'. Nor was such sorrow to be found merely in London as 'up and down the country' gay and lesbian communities ground to a halt in respect. Readers' letters more directly told a similar story of popular admiration for a 'heroine', who had touched many lives and whose death offered the opportunity to break down the barriers between gay and straight communities. In response to this 'sheer groundswell of popular opinion' (*Pink Paper*, 12 September 1997), the paper launched a campaign for construction of a memorial to Diana.

Such admiration was further demonstrated when a readership poll of 500 heroes and heroines of the gay and lesbian world saw Diana emerge with a landslide victory, relegating Oscar Wilde to a poor second (26 September 1997).

This theme, of a unified country embracing an equally united gay and lesbian 'community', has been developed, in qualified form, by a number of academic studies. Virtually all have claimed a disproportionate, not to mention highly monolithic response from gays and lesbians. Richards suggests that a close analysis of the crowds and vox-pop interviews reveals the prominence of women, ethnic minorities and 'gays who loved her for trying to dispel the fear of Aids (Richards et al. 1999: 8). Walter similarly points to the significant presence of gays who 'felt she was on their side' for this reason (1999a: 30). As we have seen, a more general theme of centre-left analyses (for example, Taylor 2000; Alibhai-Brown 2000) noted how ethnic minorities, gays, lesbians and the homeless were visible in their thousands as Diana, in life and death, extended the boundaries of citizenship to those previously excluded from the mainstream.

A number have also developed at greater length the reasons for the apparently 'close alliance with gay and lesbian styles and politics' (Johnson 1999: 36) that the princess made. She began her public life in 1981 as the fairytale princess in a royal marriage, a straighter than straight symbol of heterosexuality who was, according to the most detailed analysis, 'at best an irrelevance and at worst a complete anathema to many lesbians and gay men' (Valentine and Butler 1999: 297). But her life, they suggest, embodied a series of powerful paradoxes and took on an increasingly radical narrative with which gays and lesbians identified. This metamorphosis began with Diana's 1987 handshake. Mundane in retrospect, it came during a deeply homophobic and frighteningly ignorant mood about a 'deadly gay plague' sent from God to punish the evil deviants. Violence against gays accompanied a right-wing political agenda in which quarantining sufferers was considered a legitimate suggestion for debate. In this context Diana's '*aaah* image' (Cole 1998: 179) powerfully visualized the government information campaigns about Aids and made caring for sufferers respectable rather than dangerous. And it was followed by such high-profile work for Aids charities that it led conservative columnist John Junor to ask if the princess 'really wanted to go down in history as the patron saint of sodomy' (*Gay Times* 1998). Such campaigning also took on increasing significance to gays and lesbians when allied with later developments in Diana's story. Her comments transmitted to journalist Andrew Morton, 'I felt I was an oddball. But now I think it's good to be an oddball', were publicly articulated in her *Panorama* interview which marked the climax of Diana's queer-style 'in yer face' battles with the royals (*Gay Times* 1998; Benzie 1997; Valentine and Butler 1999).

This, as argued in the previous chapter, was allegedly part and parcel of the emergence of a 'new' feminist-friendly Diana, who 'came out', denounced the establishment and conquered the demons of self-loathing, not to mention the obsessive scrutiny of her private life. In doing so she broke away from the regulatory regimes of 'normal' family life, an action later symbolized by her unconventional relationship with a Muslim, Dodi al Fayed (Spurlin 1999). Meanwhile her close friendship with prominent gay individuals like Elton John and Gianni Versace further reinforced her position as a significant political figure in the lives of gay men (Benzie 1997), or at least someone prepared to embrace difference. In all this Diana emerged as 'the ultimate in-between', an insider but also an outsider. She had become 'a rebel with some pretty good causes' (*Gay Times* 1998), sexually straight but politically queer in the 'visible radicalism' (Valentine and Butler 1999: 301) she allegedly embodied in both her public and personal life. Such a reading of Diana's life as one of empowerment rather than victimhood places her as 'a very modern gay icon', moving beyond the traditional appeal of Judy Garland, who 'although she always managed to come back, never fought back' (*Gay Times* 1998). But her life could also fit the traditional appeal in terms of its tragedy, as well as her glamour, drama queen persona and emotional style. Meanwhile the more tolerant, progressive social order she embodied was given dramatic climax as lesbians and gays mixed freely with conservative Middle England to mourn what Valentine and Butler call a 'Queer Princess . . . the embodiment of radicalism . . . a symbol of the margins that fostered unity'. This, they suggest, was 'the true fairy story precipitated by the Royal Wedding' (Valentine and Butler 1999: 300–1).

Such analyses provide interesting speculations about Diana's increasing queer significance. But again these confident generalizations about attitudes are accompanied by a failure to examine what gays and lesbians on the ground actually thought. This can be traced, in a more specific variation of the 'problem' identified in chapter 2, to the 'over-textualisation of lesbian and gay experiences' (Plummer 2000: 54) to be found most notably in the queer theory that informs some of the above analyses (Valentine and Butler 1999; Spurlin 1999). The result is that they remain unsubstantiated in both detail and their assumptions that 'Diana was mourned with a special intensity within the gay community' (Johnson 1999: 32); or even (or especially) in the emphasis that 'while for some lesbian and gay men Diana undoubtedly remained an anathema, for many her death was experienced with a profound sense of loss' (Valentine and Butler 1999: 300). The former assertion was not confirmed by the only poll of London mourners, in which 4 per cent described themselves as gay, figures broadly similar to those which would be obtained from any general survey (Kellner 1997), while the figures for the black and Asian communities similarly reflected the national average. Given what we know of the partiality of media coverage in general, it is quite possible that a media seeking a dramatic, newsworthy story of inclusivity, may have also disproportionately emphasized the response of 'the excluded' in general, and gays and lesbians in particular. This may have conveyed more positive images of gay and coloured people, but how accurate a verdict it was on the general reactions within these constituencies remains debatable.

Less speculative is that even a close scrutiny of overwhelmingly monolithic media coverage suggests a more equivocal response. In *The Voice* a heavily qualified editorial suggesting that 'to some extent Princess Diana, despite not speaking out directly against racism, managed to break down some of the barriers between her as a Royal and the black community' implied a less positive range of sentiments, as did one reader's attack on 'idol worshipping' (8–15 September 1997). Meanwhile the one dissenting voice from the queer press came from a journalist on the Sydney-based monthly magazine *Lesbians on the Loose*. Unable to grieve for someone known only through a 'carefully crafted' media image, she angrily protested against being 'expected to mourn the loss of a straight woman who lived a life of extraordinary privilege and who dared touch a man with HIV'. The apparent gratitude for 'so little' was further compounded by the ingratitude for so much offered by others who had provided dedicated, tireless support amidst the full-time demands of their lives but who would 'not have worn Armani, or left behind $44 million' (Quirke 1997). In Britain rather more qualified initial dissent came from one reader of the *Pink Paper* who pointed out that, while Diana had done good work, 'many who will forever remain unsung have done a lot more' (12 September 1997).

Harsher criticism followed in subsequent weeks after the lapse of what one called 'a suitable amount of time'. Memorial plans were 'all going a bit far' from a paper which instead of adopting a 'mature stance', had been 'swept along with the tide of popular hysteria' in their 'canonisation' of her. One sympathizer suspected that Diana's triumph as the number one heroine of the gay and lesbian world would 'split opinion over her worthiness', a view supported by another reader left 'pretty depressed' that it could be topped by 'a dead princess who told her children that Aids was cancer' – the story Diana told them when they visited a friend dying of the disease (12 September 1997–3 October 1997). One mourning couple in London were also upset by the presence of such 'lack of respect' following her death:

My partner and I inquired at several gay pubs if the record 'Candle in the Wind' could be played as a tribute to Diana, and we even offered to make a donation to charity. We were often met with sarcasm and were humiliated. To add further insult, one particular landlord played 'Dirty Diana' by Michael Jackson instead – which was extremely distasteful – before he handed us our donation back. (19 September 1997)

Such conflict also provoked angry denunciations from others. One sceptical reader was rebuked by another asking: 'How many pictures showing Diana meeting people with Aids do you need to realise what she's done?' (5 September 1997). In Australia the fear of the *Lesbians on the Loose* journalist that she would have been 'shot down in flames' if she had dared reveal her views at a gay venue on the night of the funeral were confirmed by angry reader responses. One woman expressed 'shock that you should print' such insulting 'crap', while another was 'astonished, amazed and quite dumbfounded at not finding a tribute to Diana' but instead the 'shameful garbage' and 'small minded, badly written muck' from 'a gutless, empty, self serving, nasty, jealous little individual . . . Shame on you' (*Lesbians on the Loose*, November 1997).

The National Lesbian and Gay Survey

Shameful or not, such differing reactions suggest the need for further exam-ination of the response of gays and lesbians, among others, to her death. Part of the problem is the lack of available evidence beyond media cover-age, and M-O's Diana survey (and that by the BFI) provides little illumin-ation, with minority voices being notable only for their absence. But one non-mediated, if very small-scale exploration of popular attitudes was made by the British National Lesbian and Gay Survey (NL&GS), an organ-ization founded in 1985 by Ken Barrow, a volunteer for the M-O project. It aimed to 'give a voice to the ordinary lesbian and gay . . . the person who wouldn't have a voice otherwise' (quoted in Sheridan et al. 2000: 158) and allow them, anonymously, to offer a picture of ordinary gay and lesbian lives. Since 1985 volunteers have been regularly issued with broad, M-O style directives seeking their opinions and experiences on a range of subjects relating to their sexuality, a selection of which have been published (National Lesbian and Gay Survey 1992, 1993). Barrow died from Aids in July 1993 and since then the project has been run by former volunteer Kerry Sutton-Spence. In 1997 the organization had roughly forty volunteers and on Friday 5 September 1997 a directive, similar to, if more specific than, M-O's, was sent out asking for their views on the news, mourning and Diana's contribution in promoting acceptance towards gays and lesbians.

It received twelve replies, ranging from five lines to six pages from people from a variety of class, age and geographical areas within England. Before highlighting the themes, it is important to stress the limits of such evidence. Obviously this very small-scale, self-selecting survey does not aim or claim to offer *any* quantitative insight into the attitude of the gay and lesbian 'community', even if this was possible. And having accused others of prioritizing particular attitudes of gays and lesbians from evidence that cannot support such generalizations, it would hardly be wise to do the same. On the other hand, as with M-O, the detail of replies (averaging two pages) facilitates qualitative, empirically grounded insights into the lived experiences of 'ordinary' gays and lesbians, although it cannot, unfortunately, shed much light on the rather overlooked theme of differences between the two. Even so, these bottom-up perspectives not only provide 'ivory tower academics' with a much needed 'reality check' on their assumptions (Weeks 2000: 7), but also help nudge power relations back towards 'ordinary' people in the 'credibility struggles' (Epstein 1996) over who has the authority to speak on their behalf.

The first point to emphasize is that while media coverage of the entire gay and lesbian 'community' seemed to find only one reaction, the twelve contributors to the NL&GS articulated, collectively and some-times individually, a diverse range of attitudes. There was certainly evidence of the prioritized response. One 32-year-old female recalled: 'Ellen, my lover, and I cried and held one another all through the morning as we absorbed all the ghastly details . . . we just lay in each other's arms and sobbed for hours at the awful loss.' Yet such attitudes competed with a rather more restrained, if less newsworthy, response from others. A 32-year-old male was on holiday in Ireland with his partner and was told the news at breakfast by the owners of the guest-house where they were staying:

> I remember I thought that's quite funny, but rather a risky joke, we could have been royalists (we're not!). And there it was on the news, large as life (!) . . . 'Oh dear, that's rather sad' we said as we stood around sensing that they were waiting for us to respond. 'We're not really great fans of the royal family' we said (understatement), 'but that's very sad news.' 'Can we have scrambled egg this morning please' . . . We pretty much went about the rest of our holiday unaffected.

Such indifference was dwarfed by the contempt of one middle-aged male market researcher for 'a trivial event – as her life was trivial':

> I am writing this exactly six months after the death of Princess Diana. I have left it that long in order to cool down from my initial feelings of

anger and amazement when I received this directive. I was astonished
that the National Lesbian and Gay Survey felt this directive necessary,
felt that the death of the Princess had any more or less relevance to gay
people than to straight. In fact I am still astonished that *anyone* felt that
the death of the Princess had any relevance to their life. It was certainly
an irrelevance to mine.[2]

Other respondents, while less hostile, shared what one female described as
a 'sense of bemusement' on receiving the survey, as she wondered 'why is
this event so dramatic that it deserves an entire directive?' One middle-
aged woman was similarly 'annoyed that even in the lesbian and gay
environment this event was being assumed to have some personal
significance for me'. She had, she recalled, 'expected lesbians and gays to
have something more of a sense of proportion' in their response, a view
echoed by its dismissal in under fifty words by one 18-year-old female
who argued: 'I cannot see that this event will seem to future historians like
a key date in lesbian and gay history, nor that it merits a special directive.'[3]

Such a rejection of the relevance of Diana's story may well have been
even stronger among the large majority of volunteers to the NL&GS who
chose not to reply at all. Detailed responses more conclusively suggest a
range of opinions amongst partners and friends. A 24-year-old male cook
was unaffected while his boyfriend was 'full of deep grief', mirroring
what he detected as a broader 'strong division of opinion' among his
friends. Conflict with his partner quickly followed when, sick of the
continuous media coverage, he hired a video and 'got a lot of grief . . . for
being disrespectful'. Elsewhere a female mourner had found one of her
friends 'very upset – as though a personal friend had been lost', but also
met a 'mostly indifferent' response from her partner's gay son, which
came complete with 'some anti-monarchy joking' with his own partner.[4]

More generously, feelings of sorrow but not the devastation of
personal bereavement were combined with shock, surprise and disbelief. 'On the day itself and for some time after . . . I kept expecting her
to pop up and make more headlines', recorded one woman who noted
that the only thing that would get her emotional at all was sadness for
'the boys'. Initial thoughts and conversations instinctively turned to
conspiracy stories and assassination plots which saw the couple
holidaying in Ireland speculating 'how convenient Di's death was for
the remaining royals', allowing Charles to remarry and preventing
'mixed race half-royal babies popping up and embarrassing the
monarchy'. Most expressed largely sceptical opinions in which some
admiration for Diana was counterbalanced with considerable barriers to
identification. Again some responses defied neat categorization. One
middle-aged female was dry-eyed and hostile throughout the week, but

became briefly caught up in 'the swirling eddies of grief' on the day of the funeral before quickly returning to her 'refusal to have anything more to do with the matter'.[5]

One of Us

Three of the twelve replies emphasized a personal reaction that was to some extent 'caught up in the universal grief' following the news. Their common explanation for this was the 'world of difference' Diana made 'in the area of gay and lesbian acceptability in society'.[6] A particularly rich insight into such identification was offered by one middle-aged female lecturer who was 'captivated' by the week of mourning, despite her 'inner reluctance . . . political instincts and better judgements'. She was among those who were 'ambushed by their own emotions' (Ignatief 1998: 187) in their response:

> I still do not understand the strength of my emotions or the sense of loss. It still does not seem rational – I am a socialist, a feminist, a lesbian woman, anti-monarchy etc. I spent the days of Royal Weddings on remote Welsh beaches! I spent the day of Diana's funeral enthralled and absorbed by the T.V. coverage. I have to say that I *would not have missed it for the world.*

The reason for this dramatic change in the story since 1981 were illuminated in a reply which viewed Diana's life as 'a real paradox' of two contrasting stories:

> here is an Insider (beautiful, rich, privileged, not one of us) who also appears to be an outsider (bulimic; divorced (from husband and The Firm); a supporter of other outsiders; perhaps in some ways one of us after all). I think at some level we were grateful that she *included* the *excluded* . . . those disabled through mines; those with AIDS. Although as a feminist she was not my sister (she was after all a member of the elite) yet she was also my sister (she knew what it was like to be abused and used as a woman) in her defiance of conventions . . . Little wonder that she held some fascination for those of us who remain outside even when we appear to be on the *inside*.

The competing pushes and pulls of such a double life and death generated a deep 'ambivalence' and 'confusion of feelings' after the news. But she became quickly sympathetic towards a woman who 'led the establishment on an unmerry dance' and whose mourning symbolized a post-

Thatcherite hope for 'a more caring, loving, charitable approach to people – especially for those of us on the outside – women/gays/those with "positive" status'. This peaked with the funeral as the respondent, watching on television, 'experienced a kind of loving connection' with the crowds. The flowers and the applause of Earl Spencer's anti-royalist speech signified a popular, participatory anti-establishment 'collective resistance', embodied by a woman who was:

> at the end of the day an anti-hero not a hero . . . For me her funeral became a celebration of those who are defiance – those who 'kick up a fuss' who 'won't go quietly'. She was a victim true – but she was also a survivor and a resister. No wonder gays, lesbians, black people etc came out for her on the day of the funeral. As one punk commented 'she was a rebel' and he liked rebels.[7]

She also hinted at the way Diana's death allowed her 'to make sense of private unresolved grief' in a pattern similar to the response of others in September 1997. Those manning the National Lesbian and Gay Switchboard found that callers were grieving over personal losses as Diana's death gave them 'the opportunity to open up' over past losses (Teeman 1997). Such a connection was also made by one middle-aged man, whose 'very first thoughts' were 'not again', as the news triggered a comparison with the early deaths of his two sisters at the ages of 18 and 21. On a different but equally personal level, one younger woman's sadness at the loss of 'an icon of everything I love and find attractive in my own sex' provides a glimpse of Diana's sexual appeal to at least some lesbian women (Valentine and Butler 1999: 300).[8]

One of Them

Such evidence illustrates how some gays and lesbians increasingly identified with the Diana fairy story. Others, as we have seen, were not convinced by such a tale and offered a number of explanations why. For some Diana simply remained, as one woman put it, the 'classically heterosexual icon'[9] that had emerged in 1981, an obvious alternative reading which is made even less surprising given her lukewarm image among lesbians and gays between 1987 and 1997. Assessments of Diana's campaigning for Aids charities, for example, were almost as grudging during her life as they were flattering after her death. Diana's gesture in 1987 was not viewed as particularly important by the gay press at the time but was, as the editor of *Gay Times* recalled, seen as 'a drop in the ocean' of homophobia, 'a pleasant but not terribly significant gesture' (D. Smith 1997).

The result, as one sympathetic analysis concedes, was that 'during most of her life, except for that brief period following her separation from Charles, the queer aspects of Diana's image were difficult to ascertain as they were often socially obscured by official images of her connections to royalty' (Spurlin 1999: 156).

Even then, they remained far from clear. In 1994 two newspaper surveys of gay icons did not even afford Diana a mention (*Guardian*, 23 September 1994; *Observer*, 18 September 1995). And as late as the edition before her death one reader of the *Pink Paper* (29 September 1997) had protested about Diana's inclusion even in the paper's list of 500 heroes and heroines asking, 'What has she done?' While her death certainly led gays and lesbians to reflect on Diana's life more positively, these competing sentiments did not vanish from thoughts, even though they vanished from view. One middle-aged woman evoked precisely these 'longer memories' of how Diana 'had been rebuked in the past for speaking at a convention supporting "family values" – remember the placard-carrying dykes and gay men?' Her resultant belief that 'Diana did nothing for gay issues' was shared by others rather more sceptical about her impact and efforts in promoting tolerance of homosexuality. Even the famous photographs of her shaking hands with an HIV-positive man generated an oppositional stance from the male market researcher who wrote of his

> annoyance that she has been elevated to the status of a 'gay icon' on very little evidence that the (very, very little) work she did for gay charities was of any lasting value. I am absolutely certain that the front-page photos of her shaking hands with PWAs had no lasting effect on the public intolerance of AIDS. The photos did a lot of good for her own image (which seems to have been the driving concern of her whole life) but I know that far from dispelling they did as much to *reinforce* the disgust and fear that many people still feel.[10]

Featuring prominently in such detachment was a fundamental barrier to identifying with Diana's life among these volunteers – her continued close association with royalty. We have seen how Diana's story tapped into the identity of one respondent as 'a socialist, a feminist, a lesbian woman, anti-monarchy' – although only with some difficulty. Part of this, indeed, inclined her to the sceptical view of her partner's gay son, who had worked for an Aids charity. Like his partner and colleagues, he still viewed the princess as 'intimately bound up with the monarchy and thus beyond much consideration'. Others shared these views. One younger man explained that his bemusement on receiving the directive stemmed from the fact he was 'instinctively not a monarchist'. 'I didn't want to be bothered with it at all', agreed one woman; 'she was part of a royal idolatry this country practices and I couldn't give a toss really.' One middle-aged female who had been 'very detached and puzzled by the whole of this event' recalled that on the day of Diana's wedding she had been riding on a motorbike along the empty roads of Gloucestershire. She evidently felt nothing had changed to demand her attention towards a woman who symbolized 'an outdated and useless class system that serves only to keep the rest of us down'. Diana's position as a rebellious royal insider rather more than a fellow outsider helps explain why most of these responses failed to even show awareness of, much less sympathy for, the 'visible radicalism' of the post–1987 fairy tale detected by academics. Rather more visible was a continued reactionary horror story starring what one man described as 'a spoilt, vain, immature, self-indulgent product of the upper classes', who, having opted out of her marriage, 'continued to exploit the position of privilege to which she no longer had any right'.[11]

This level of hostility was not replicated by others, but it does illuminate a broader class barrier to identification that stemmed from the enormous gulf between Diana's life and that of 'ordinary' gays and lesbians. We have seen how, even among those sympathetic, lack of affinity for Diana's position as a member of the elite competed with admiration for an 'anti-hero'. For others this position served to transcend or qualify any queer identification. As one female argued:

> Diana, like any other celebrity, lived a life which I cannot imagine: a life of wealth and privilege . . . If she had gay friends – Elton and Gianni – then that was not a statement to the world, in my view. It was a private friendship between seemingly extraordinary people; unreal people; people who cannot be like the 'poofter down the road'. I can imagine gay-bashing thugs sweeping through the streets holding posters of 'We love you Diana' in one hand and beating the crap out of gays with the other, never thinking that the person they are brutalising is like the friends of the woman these thugs profess to love.

While one man offered more praise for the way Diana had gay friends and 'did use her privileged position to good cause', this very position provoked him to wonder 'how much did it really affect her given that on the day of her death she had just received a ring worth £250,000'. This led him to conclude: 'In the unbelievably wealthy circles that they moved in money speaks very loudly and I don't really think her friendship encouraged tolerance or acceptance except in the broadest scheme of things.' This lifestyle also served to neutralize any anti-establishment sympathy for Diana's battles with the royals. One younger man noted a widespread view among his friends that 'she had status and a lot of homes and money, and the ability to still have affairs so why was she complaining'.[12]

As for her contribution to Aids awareness and other causes, this had to be placed in its proper perspective. 'I suppose if we must have celebrities they might as well do something useful and there is no doubt that she did her bit', one woman grudgingly conceded. But 'no more however than many unsung heroes and heroines' within an unfair system where fame worked 'to falsely inflate the contribution of some over others'. One of the twelve respondents had met Diana ten years previously, but unlike the many accounts which profess to her alleged magical appeal, she had not been impressed: 'All I remember is that she wore a turquoise suit and looked very thin and rather bored and I couldn't understand what all the fuss was about.' She detected in her subsequent attitude

> an element of resentment that any woman can command so much adulation because she . . . happened to be born into a privileged family . . . I have far more time for the ordinary, unbeautiful people who work with homeless people or people with HIV/AIDS all the time and without even a percentage of such praise and admiration.[13]

The Mourning After

Such responses show close similarities to those found elsewhere in this book and the same is true for responses to the mourning after. 'Her death was not a great period of grief for me as I never knew her', noted one man simply. The strength of this common-sense attitude could transcend identification with Diana's campaigning on gay issues. As one man noted:

> As an individual I respected Diana's excellent work with HIV and AIDS . . . I think her work did make an impact and yes, I do feel that her open-ness helped in terms of gaining wider societal acceptance . . . But the mass reaction to a death of someone who the vast majority of us had never met and did not know, I simply couldn't relate to . . . I am sorry but I would be lying if I said I felt anything on an emotional level.[14]

This again meant that people saw little to identify with and much to deride in the 'bizarre and worrying' public hysteria. Cynics also thought it 'highly ironic that it was probably the very thousands "mourning" her who had bought the newspapers and magazines . . . which generated the harassment' in the first place. Others considered that the public 'obsession', far from being sexually progressive, offered a deeply depressing illustration of 'the moral, emotional and political poverty of our society'.[15]

This suspicion of the emotions stimulated towards a stranger also extended to those who were upset. The most sympathetic woman was, like her friends, filled with 'a deep distrust of emotions . . . As my mother was to say after the funeral (she watched it in tears with a friend, sipping sherry and laughing at herself), it has "made ninnies of us all".' And while some within a gay community often associated with expressivism hailed the apparent demise of 'Prince Philip's stiff upper lip' (D. Smith 1997), not everyone wanted to 'break out of the emotional straightjacket and cry' (Teeman 1997). For some its removal was a source of severe discomfort for their male and/or national identities. 'Maybe I'm too English or too male but I found the whole thing very embarrassing', noted one man 'taken aback by the mounting tributes and the mounting bunches of flowers'. Or as another man, 'nauseated (not too strong a word) by the media-fed hysterical public reaction', suggested: 'It was disgusting and made me embarrassed to be British.'[16]

As these comments suggest, media coverage was also a source of criticism, suspicion and cynicism – but also fascination. On a nurses ward staff commandeered a television on hearing the news but initial fascination turned quickly to annoyance. 'Their low hushed voices, oozed sadness, seemed insincere and rapidly got on my nerves.' Diana's post-death sanctification – mocked as 'Diana for Queen of Hearts. Diana for a sainthood. Diana for God' – also provoked unease among those who were 'not uncritical of her during her life and would be more comfortable with a more balanced appraisal'.[17] Even sympathizers agreed 'that the media overhyped everything' but nevertheless produced 'very addictive viewing', in an ambivalence well captured by one middle-aged man:

> I watched a lot of coverage over the next week but I very often found myself annoyed when I wanted some relief and my favourite programmes had been cancelled. I do feel that the coverage was too extensive and the media helped to stoke the nation's grief.[18]

And while even those upset were sometimes critical of media coverage, those who were not sometimes found that they 'wanted to be aware of what was happening' during the course of 'a unique event' which they had been 'unable to ignore'.[19] This peaked with the funeral, with one female cynic becoming momentarily engrossed and upset after a 'breathtaking and marvellous' eulogy from Earl Spencer, even if Elton John's tribute was less generously dismissed as 'crap'. Rather less complex, if more flattering for the singer, was the motivation of one 32-year-old man, who offered proof that, while Diana's mourning may not have embodied an 'alternative fairy story' for everyone, it could still remain an entertaining one:

> I ended up spending pretty much the whole of Saturday watching the funeral on telly. I had intended to just catch a bit at the beginning and then do something else, but how often do you see a royal funeral on television? Especially one with Elton John singing at it?[20]

Unravelling the Fairy Story

Clearly the NL&GS respondents were very far from being 'united in grief' in response to a life and death which generated a range of conflicting and sometimes ambivalent reactions. Some were drawn to the story of a 'queer princess' who had transcended traditional boundaries to become 'one of us', an outsider who worked for and symbolized the position of marginalized others. But for others detached by Diana's heterosexual image, wealth, 'unexceptional' charity work and royalty, such a fairy tale was seen as precisely that. Meanwhile the story of her mourning provoked identification on personal and political grounds. But its dramatic departure from a culture of private, personal grief also generated disbelief and alienation, tinged with fascination. Such responses closely replicate the key themes found throughout this book – indeed there was little that was particularly unique about the above attitudes. While the response to Diana's death may have united some within the gay and straight communities in mourning, it also united others in apathy or hostility. This also demonstrates the pigeonhole simplicity of accounts that have explained the response of gays and lesbians as determined solely (and positively) by their sexual identity with Diana. This, negative and mixed as well as positive, was only one element among other, sometimes conflicting or more important multiple identities and influences in shaping individual attitudes. Even when writing within a context in which their sexual identity was prioritized, this was only one, albeit important, feature of the broader attitudes of gays and lesbians.

It would be foolish to overinterpret such small-scale evidence. But arguably it is the very range of views generated by just a dozen responses that so very clearly illustrates – indeed undoubtedly understates and oversimplifies – the complex and contrasting reactions to the Diana Events from gays and lesbians, to say nothing of the differences between them. And it seems highly plausible that Diana's paradoxical life should have produced such responses to her death from pluralistic and divided gay and lesbian communities, not to mention the range of views that the extraordinary events of the mourning stimulated. The existing emphasis on Diana as a 'queer princess' is important in explaining the remarkable fact that she was mourned at all by some lesbians and gays. But it would be wrong to oversimplify or ignore the diverse responses suggested here. To do so really would produce a fairy story.

9

Mourning News: The Media, the People and the Veil of Tears

Media Power and the Myth of Mourning

The above chapters have demonstrated a range of complex and sometimes contradictory popular reactions during Diana's mourning, as competing attitudes and identities drew people in towards the mourning but also alienated them across a range of themes. But above all they demonstrate a reaction that differed markedly from the media impression of the response of 'the people'. For the myth of the mourning, of a nation united in deep, tearful, adulatory grief was precisely that. The vast majority of the country did not visit mourning sites, place flowers or feel personal grief in the way that was widely emphasized. Meanwhile even among the minority who signed the books, placed flowers or went to London, there were proportionately few reacting in a deeply tearful, adulatory, grief-stricken way, and attitudes and motives were frequently complex. The behaviour widely attributed to 'the people' was in fact the preserve of merely a small minority within a minority, perhaps shared by, at the very most, 10 per cent of the population.

Yet while unmediated popular experiences were very different from the mediated message, what is striking is the extent to which people's perceptions of the public mood corresponded with media images. Such an apparent paradox fits in more broadly with research on media effects which has demonstrated that just because audiences are active does not mean that they are immune to media power (Philo 1999). So we have seen how people resisted the sanctification of Diana or the pressure to grieve or consumed media coverage in a frequently less than reverential manner. Yet while there were serious limits to the way media coverage could influence individual reactions,[1] at the same time it was able to profoundly influence perceptions of how others were reacting.

Throughout this book we have seen how people made generalizations about the reaction of 'the public,' 'the nation' or 'the people', and there was little doubt about what it actually was. There are two points notable in this regard. This study supports other research (for example, Philo 1990; Kitzinger 1999) in challenging assertions that alleged 'polysemic' media texts can be manipulated by audiences to mean totally different things to different people. People were in fact virtually unanimous in correctly reading what the preferred meaning actually was. There was no one who argued that the media was not sanctifying Diana or not suggesting that the population were united in deep, tearful grief. Secondly, what is even more notable is the extent to which people saw media coverage and the response of the people as one and the same. Media messages helped create, in two interlinked ways, a striking 'reality effect' about the popular mood (for similar conclusions see also Turnock 2000: 82). Very few rejected these images and when they did, their challenge was distinctly partial or equivocal. First, media messages were important in conveying the impression that everyone, almost everyone, or at least the majority of 'the people', was in mourning. Even when people resisted the message that everyone was grieving, they tended to suggest that non-mourners were in a minority. Secondly, the reality effect was as, if not more, pronounced in the way the media influenced perceptions of the *nature* of the popular reaction, characterized by deep, tearful, adulatory grief. But in both these cases the popular reaction was a media myth, not representative of the widespread unmediated reality.

We judge the 'climate of opinion' from two sources, personal observation and the impressions gained from the media (Noelle-Neumann 1993). Previous explorations of media power have demonstrated that personal experience could be a highly potent source of resisting media messages (Philo 1990; Kitzinger 1999a). Given that very few M-O volunteers reacted according to the dominant mood, one might expect this to be a powerful source of opposition, perhaps unusually so given the explicit task of volunteers to observe the attitudes of others. Certainly this could be found among the few who did not accept the message. One man argued:

> The media has usually referred to 'a nation united in grief'. This is untrue. The nation has been sharply divided. On the one hand, many people – probably a great majority of the population – became obsessed with grief. On the other hand, a proportion of the population remained strictly aloof from this popular wave of sentiment.

He backed up his views with details of the personal experience with over 300 people he had come across during the week, all but two of whom 'firmly held the alternative view and derided the "mass hysteria" – a phrase which had soon caught on'. Where was 'the nation united in grief', he wondered?[2]

But the significance of personal experience was significantly limited in September 1997 because the two sources were not viewed equally. Even the above man noted how 'probably the great majority' were 'obsessed with grief'. Faced with the unequivocal media impression of popular opinion, the local reaction, of friends, family, work colleagues, even of the community in general, was felt to be precisely that rather than being representative of the broader 'climate of opinion'. Alternative unmediated experiences were defined in parochial opposition to the national mood as conveyed through the media, rather than viewed as undermining their impression. The following account conveys this contrast graphically:

> As the week went on it was apparent going by the television coverage of events that everyone – apart, it seemed, from me and my partner and a few friends and acquaintances – was in mourning for the dead princess . . . the whole nation, we were told, was totally united in its grief! Dissension! There was none! And reading the newspapers, it wasn't difficult to believe it. I was beginning to wonder if there was something wrong with me and my partner and our small group of like-minded friends, who all felt nothing. Or was it that we were the only ones that had not contracted this peculiar virus, that seemed to have infected the whole of the UK? By Wednesday I was beginning to think so and when three of us 'heretics' had what we felt like a clandestine meeting in the local pub, we talked in hushed tones as we all reached the same conclusion. Yes, there was a madness in the land. It was very disturbing. Would the thought police soon be stalking the countryside rooting out non-believers for not showing due respect?[3]

Sometimes the power of media images worked in tandem with unmediated impressions of the *visible* local public response to isolate alternative equally visible unmediated evidence of the mood. One woman reported:

> As the week wears on, flowers pile up everywhere, including around our market place and we see people queuing for hours in London to sign books of condolence. I can't understand how so many people who have never met the Princess seem to feel her death so personally . . . Office debate rages – all ages from early 20s to late 50s – agrees that we can't understand this outpouring of emotion. Yes it was an appalling tragedy but, no, it wasn't a personal one. So far, I haven't found anyone who has left flowers or who doesn't feel the whole thing is going over the top.[4]

In this case, the flowers piling up locally, when seen in conjunction with the television images, were viewed as evidence of this developing 'outpouring of emotion'. At the same time the alternative reaction that she had discovered from 'everyone' counted for little in countering this combined media and social picture of the reaction of 'so many people'. This suggests that local images were more likely to be seen as representative of the national mood when they reinforced the media impression, but when they directly contradicted this they were dismissed as unrepresentative.

Secondly, in terms of influencing the nature of the response, even those who resisted the image that everyone was in deep grief, made generalizations, based entirely from media coverage, on the feelings of mourners. In doing so they often presented a two-dimensional view which contrasted (a minority of) aloof non-mourners with (a majority of) hysterical, adulatory mourners. As one man put it:

> As an observer I came to the conclusion that in the main, people reacted in one of two ways, either *over the top as seen on TV, radio and newspapers*, and like me and many of my friends, a feeling of pity and sorrow for her sons, family and friends, while not feeling any special feeling of loss themselves [my emphasis].[5]

Similarly the first man above (p. 154) talked of how the nation was divided between non-mourners and those who became 'obsessed with grief', a verdict which is widely reproduced throughout this book and which the following comments further illustrate (my emphasis):

> As the days went by, I became more and more disgusted as well as bemused and bewildered by what I was *reading in the newspapers and hearing on television*. More than this I was disturbed and even frightened by the attitudes of other people. *We kept hearing* about an outpouring of national grief and how people felt that Diana was a member of their own families.
>
> During the next few days *I watched with amazement* the almost hysterical reaction to her death.
>
> *The public* reacted in what was, to me, an extraordinary fashion . . . it did seem to be hysterical . . . *There were people reported* as saying that they did not weep for their husband or wife, or for their father, as they wept for Diana.[6]

What is again notable here is that people got their images of the 'mass hysteria' from the media and not first-hand experience. This was the most common phrase used by correspondents. But there were no instances of people referring to 'mass hysteria' on the basis of what they had actually seen with their own eyes. There were no accounts of people deriding others they had witnessed hysterically breaking down in tears. Indeed the small number with first-hand experience of visits to mourning sites further confirmed the reaction as one of quiet restraint. Equally there were no examples of people coming across others eulogizing Diana as a saint. But it did not make these images any less powerful, even among those who did gain first-hand experience of the reaction. It was a point well illustrated by the experience of one woman who returned from holiday abroad just after the funeral and went to Kensington Palace before returning to her home in Yorkshire the following day. She reported how in London 'there were still many people quietly walking about and piles and piles of flowers and hundreds of messages . . . One could not but be impressed by the feelings afoot'. But such a favourable personal impression did not last and returning home the following day she 'found everybody talking about it. All took the same line as me – shocked and sad, but thought the popular display of grief had gone over the top'. It was, she believed, a worrying popular 'state of hysteria and idolisation. It's all very well to say that the People must speak – the people must be listened to, and so on. But what if the People lose their heads?'[7] Her views on a pathological popular response demonstrates that while people may have expressed contempt, derision, anger, worry or puzzlement at the perceived reaction, the reality effect – that this *was* 'the people's mood' – was unchallenged. Even the feelings of 'everybody' she knew that was not mourning, along with personal observation of the 'impressive' reaction of mourners, could not alter the power of these images.

Personal experiences of seeing mourning sites certainly reinforced this image of the national mood and the intensity of the response. But popular understanding of what was going on and how exactly people were reacting and feeling was gained primarily from the media. After all, there was a comparative lack of first-hand experience of those who were grief-stricken, not least because so few people were actually reacting in this way. Paradoxically, the very fact that most people did not visit mourning sites actually increased the power of the media to define the response of 'the people'. And even those who did – as in the case above – got their images of how others were reacting predominantly from media messages. Such a point explains why even those we might class as 'mourners' were also to be found deriding 'the mass hysteria of so many', or cautioning against 'the public' turning Diana into a saint. Seeing at first hand the flowers, books of condolences and queues could powerfully reinforce this impression of an adulatory, hysterical mass response. But it was the mass media that framed the understanding that all these gestures powerfully *signified* this response – there was nothing inherently emotional, for example, about placing flowers or signing a book of condolence (Biddle and Walter 1998).

In addition to personal experience, some people, as again noted in previous studies (Philo 1990; Kitzinger 1999), could use logic to challenge media images. But again, even when they did, the strength of the perceived mood meant that the usual images kept cropping up to compete with and undermine them. One woman suggested:

> Why did she have this effect on some people? I don't say most people. There must, surely, be many others who felt as I did, that the whole life and death of Diana was a roller coaster of high and low tragedies and that so much attention from so many onto one person cannot be anything but extremely unhealthy.

Already we see the challenge to the idea that this affected 'most people' competing with the awareness that 'so many' were showing such attention. This latter view remained predominant despite her doubts as she talked about how 'the massive outpouring of grief from the nation shocked and indeed, rather frightened' her and wondered 'should the population really have such adulation for a person with such human faults and foibles as Diana?' This was further reinforced by a retrospective comment of how she felt 'extremely angry and . . . unutterably depressed by the public reaction', illustrating how assumptions of adulation and a mass response from 'the public' still dominated despite her earlier doubts.[8]

Similarly another man stood out virtually alone in his correct suspicion that 'most people have not been greatly moved by the death and that the flower donators and the like are a minority of the public, albeit a very large minority'. His direct experience on a holiday with a party that included many readers of the *Belfast Telegraph* reinforced this logic: 'I would have expected that amongst the latter there would be many who were distraught by the death, for that paper is chiefly read by the Loyalist community in Belfast. Not one of them made any mention of the event.' However this speculation about the popular mood was challenged by the more concrete images visible on arriving back in Britain as he noted: 'It was only when we returned home that we began fully to appreciate the mass national hysteria that had been generated . . . I did not share the national grief.'[9]

The Media, Popular Attitudes and the Spiral of Silence

The above section illustrates how one particular response came to be accepted as the popular reaction despite the fact that it was held by only a small minority of people. The massive discrepancy between opinions aired in private and those found in public was above all due to a media-generated 'spiral of silence' (Noelle-Neumann 1993) of popular attitudes in the week following Diana's death. The spiral of silence is a theory developed in the 1970s by Elisabeth Noelle-Neumann, although its origins go back much further to now unfashionable 'mass society' theories of the media (Beniger 1987), and also to the work of M-O founder Tom Harrison (Splichal 2000). In an article in 1940 Harrison suggested that 'at all ordinary times, there is a tendency for most ordinary people to follow what they believe to be the majority, to voice in public mainly those sentiments and opinions which are generally acceptable and respectable'. Public opinion, he argued, was 'what you will say out loud to anyone' and was only a part of private opinion that would 'dare show itself at any moment'. Crucial to socially sanctioning attitudes as 'generally acceptable and respectable' was a press which presented 'their own opinions and wishes as if they were held by a large number of the population'. The result, as at the Munich crisis, was that people tended to voice attitudes which were 'generally acceptable and respectable', while hostile reactions, lacking social and media sanction, retreated into privacy (1940: 370–81). Such a process, as theorized by Noelle-Neumann, is based on four main propositions:

1 Society threatens deviant individuals with isolation.
2 Individuals constantly experience fear of isolation.
3 Because of this fear of isolation, individuals are constantly trying to assess the 'climate of opinion', the strength and distribution of attitudes towards a subject against their own.
4 This estimate of the climate of opinion in turn affects their behaviour in public, especially their willingness to express or conceal their opinions. If they consider that their views are dominant or 'on the rise', they will be willing to express their views publicly. If they sense that their views are the minority, they will be more likely to remain silent.
   (1993: 202)

This can produce a spiralling process, resulting in the views that are perceived to be dominant gaining even more ground and monopolizing the public scene while alternatives disappear from view as supporters, fearing isolation, stay silent. The result creates a situation of 'pluralistic ignorance', under which people develop a mistaken view of how most people feel, overestimating the strength of the majority view and underestimating that of the minority (Noelle-Nuemann 1993; Shamir and Shamir 1997). In some cases, as during Diana's mourning, an extreme case of 'pluralistic ignorance' can mean the public wrongly perceives the majority view to be that of the minority and believes the minority view is that of the majority.

Such a process has been confirmed, for instance, by numerous studies in social psychology which demonstrate that people tend to conceal views if they feel they are in a minority within a group and more willing to express them if they consider their views dominant (Abrams 1997). Even in normal circumstances this tendency to 'go with the majority' is a regular feature of opinion expression that explains why opinion polls, for example, regularly tend to overestimate the lead of the party perceived to be ahead (Turner and Sparrow 1997; for an overview of research see Glynn et al. 1997).

Such a theory is not without its critics (Splichal 2000), but arguably in times of 'crisis', such as during wars and catastrophes, the spiralling of one opinion and the disappearing of others can become even more pronounced. Whether this will occur, it is argued, is based on three factors (Scheufele and Moy 2000). First, perceptions about what opinions are gaining strength and which ones are disappearing will affect the tendency to express attitudes publicly. In Diana's mourning the mountains of flowers, long queues, books of condolences and shop shrines all over the country offered striking visual reminders, both mediated and unmediated, of the growing strength of perceived popular feelings. Indeed it would have required a particularly perverse logic to suggest the reverse given the visible public reaction. Meanwhile non-mourning sentiments were invisible, as routine, unremarkable and unnoticeable as mourning feelings were not. Secondly, for opinions to spiral and one to disappear, the issue has to have a strong moral or emotional component, which was certainly highly prominent in this case. It was about showing your respects on the death of a 'royal' and to fail to do this was widely presented as simply lacking in humanity, decency and patriotism. Those who disagreed were silenced as an indecent majority.

As this suggests, thirdly and most crucially for this process to occur, the media must take a clearly defined stance on the subject. As we have seen, on this occasion the media could hardly have been more monolithic about what was and indeed should be the popular response. The media are the most important source for assessing the climate of opinion and if a certain view predominates in coverage it will tend to be magnified in opinion expression, influencing perceptions of what can be said without fear of isolation, and giving people words and arguments to defend their views. For the fact that individuals are aware that their opinions are supported by the media is important in influencing their willingness to speak out and 'not in a single instance has the process of the spiral of silence run counter to the line taken by the media' (Noelle-Neumann 1993: 201).

This is exactly what happened in September 1997, an out of the ordinary period of 'liminality' that saw everyone initially unsure of how to act and learning from others, and most crucially from the media, about what was acceptable, normal social behaviour (Walter 1999a). There were two broad conflicting opinions that were initially prominent. In many ways the dominant, culturally normal reaction was that, while Diana's death was a very sad personal tragedy, you could not feel grief for a stranger known only through the media and to do so was a weird, pathological act. On the other hand was the perception, based both on alternative traditions of communal mourning and a less suspicious view of media 'reality', that the normal act was to feel sadness and even grief and indeed it would be uncaring not to feel this way (Giles and Naylor 2000).

We have seen how the former view remained the central private explanation among those who could not join 'the public grief'. And immediately following Diana's death even some of those upset were initially reluctant to express their feelings publicly or even privately for fear of social isolation and mockery. One younger female was deeply upset by the news but was unwilling to admit it to her friends: 'We were due out at a B-B-Q, and I wanted to cancel, and yet I didn't for fear of it seeming stupid, I mean, I didn't know the woman for God's sake.' Meanwhile one 48-year-old woman had broken down after hearing the news on the radio while driving to her local pool for her regular Sunday morning swim:

> I began to cry quite spontaneously and without warning – I surprised myself that I could react so immediately and unselfconsciously and without warning. I must go back home. But they might think I was over-reacting a bit mightn't they? I mean, *I* knew I was right, that Princess Diana had been someone who spoke for women, for the oppressed (one and the same often), she had a heart that she was happy to share, emotions to express publicly, beauty, purity of soul, she spoke to and for mothers and wives, and children of broken marriages. All that and somehow a lot more, but that's how I saw her. Others might think it was strange that *I* could cry about something so far off (her emphasis).

She decided to get through her tears by having a swim instead. In the changing room she met two women friends who did not appear to be affected: 'I wondered why they weren't as upset as me. I felt very alone, as if my reaction was quite uncalled for.'[10] Being upset at the death of a stranger was at this point viewed as a deviant act which was not legitimate for someone 'so far off' and people were reluctant to advertise their feelings because of the perception that they would be socially isolated, made to feel 'stupid'. But very quickly the media, backed socially by those who shared such feelings as well as from above by the elites, legitimized this reaction – indeed behaved 'as if any other response might get you put in jail' (Pearson 1997). Over the course of the week there was an inversion of the above assumptions. Not to be upset, even not to mourn in a particular way, was now constructed as the deviant reaction that was not shared by 'the people'. One female mourner in Cardiff had initially felt 'silly' about her reaction but after watching television and seeing 'so many people' share her thoughts, no longer felt on the defensive:

> I knew she was popular but I had no idea that everyone felt as strongly as I did and even more strongly than I did. All those people, all those flowers, all those people waiting to sign the books, its unbelievable and very, very moving . . . When I felt my reaction to Diana's death I did not dream that so many people felt like I did. I felt I was silly to feel this way about someone I never knew . . . Now I know that I wasn't stupid, the majority feel the same.

Her confidence that she was part of the majority meant that by the Tuesday after the news she had taken flowers to the local Princess of Wales Hospital, having 'heard that other people had'. Meanwhile after her sad swim, the woman above returned home to find her reaction shared by both her family and, even more crucially, media images that suggested most people, the entire nation and even 'the world' felt the same (notice also how her language changes from I to We):

> I felt so devastated still, but relieved and happy that yes many, even most, shared the way I felt. I was pleased because I wasn't alone. My reaction hadn't been isolated . . . All that day I never left the TV for more than a few minutes . . . People were starting to gather in London – bring flowers – they, like me, felt the strong urge to do something. Only I never got further than the sofa. I became fascinated by the historic grief which was unfolding before our eyes. I felt somehow proud to be a part of it . . . And I felt proud to be British . . . We were suddenly all crying in public . . . the stiff upper-lip British . . . It was truly a national catharsis. Out they came – young and old, rich and poor, black and white, men and women and children . . . The reaction all over the world had been instantaneous and uniformly heart-rendering. [11]

Media coverage certainly did not cause people to feel like this. But it did serve to legitimize what were previously perceived as culturally illegit-imate emotions by suggesting that 'many, even most' were feeling that way rather than just individuals, families or friends. As one woman surveyed by the BFI commented: 'I was so relieved to find that I was not alone. My reactions and hurt were obviously the same as millions of others' (Turnock

2000: 15). Also crucial in this was Blair's early tribute. By suggesting that 'like everyone else in the country' he was 'utterly devastated', in 'grief that is so deeply painful for us', he not only gave prime ministerial approval to grieving for a stranger but insisted that this was and should be the nation's response.[12] On another level the presence of tearful reporters meant, as one woman put it, that 'right from the start, there seemed to be a feeling that "We're all in it together"' (Turnock 2000: 26).

As we have seen, the population was very far from being 'all in it together'. But the emergence of a highly authoritarian media and social communal mourning which essentially stated 'We all feel the same – we are all upset' served to mask this. Social traditions of respect for the dead and those upset alongside fear of the intolerance of the living ensured, increasingly, that all but the most pro-mourning sentiments were deemed 'inappropriate' for public airing while alternative or even mixed opinions, even among mourners, retreated into privacy. As one sceptic, referring to a comment from her window cleaner about a 'sad, sad week', noted: 'I was even more careful not to state the views I had as I certainly wouldn't want to offend anyone who felt strongly about it.' Such pressure to conform to the dominant mood was found across diverse experiences during the week:

My middle son's class were asked to write an account of what the things they liked about Princess Diana as part of their homework. This was rather difficult. All F [son] could think of was that she had taken her sons down the water slide at Thorpe Park. So he wouldn't feel left out, we came up with a few other offerings.

My hairdresser, who operated independently within a large garden centre, which was closed all morning for the funeral, had a dilemma. She is still building up her business but decided after pressure from customers and the garden centre to close at 10.30 a.m.

My 29-year-old daughter in law was berated by her sister for not signing a book or laying flowers. When asked why she felt so strongly that she should have done so, her sister could only answer 'Well everyone is and you will be a social outcast'. My daughter-in-law said that for a moment she felt like she was destined for the Tower.[13]

As the last comment suggests, the darker side of this expectation of respect was deep intolerance towards those who failed to show it, both from the media and the vocal minority. Dissenting media coverage provoked angry complaints from those who thought such coverage was simply illegitimate. Some *Private Eye* readers denounced 'a truly shitty magazine' and considered that 'a more fitting response would have been for you to have kept your gob shut for once in your life' (3 October 1997). Meanwhile a distinctly grudging obituary in the *Economist* provoked readership praise for its 'restrained' approach, but complaints that its 'entire diatribe' was 'vicious, salacious and reprehensible' (6–20 September 1997). Similarly, sceptical letters in the quality press left other readers and even columnists complaining against such 'clever-clever' 'sneering' (*Guardian*, 3 September 1997; Grant 1997b). One woman considered that A. N. Wilson had written 'witheringly' about the Princess (albeit in the week after the funeral) as she recalled: 'I was so angry that I wrote telling him . . . that it was totally inappropriate and out of order to write this at this time.' Meanwhile the woman above who had been initially so reluctant to express her views on the Sunday was rather more confident in doing so by the following day, after seeing her reaction shared with – and now supported by – 'so many others'.

> On Monday night we talked about her in the pub after choir. One friend remained silent and I remember how dismissive he had been about our reading of Andrew Morton's book, decrying all royals and monarchists. As we eulogised he looked more and more pained until I asked him what he was thinking. He had not been moved, and neither had his work colleagues, by the death of such a deceitful, manipulating, spoilt brat. And, speaking directly to me, he did not comprehend how any rational, intelligent person could possibly think otherwise. I couldn't let her take that and I went for him verbally. I felt sorry for him, I said, really sorry if he failed to see what so many others had seen . . . There was a silence as we stared at each other. A man next to me whispered 'we're right with you'.[14]

In one sense there is a long history of such sentiments in policing and suppressing dissenting attitudes towards the monarchy. In 1897 republicans faced the verbal and physical wrath of 'Jubilee Bullies'. In the 1950s when John Grigg made (by today's standards) an incredibly mild critique of the Queen, he was physically attacked, received virulent hate mail and was banned from the BBC. Labour MP and Republican Willie Hamilton faced similar abuse for his stance in the 1970s, while during the 1977 Jubilee the Sex Pistols were violently assaulted in action at least partly sanctioned by press demands to 'Punish the Punks' for their suggestion that the monarchy headed 'a fascist regime' (Taylor 1999; Ziegler 1978; Savage 1992).

Of course by the 1980s this old media taboo against attacking the royal family had partially, if very far from completely, broken down. But within hours of Diana's death 'a new one seemed to have sprung up around the monarchy's renegade daughter' (Nairn 1998: 223–4). Those who even much later offered critical perspectives on Diana's life (Junor

1998) or mourning (Jack 1997) received the media abuse, hate mail and even physical threat that replicated past patterns. This offered merely a pale imitation of the authoritarianism of September 1997 which saw people complaining of 'a kind of floral fascism' in 'a country patrolled by the grief police' (Jack 1997: 18), and manifested in verbal and even physical attacks on the mildest form of dissent. Dissenting writers to the press, and many more subsequently, complained that it was 'like living under fascism', you felt afraid to say what you thought.

Such a climate of intolerance led those who did not conform to the perceived mood to hold their tongues. One woman reported how neighbours who were incensed by the behaviour of the royals 'got quite angry' when she did not agree with them before adding: 'They brought the subject up, not me, I have not been raising the topic with anyone since it generates such high emotions.' Others were even more reticent in the face of the strength and perceived intolerance of the popular mood:

> My husband objects to it all and so do others he knows, but from some colleagues aggressive reactions to criticisms of what's happening in the country they've decided not to voice their opinions any further . . . I keep meeting people who say in quiet corners that the nation has gone mad, but who feel that they daren't say it aloud for fear of other people's reactions (I recall that Nazi Germany had much the same problem with people not daring to say they weren't great fans of Adolf Hitler).

> Those of us who were sorry, but no more so than for any other person tragically killed . . . began to feel intimidated . . . I have heard people say they did not like to be the first to say how exaggerated the whole thing was, how unreal and even frightening.[15]

The way opinion spiralled in public now meant that the normal demand for balance was jettisoned so that all but the most absurdly romantic and one-sided pictures of Diana's life were now deemed illegitimate and inappropriate. This, a number of sceptics later noted, went well beyond the conventions of obituaries that entailed honouring the dead 'not only with generosity but with some semblance of accuracy' (Heller 1997). No one would wish to focus overtly on Diana's faults at this delicate time, noted A. N. Wilson (1997) the following week, but was it 'really necessary' to make up so many lies? Perhaps of more concern to those alienated by the week was the way the demand for communal mourning took on such a momentum that everyone was expected to grieve, and be seen to grieve.

This effect also extended to journalists themselves, which is not surprising given that most of them, like the people, got their story of the popular reaction rather less from first-hand experience and more from the media messages that they tend to consume more voraciously than anyone. 'Am I alone in thinking that the country has momentarily taken leave of its senses?', asked A. N. Wilson repeatedly after the funeral, while later some journalists were to admit to the 'contemptible journalistic cowardice' (Lawson 2002) of self-censorship in the face of this perceived mood. A month after Diana's funeral, in an article entitled, revealingly, 'A Nation in Mourning (and if you weren't you had to keep quiet)', *Independent* journalist Miles Kington recalled how he was

> one of that silent number who were not caught up in the mood of national grief for someone I hadn't loved. I don't think I was the only one to feel, as the mood of national woe grew, that the whole thing was getting out of hand. Yet the national mood was such that you could not express your dissent without being thought unpatriotic, unfeeling or tasteless . . . I didn't even trust myself to mention any thoughts about the Princess in this space, for fear of being thought a monster of stone. I am sure other writers and commentators have similarly kept quiet and written about more important things. Which means, quite possibly, when posterity comes to look back . . . it will conclude that the whole nation succumbed, because those who abstained said nothing. (Kington 1997)

Even those who had earlier managed to break this mood noted how they were battling against a monolithic 'climate of opinion', in which 'the zeal of the grief police' even extended into the newspapers themselves (Reid 1997; Ferguson 1998). At the *Evening Standard*, the paper's editor asked each of its columnists for a tribute and when one writer, Brian Sewell responded by instead revealing that he 'could feel no grief for . . . a promiscuous playgirl who died in a foreign lover's arms in a Paris underpass', his editor responded, 'I can't print this. They'll break your windows and poison your dogs!' (Sewell 1999). The offending article had to wait a year before it was published, and even then it was accompanied by a half-apology that 'it will upset some' (Sewell 1998). A week after the funeral the 'united in grief' popular mood was still leaving little room for dissent, as one journalist on the broadsheet press noted:

> Those of us who are not willing to pretend to emotions we don't feel have been getting an ominous message – that we ought to keep quiet – it's a message which is not easy to defy in the face of repeated assertions about the whole country being united in grief. (Smith 1997b)

Again respect for the dead and those feeling 'bereaved' played a part here, to quote one dissenting article, in ensuring a contrast between 'those participating in the carnival of grief and those who kept their thoughts decently to themselves' (Waterhouse 1997). And perhaps sharing these sentiments, almost all similarly sceptical journalists chose, or were allowed, to air their views only after the due 'respect' of the funeral. Indeed paralysing alternative public views during the mourning was the awareness that certain opinions were less legitimate at this point. There also appeared to be nothing really at stake in this repression of alternative views – this was not a war or a serious political incident but a tragic death in which dissent was not important. Meanwhile the spiralling of demands for 'respect' also made it difficult for journalists, even if they had wanted to, to scrutinize critically the feelings of those perceived to be deeply upset. This in turn further made it difficult for mourners not to participate in a performance in front of the cameras where deep grief became the order of the day, rather than the sometimes more equivocal and certainly more complicated views that they held. The demand was for a tearful tribute to the 'Queen of Hearts', nothing less and nothing more.

More broadly, whatever the inclinations of journalists within these somewhat elastic customs of respecting the dead, a context which saw the media widely blamed for 'killing' Diana led most to veer on the side of hagiographic caution, hoping perhaps that the current eulogies might eradicate memories of past hostilities. The legacy of the Hillsborough disaster, when the *Sun*'s attacks on those killed had seen the paper publicly burnt and boycotted on Merseyside, may have further reinforced the commercial imperatives behind this approach. At the *Daily Mail*, and no doubt elsewhere, such a policy was directly imposed by senior executives. Columnist Simon Heffer had written some hostile articles about the Princess of Wales before she died and later recalled:

> It was deemed that my views should be kept in their place, which was not in the paper, not at the time. Many hacks would now cite the Nuremberg Defence and say, 'I was only obeying orders'. They wrote things which looking back they would not have been very proud of. (Hitchens 1998)

Indeed even some of those journalists who were in the vanguard of questioning the popular reaction at the time also played their parts in shaping perceptions of it. *Guardian* journalist Elizabeth Hilton (1997) had been one of the first to break ranks to attack the media hagiography on the Tuesday, but she had also contributed to it the previous day when she presented a Radio 4 programme of tributes (Karpf 1997). In *The Times*, Nigella Lawson's post-funeral attacks on the 'grief police' contrasted with her pre-funeral comments about 'why the nation is right to share the royals' grief' and her explicit assertion that it was 'appropriate to say only positive things now'(1997c/a/b). And presumably Heffer would also cite the Nuremberg defence given his role alongside his fellow shamed 'hacks' in reporting 'How Diana has Truly United Our Kingdom' (Heffer 1997). Such levels of self-censorship were only topped by A. N. Wilson, as his post-funeral attack 'This Cult of Diana Makes me Shiver' contrasted with an unequivocal earlier alignment with the mourning mood. 'The British people', he wrote in *Time* magazine, 'was in love with Diana . . . It's as simple and as personal as that. And that is why we weep for ourselves and for her' (*Private Eye*, 3 October 1997).

Faced with this relentless emphasis on one viewpoint, people estimated, principally from the media, that there was a 'climate of opinion' in which their views were best kept to themselves. Indeed the power of the perceived national mood left many feeling isolated and atomized, a pattern of behaviour more reminiscent of life under dictatorship (Peukert 1989):

> I feel as if I am the only person in the whole country who has not shed a tear over the death.

> I appear to be the only person in this country not suffering from the mass hysteria which has been apparent from the moment the news was announced.

> I feel as if I am the only person in the whole country who has never shed a tear over the death.[16]

The result was a retreat of opinion deep into the private realm, as people estimated that their opposing views would, to say the least, 'not be popular' (see the comments in chapter 2 to this effect). Chapter 7 noted how one woman had been tempted to disrupt a radio eulogy to Diana by ringing in to mention her role in the break-up of Will Carling's marriage, but her husband had advised that they 'ought to lie low!' On another more worrying level, the power of the perceived mood penetrated deeply into her psyche: 'I felt guilty because I wasn't upset . . . By the Thursday we were beginning to think that there was something dreadfully wrong with us and our friends or else the nation was in a state of mass hysteria.'

Or as one arch-sceptic admitted: 'I once crossed London Bridge in the rush hour, when everyone was going the other way and I felt WRONG!'[17] As this illustrates, even routine actions that transgressed the totalitarian demands of mourning were felt to be deviant. One man had 'felt quite guilty' when he bought flowers for the house instead of joining the mourning queues, while a woman who had listened to the funeral after going out blackberry-picking recalled: 'I felt guilty doing even that, as though we ought to have been prostrated with grief in a darkened room or something.'[18] Another woman had struggled to wash her outside windows before the funeral began. Her street had seemed 'unnaturally quiet' and she had 'felt some kind of pressure to be inside by then, not to be seen ignoring the event'. Her new partner, a music teacher, had been working but had also managed to see it:

> It was simply a naturally occurring break in between lessons, but she said she'd been glad to have it because one parent had wondered rather accusingly at her having lessons at all that day. She was able to say she'd watched the funeral and that seemed to make the parent feel better. I told her about my finishing the windows by 11 and we agreed that it was almost like being spied on; we would have been informed upon if we'd gone against the moral consensus.[19]

Others were similarly left feeling 'profoundly uneasy', wondering if there was 'something wrong' with them for 'not feeling as moved as so many others appeared to be' and being so 'callously lacking' in grief.[20] One woman was worried about the character flaws her reaction had revealed when compared with the 'majority' response:

> I have been quite concerned by my reactions. I feel completely out of step with the majority . . . I don't feel *personally* touched by her death and am unable to identify with the millions who do. I have levelheaded friends (and a levelheaded husband!) who are completely cast down by her death. Over the last couple of weeks I have felt quite isolated and have wondered why I don't share these feelings. Is it a coldness, a lack of emotional warmth?

She did, however, take some comfort in the fact that, like others, she found the 'Mummy' funeral tribute 'very moving' and 'shared everyone's reaction to her brother's speech'. 'So perhaps I am not totally heartless', she added hopefully. One of the above men had meanwhile been 'comforted' to find that his work colleagues shared his sceptical feelings[21] and people looked to family, friends and colleagues, testing the waters perhaps with ambiguous comments, determining the 'climate of opinion' within their particular circle before deciding to air their views. Matthew Parris (1998) later noted how he and other like-minded individuals had 'learnt to sound out fellow sceptics gingerly on social occasions, for fear of offending'. One man similarly reported: 'Various friends asked me politely what I thought about the tragedy and when they saw that I wasn't greatly moved by it, they visibly relaxed and all agreed (without prompting from me) that she wasn't the saint people were cracking her up to be.'[22] But although social isolation may have been reduced in private, only the hardest of the 'hard core' (Noelle-Neumann 1993: 170) of dissenters were prepared to risk the wrath of a public mood perceived to be deeply intolerant of negative views. Perhaps the most hostile comments came from a woman who did not share any of the self-doubts or guilt of some of those above and was supported in her views by an equally hostile family. She recalled her experience on the first day of the mourning:

> On Monday 1st September, I happened to go for a day out to Nottingham. I was very impressed by Nottingham's Council House but less impressed by the crowds heaping flowers in front of it – and queuing up to do it! I said 'God! Is this for that bloody leech?' My sister jabbed me sharply and said: 'Shut up! You'll get us lynched'.[23]

And in the face of the perceived mood, she decided that silence was the best opposition, remaining privately venomous but publicly quiescent to the extent that she could even, perhaps, have been mistaken for a mourner. She was ultimately powerless in the face of the dominant mood as alternative views, for the most part, remained firmly within the confines of private conversations and thoughts.

The Game of Shame

Another way of demonstrating the role of the media in shaping the public climate of opinion is by examining acts of 'dissent' – if they can be termed that – during the week. Enough has been said about media hostility to the failure of the royals to grieve with 'the people'. But perhaps the only public 'opposition' to the mourning came in the attempt, subsequently abandoned, by the Scottish Football Association to continue with an international football match on the afternoon of the funeral. The overwhelming media and social message was that there was simply no question that the game should not be played. On the day after Diana's death, veteran *Daily Mail* sports reporter Jeff Powell was already heaping 'shame on the sports that kept playing' the day before while describing the cancellation of football matches as 'the only proper, the only decent, the only human response' (1 September 1997). Such a 'proper' reaction appeared confirmed by news that sport was planning 'a day of rest' for the funeral. That the Scots were going to carry on, however, provoked such fury that one could have been mistaken that they had somehow engineered Diana's death themselves. Scottish Secretary Donald Dewar joined with Tony Blair and William Hague in denouncing an 'utterly inappropriate' and 'disgraceful' decision that had provoked 'widespread anger amongst the public'. A Scottish Labour MP called for the immediate resignation of chief executive Jim Farry who had 'brought shame on the nation', while the Rangers' vice-chairman Donald Findlay demanded nothing less than a full independent judicial investigation into a 'quite appalling' decision. Meanwhile several Scottish players announced that they were too upset to play on the Saturday, a decision led by striker Ally McCoist who stated: 'Tears have been shed from the corner of England to the top of Scotland. It is only proper to pull out and show our respect.' Fans, meanwhile, weighed in with their condemnations and the offices of the SFA were daubed with slogans demanding 'cancel the game'.

Supporting such a position, media coverage combined virulent denunciations of a 'shameful' decision, character assassinations of Farry and an unequivocal reading of the popular mood. Under the headline 'You're a Disgrace: Scots Shame for Funeral Day', the *Mirror* considered: 'the decent people of Scotland will hang their heads in shame this morning over the revolting antics of their football chiefs' in a decision that had 'insulted the entire nation'. The refusal of the 'fiercely patriotic' Ally McCoist, pictured with his CBE alongside the other dissenting players, to play in the 'Game of Shame' was commended as the only possible response:

> They rightly asked how any respectable soul could consider gathering for a trivial football match, against tiny Belarus of all things, at the very time when Princess Diana's body was being laid to rest. The thought is so abhorrent it makes us shudder. But Farry did everything he could to stage the game nobody wanted. (*Mirror*, 3 September 1997)

'How DARE they go against what a nation feels and wants?', asked the *Mirror*'s sister paper the *Daily Record* angrily. Denouncing the 'Shower of Scotland', it printed pictures of 'the seven men who took the decision which stunned a grieving nation' and 'flew in the face of public opinion' as 'furious supporters said it was a WRONG decision'. Demonstrating this, seventeen printed letters saw fans all condemning an 'absolutely disgusting' decision which was 'going against national opinion' as 'everybody is against it' (3 September 1997). Juxtaposed against this interpretation of popular opinion were depictions of Farry as 'a dictator' and 'dour official' (*Scotsman*, 4 September 1997), an out-of-touch petty bureaucrat who 'spoke coldly of logistics while everyone else wiped away a tear' (*Record*, 4 September 1997). 'For a pumped up official to defy public opinion so, shows a callous lack of understanding. He's heartless and uncharitable', considered the *Mirror* (4 September 1997).

Farry also had had the temerity to deride governmental pressure by commenting that one of the Scottish defenders was out injured 'so big

Donald [Dewar] would be welcome in the back four'. But in a week of prescribed mourning a joke, however mild, was no laughing matter. Amid public calls for Farry to apologize, the press denounced such 'tactless, tasteless lack of compassion' (*Mirror*, 3 September 1997) from 'a soulless man of amazing insensitivity', a 'shockingly flippant . . . monumental insult'. The only proper course of action, the tabloids agreed, was resignation. 'This Man Shames Our Game' said the *Mail* (4 September 1997), 'Go Now' agreed the *Record*. 'Off – So Should You Be, Farry' demanded the *Sun*'s Scottish edition (4 September 1997), following the belated decision on the Wednesday evening to call off the game in another triumph for 'the people', after which 'a lifetime's silence from Farry might pacify an outraged public' (*Mail*, 6 September 1997). Nor were the broadsheets any different as, from right and left, they called on Farry to bow his head 'in shame' (*Telegraph*, 3 September 1997), and considered that such was 'the intensity of the national grief . . . there was clearly no question of playing football' (*Guardian*, 6 September 1997).

This was contrasted with the way sport in general and football in particular was setting 'the proper tone for grief' in their 'touching show of respect' (*Mail*, 3 September 1997). 'We'll Do it for You All' (*Sun*, 4 September 1997) said England football manager Glenn Hoddle as he promised 'to lift a nation in grief' with England's World Cup performance the Tuesday after the funeral. The team's problems, Hoddle commented, were 'purely emotional' after an event which had had a 'profound effect' on them (*Sun*, 10 September 1997). Details duly followed of how 'Wembley Weeps: 75,000 in Tears' (*Express*, 11 September 1997) as they said 'Goodbye England's Rose' (*Mail*, 11 September 1997) before the game. Nor was the sporting grief confined to English footballers. Reports spoke of rower Steven Redgrave's 'inner turmoil', racing driver David Coulthard dedicated a victory in the Italian Grand Prix to Diana, while British tennis player Greg Rusedski was urged by his coach not to watch the funeral for fear that he would turn into 'an emotional wreck' before an important match.

In the face of this overwhelming story of a dominant 'proper' and deviant 'improper' response, the only real alternative coverage came in the *Herald*. In keeping with its philosophy that 'life goes on', the paper argued: 'for the life of us we cannot understand how attending Pittodrie on Saturday afternoon would have demeaned the memory of the Princess.' It was 'simply wrong' to railroad people so that those who had little emotional engagement were made 'to feel that they are somehow deficient or out of step'. A series of articles supported Farry's position, suggesting that 'dignity and respect' was 'being carried too far' in demands for mass cancellations that were 'way over the top'

(2–5 September 1997). Such views were notable for their absence in the mainstream media, with the exception of two dissenting articles, albeit published after the game had been postponed. Denouncing 'the torrent of abuse' unleashed on the SFA, *Times* journalist Magnus Linklater (1997) considered that the reaction said 'more about press hysteria than the real state of our feelings about Diana's death'. Meanwhile *Mail* columnist Richard Littlejohn was, perhaps surprisingly, allowed to air his views that 'No Disrespect, but Scotland should have Played'.

There were several points notable about such coverage. Most importantly it was framed by the assumptions that playing the game was a legitimate proposal and the picture of public opinion was more complex than was widely presented. Unlike the monolithic attitude detected by the *Record*, for example, the *Herald*'s letters page offered a more divided response. Some attacked the decision to play the game, but others praised the authorities 'for once' having 'represented the fans in the wake of the media' that had gone 'stark raving bonkers' and was 'entirely unrepresentative of the general Scottish feeling'. The result, one journalist subsequently suggested, was that a man who was deeply unpopular among Scottish fans had been transformed into 'the people's champion . . . a kind of anti-establishment figurehead for the sizeable but silent section of the population resentful at the enforced sadness' (McAlpine 1997).

Secondly such coverage drew on news sources, information and arguments that were firmly absent from the mainstream media. Most of the tabloid coverage was filled with two-page spreads on the views of Ally McCoist and accompanying condemnatory quotes from various politicians and fans. The *Herald*, on the other hand, featured former Scottish manager Tommy Docherty arguing: 'Would I have played? Of course I would. All professionals have had to play after family bereavements at some stage during their career. How is that easier than after a Princess has been killed?' Of the players' rebellion, he was 'amazed at their attitude', as was former international footballer Willie Miller who agreed that 'as a professional you must get on with the job of playing football'. Elsewhere the Scottish Liberal Democrat spokesman Menzies Campbell attacked calls for Farry's resignation as a 'gross overreaction' (*Morning Star*, 5 September 1997), a spokesman for the Roman Catholic Church in Scotland said they had no objection, as did the Bishop of Edinburgh. Advice had been sought from the palace, who had approved the game, as apparently did the sports minister Tony Banks before the government started drifting with the perceived tide of opinion (McAlpine 1997).

Such sources also publicized and supported Farry's defence that the game was to kick off, contrary to the general media impression, long after the funeral, with an appropriate show of respect, and an hour after the shops reopened at 2 p.m. One *Herald* columnist denounced the pervading 'atmosphere of certain madnesses and absurdities', as he wondered:

> If it's all right for shops to open in London why is it all wrong for Scotland to play football one hour later and 600 miles away in Aberdeen? Is buying a pair of knickers in Marks and Spencer's more respectful than watching a game of football? A game that was to be preceded by two minutes silence by all who were there. The players were to have worn armbands as a mark of respect. Is getting pissed in a pub more decorous than this? (Reid 1997)

This alternative coverage not only presented a more complex picture of popular attitudes, but drew on common-sense cultural norms that there were limits to how much you could grieve for a stranger, while people should not be forced to if they did not want to as life went on. In any case due respect was being shown, even after the funeral. In the latter argument there was also the powerful appeal of precedent. Littlejohn compared the cancellation of sport to Winston Churchill's Saturday state funeral when thousands lined the streets to pay their respects and then went off directly to watch sporting events. He pointed out that 'none of those who attended were accused of lacking respect' and 'what was good enough for Churchill, should be good enough for Diana'. Others similarly pointed out that Dunblane, Lockerbie, Piper Alpha and Hillsborough had all left greater scars on the popular psyche, but none led to such a mass shutdown.

These alternative perspectives are valuable less for themselves – they played virtually no part in, much less had any impact on, the public 'debate' at the time. But they illustrate the powerful alternative arguments and opinions that were excluded from mainstream coverage as one opinion was systematically legitimized as the only proper response while all others were presented as illegitimate. And the 'game of shame', it has to be remembered, was hardly a subversive act but a mere expression of loyal communal mourning. It is a measure of the intolerance towards alternative opinions that the decision to mourn Diana through a two-minute silence and all the players wearing black armbands can even be explored as an act of dissent.

The inevitable result was a spiralling of one particular very rigid pro-mourning view at the expense of others during the first half of the week. Such a fact perhaps explains why it was considered appropriate for sport to continue and for BBC2 to televise it on the day of Diana's death, but it was considered deeply inappropriate to play a football game after her funeral. The pattern of calls to the SFA provides a glimpse of this process. By the Tuesday they were, despite the demand for mass mourning, 'perhaps surprisingly split evenly between those who wanted the game postponed and those who wanted it to go ahead' (*Herald*, 3 September 1997). By the following day, in the midst of this relentless social and media pressure against the 'game of shame', *public* opinion had radically altered and alternative views, always on the defensive, had retreated still further. Only a quarter of the calls to the SFA were now favourable, while a telephone poll for Scottish television of 35,000 callers found 89 per cent calling for the game to be switched. As Farry, justifying the belated decision to switch the game in the face of 'the escalating mood' noted, 'the national mood on Monday was not the national mood as of Tuesday'. That this was the case was a classic illustration of the media's ability, in tandem with elites and vocal minorities, to construct (Lewis 2001), distort and suppress rather than reflect popular opinion, manufacturing and imposing a pseudo-consensus rather than reflecting a real one.

Lifting the Veil

In this process it is virtually impossible to separate media and social pressures. Indeed the whole point is that they worked together in a symbiotic spiralling process so that a reaction of a very small minority became elevated and widely accepted by people as the national response. This simply could not have occurred without media coverage. Silverstone is right to ask 'Who Placed the First Flower?' and emphasize social experience rather than media messages in influencing initial responses – even if this ignores that the response had been largely 'learnt' from seeing media images of previous disasters (Walter et al. 1995), as well as for a woman known through the media (Merrin 1999). But leaving these qualifications aside, the key questions to explaining the popular reaction as a whole and the way it was widely perceived are: 'How did we learn of who placed the first flower and did we ever learn of the majority who did not?' It goes back to the old cartoon of a boy pestering his father with the unanswerable question: 'Dad, if a tree falls in a forest and the media are not there to report it, has the tree really fallen?' For if the media do not report that some people are not in mourning but instead insist, in a strikingly powerful way, that everyone is and this is the only 'normal' response, then the chances of alternative opinions becoming part of the perceived reality of the experience are limited.

What happened during Diana's mourning was that the media ensured that the response of a highly vocal minority was magnified and indeed further distorted into a reaction of adulation and emotion – an attitude that amounted to no more than a minority within a minority. In doing so, this excluded the far greater, more complex and diverse alternative realities being felt and experienced by the silenced majority. Throughout the country there existed a separate 'climate of opinion'. But there was nowhere for people to discover this climate apart from through local experiences, and they, for the most part, were not seen as representative of the national mood. The result was the paradox that, while proportionately few people responded in the way media coverage emphasized, the truth of these messages was widely accepted.

Without the media this would simply not have happened. Consider the reverse process in which the media had instead socially sanctioned the types of attitudes found widely in private, even initially among mourners, that while it was a sad event, feeling upset for a stranger was abnormal. Coverage had insisted that everyone felt like this and that this in fact was the only normal reaction to have. Meanwhile the prime minister and other notable figures were prominently featured denouncing such 'inappropriate' grief and those who wished to show it were demonized as 'sick' individuals who were no longer part of 'the people' and 'the nation'. The result is that those mourners who 'felt differently' would have retreated, ashamed, worried and isolated by their feelings for a stranger. Their views would have been confined to friends, families and colleagues, while the more sceptical views found throughout this book would, thanks to media coverage and social legitimization, have dominated in the public domain.

To a limited extent this was what happened in the aftermath of Diana's death, as all the factors that made up the spiral of silence slowly began to unravel. As the flowers were swept away, the tears dried and politicians, pop stars and princes all called for an end to the grieving, the only possible perception was that the strength of feeling on the subject was decreasing, if only slowly. Moreover, Diana's burial removed the need for respect for the dead and the intense demands of communal mourning. The absence of media and social pressure to mourn for a stranger led to the re-emergence of the initial, culturally dominant position, present throughout private attitudes, that it was pathological to grieve, especially so intensely, for someone you did not know. Even when the media made people feel guilty for not mourning, they often advanced two alternative propositions, that either there was 'something wrong' with them or else 'the nation' was in a state of 'mass hysteria'. And it is this latter view that has increasingly predominated in the aftermath.

This was further facilitated as the social isolation and atomization that the media produced gave way to a greater variety of alternative messages. This began just before the funeral, and slowly accelerated afterwards. Only a minority of M-O respondents gained access to alternative messages during the course of the week (and given the higher proportion of broadsheet readers among them this overstates this effect more generally). But for those who did so, the feelings of validation of their views that media coverage provoked could be quite striking. Consider the views of the following man, which followed directly from an extract above (p. 155) in which he had vividly conveyed his feelings of isolation the day earlier:

> But then a breath of fresh air! On Thursday, the first crack of dissent began to appear in the up-to-then solid walls of press correctitude. Admittedly it only came in the letters page of the *Independent*, where two correspondents expressed their bewilderment at the frenzy of Diana-itis. Then the following day, a small article appeared which matched my thoughts pretty closely. The writer [Maitland 1997] – an occasional contributor, clearly not constrained by the general editorial policy of the paper, which continued to push the universal 'Her like will never pass this way again' line – objected to being made to feel like a leper because she did not feel particular grief for the 'late lamented' Princess, for whom she had little respect in life.

Others similarly took comfort in media coverage that gave them the knowledge that there were others who shared their views:

> I got very tired of the huge coverage . . . I did not read a lot of it and began to wonder if my husband and I were alone in being saddened by the lack of perspective . . . It was not until a few days later that a few letters from readers and a few articles from journalists appeared, which echoed our feelings and impressions, that we realised that we were not alone. We refused to feel *bad* because we were not devastated.

> I enclose copies of *Private Eye* covering the period which brought a welcome change from most of the media coverage. I was pleased my feelings were shared by so many others.

> All week the headlines were ghastly. The queues of people waiting for nothing in particular, or to sign the books, or to leave flowers. Thank goodness the *Independent* came to its senses on the Thursday or Friday and started printing editorials and opinion pieces echoing the first trickle of letters asking who else in the country felt like the tabloids (including *The Times*) said they ought to. I felt it was back with the sane again.[24]

Noelle-Neumann writes that 'the media provide people with the words and phrases they can use to defend a point of view' (1993: 173), and this was particularly true in this instance given the dominant view that everyone should mourn and it was inhumane not to. One woman, for example, quoted extensively from:

> a cutting from the *Daily Telegraph* [Pearce 1997] which summed up to me a lot of what I felt. The Diana cult was 'sick – a feeding frenzy – an obsession, a deeply unhealthy yearning to live somebody else's life' . . . The article goes on to say that this is unspeakably sad and how I agree. People, ordinary, down to earth, nine to five working people should have lives that satisfy them. 'The only emotions worth having are private ones – private love and private grief'.[25]

In this way alternative media coverage validated non-mourning reactions, reduced social isolation, and encouraged people, including journalists, in their views. One letter-writer to the *Herald* (5 September 1997) who had thought that he was 'at best an unfeeling and cold-hearted bastard', felt 'mighty fine' to know from his paper's coverage that he was 'not alone in the closet of bemusement'. Meanwhile dissenting columnists wrote how they had received sometimes record postbags supporting their columns, with many expressing the sentiment, even some time later: 'Thank God someone thinks the same as I do' (Littlejohn 1998; Waterhouse 2000). 'I felt like Lynda Lee-Potter' wrote *Observer* journalist Euan Ferguson (1998) after receiving almost 200 letters, almost all supportive and most of which simply began 'Thank you'. Even letter-writers received large sackfuls of mail. One man who protested in the pages of *The Times* received an astonishing eighty-seven letters in reply, half of which saw people state that they 'felt afraid' to express their opinions (Hitchens 1998).

It would be wrong to exaggerate the number of people who had access to these views during the mourning. As chapter 1 notes, it was only in the weeks and months that followed that media message became steadily less monolithic. By 21 September, one woman who had subsequently listened to Radio 4's *Feedback* programme had this to say about the changing response:

> In fact as the days have gone past and people have quietened down – and a greater variety of responses have been reported – it seems that many, many people did not join the outpouring of grief, but kept their distance and their sense of perspective! I was not alone after all.

Others also detected a shift in the popular social and media mood:

> Since the funeral, on the phone-ins on radio, you hear other views, and people saying that she was not the only one to do 'good works'.

After the mass hysteria someone commentated on the intolerance of the people at the Palace gates; how rude they were about the press and the Royal family, how they were looking for someone to blame.[26]

The pace of this de-spiralling of views and the challenge it posed to perceptions of the popular mood should not be exaggerated. As one woman quoted above put it in the December: 'I am still alarmed at the strength of feeling engendered by this tragedy and realise that I must keep my somewhat "negative" views to myself. Diana fans are everywhere.' But among readers of the quality press at least, Ian Jack's article at the turn of the year seemed to have had a substantial impact, judging by the number of people who attached reviews of his article and other anecdotal evidence. For one man quoted above, for example, it was the first public explanation of 'the alternative view' he had come across in public.[27] By the turn of the year, indeed, views were certainly changing socially, as increased defensiveness about the 'insincere' mourning were now combined with greater confidence in condemning an 'over the top' reaction:

January 6th 1998. There was nothing insincere about the mass outpourings of grief. To my mind, they were spontaneous and sincere.

January 12, 1998. Opened the typewriter to start the autumn directive and found this still in the roller! So I'll add that, in the past two or three weeks, an increasing number of people, looking back over the year and also discussing the tickets to view the burial site, have been taking the view that the whole thing went OTT. A columnist in our local daily paper calls the Althorp burial site 'the Maudlinorium' and a local radio DJ is refusing to back down after saying that those who had bought tickets were sad souls.[28]

Once the particular social and media constraints on opinion in September 1997 were removed then what was actually the majority private opinion during Diana's mourning now, in the months and years that followed, increasingly predominated in public (see chapter 1). Within this process, media coverage had a striking but very double-edged impact. On the one hand, people could not challenge the reality effect of what happened as conveyed through the mass media. On the other hand, the very power of these images of widespread, hysterical, adulatory grief for a stranger provoked a popular backlash, based on dominant cultural norms, against an abnormal case of 'mass hysteria'. People accepted the media images of the mourning but at the same time were repulsed by them. By conjuring up an imagined nation of deep grief, the media created a polarization that saw even those upset deriding the mass hysteria of others. Ironically, if the media had been more accurate in conveying the nature of popular reactions, it is unlikely that the event would have been viewed in such negative terms. But whatever the post-mourning backlash this caused, this illustrates how the images of the perceived popular reaction remain as powerful as ever. For as noted in chapter 1, mass hysteria is a negative explanation for what was perceived to have happened, not a challenge to it.

Media Power – Not People Power

In all this, the media's failure to reflect the diversity of attitudes that Diana's mourning inevitably stimulated, and its role and power in shaping a deeply misleading perception of the popular mood, offers ground for serious concern. In 1940 Tom Harrison had written:

> There is no getting away from this fact: the Press and Parliament version of public opinion is frequently miles away from 'real public opinion', let alone private opinion. For first we have the falsification between the person's actual (private) opinion and the version he gives out in public (public opinion), and second we have the falsification between public opinion and the version published (published opinion). (1940: 375)

How successful the media could have been in getting to 'private' opinion in September 1997 remains difficult to establish. But the point is that for the most part they did not even try. Far from seeking to penetrate the mourning veil, the media was central to its construction, thereby covering the nation's real views 'under a large monolith called GRIEF' (Jack 1997: 17). Even on the basis of the public opinion freely available, the version of popular reactions that they presented was 'miles away' from the truth. During Diana's mourning the media not only abandoned its much-trumpeted critical role of reporting and reflecting the public mood, but instead began telling people what they were and even should be feeling. Pollster Robert Worcester (1997) wondered whether no poll was taken during the week because the media did not want the facts to get in the way of a good story. And certainly the amazing ability of Diana to attract viewers and readers, coupled with the dramatic images of her mourning, created a widespread fascinated horror that saw viewing, reading and profit figures soar. Meanwhile the media's symbolic alignment with 'the people' in mourning also helped defuse a potentially dangerous public backlash against their behaviour. The one downside to this, as journalist Joan Smith later pointed out, was 'a culpable failure on the part of many journalists' when faced with such a dramatic story to also provide an accurate one:

They were so busy interviewing individuals in the crowd outside Kensington Palace or in the Mall that this transparently self-selecting sample was somehow transformed into the voice of the nation. I knew something was awry when I heard an uncritical radio interview with a man who had a 14-inch portrait of Princess Diana on his thigh. On his what? It is harder to get a full range of opinion. But I have been unable to square my experience, which is that I know of almost no one who feels personally bereaved, with what I have been reading and hearing on a daily basis. (Smith 1997c)

Emphasizing the views of 'ordinary people' and serving as a participatory forum for people to mourn was superficially democratic but in reality profoundly anti-democratic. For it was a forum that gave access to just one particular response, as the 'people who scream the most . . . the louder, the less controlled, the better' (Liebes 1998: 80), were presented as the representative voice of 'the people', while all other responses were systematically excluded. In doing so the media served massively to distort perceptions of popular responses, both at the time and subsequently, to the extent that the popular memory of what happened is fundamentally a false one. And just as the myth of the blitz has survived virtually unscathed by academic assault (Smith 2000), so it seems highly likely that the myth of a British nation in widespread, emotional, adulatory grief will remain dominant, in negative and positive forms, in popular memory. For the media myth is not only stronger than the unmediated reality of popular experience, but *is* the widely accepted reality, for good or bad, of 'the people's' response. That this is the case is a striking illustration, not of a democratic week of people power, but of a dangerously undemocratic week of media power.

Notes

Chapter 1

[1] C2761; this refers to the Mass-Observation number given by the archive to each volunteer. In identifying correspondents throughout the book, I have usually, although not always, offered their sex and sometimes age as contextual information. Except when discussing regional differences, geographical location has tended to be excluded, although on occasion it has been added to offer a more vivid illustration of the experience. While this lays the approach open to the charge of inconsistency, the simple rationale has been to offer a reader-friendly text in which the contextual information performs a descriptive function unless otherwise noted.

[2] Newspaper titles, if preceded by '*Daily*' (e.g. *Daily Mirror*, *Daily Mail*) have been shortened.

Chapter 2

[1] Drawing on the media to criticize media bias (which this book does throughout) raises, as Herman and Chomsky note, the obvious accusation that such criticism is self-refuting. Particularly in this case when many dissenting articles and letters were written precisely in response to or explicitly criticized media bias, their counter has considerable weight: 'That the media provides some facts about an issue, however, proves absolutely nothing about the adequacy or accuracy of that coverage . . . That a careful reader looking for a fact can sometimes find it with diligence and a sceptical eye tells us nothing about whether that fact received the attention and context it deserved, whether it was intelligible to the reader or effectively distorted or suppressed. What level of attention it deserved is debatable, but there is no merit in the pretence that because certain facts may be found in the media by a diligent and sceptical researcher, the absence of radical bias and de facto suppression is thereby demonstrated' (1994: pp. xiv–xv).

[2] The practicality of accessing the material, lack of awareness of it and the lingering of old suspicions about M-O's value are perhaps all factors, as

is the fact that the ethnographic turn generated plenty of conceptual discussions but 'remarkably few serious forays into the field' (Lewis 1997: 85).

3   C110; P1730.

4   One note of caution should nevertheless be sounded for it would be wrong to romanticize or exaggerate this process. For in this particular democratic collaboration, as with others, some are more equal than others and it is the author that in the end controls what is presented. This cannot and indeed should not be avoided in favour of the relativist free-for-all implied by 'post-modern ethnography'. For it is 'precisely the necessary responsibility of the analyst', arguably the whole 'point' of academia, to provide an explanatory framework that gets, as far as is possible, to the truth of what happened; see the sensible discussions in Morley (1992, 1997).

5   H1709; B2240; B2752.

6   T2203; C2053; C2722; B2258.

7   B1120; P1730; B2785.

Chapter 3

1   D2051; E1510; A2212.

2   H276; A2801; B736.

3   B2810; W1918.

4   B2638.

5   M1544.

6   M1498; C2722.

7   G2089.

8   B2258.

9   C2654.

10 B1424.

11 A2891; H276.

12 D2123.

13 G1041.

14 B2258; W565.

15 B1989; B2785.

16 P1743; A1646.

17 H2637; R450.

18 B1120.

19 J2187; B2066.

20 J2187; B1989.

21 S1383; M2443.

22 P2494; M2443.

23 Details of these engagements can be found announced in *The Times* at the start of January every year.

24 H1705; G1041; B2154.

25   N1592; M1498; A1783.
26   P1278; W1893.
27   H1709; H1263.
28   D2123.
29   B2240; K2241; W565.
30   C1713.
31   N1484.
32   A1783; B2154; E1510.
33   R2065.
34   L2393; B2154.
35   K1625; R450.
36   B1509; M2164.
37   J2799; B2760.
38   B2154; J1481.
39   D1602; M1544.
40   R450.
41   M381; P1730; C2722; B1386.
42   P1637; L2393.
43   F1373.

Chapter 4

1   C579; M2811; H2603; R1321.
2   C2761; B1215; T2003; P1730.
3   C2722; G1041.
4   K1321.
5   J931.
6   Quoted in P1730.
7   B89; B1386.
8   A883; B2258.
9   L1477.
10   D2239.
11   BARB.
12   R1468.
13   B1426; B1442.
14   S2211; B2258.
15   B2785.
16   Mass-Observation Topic Collection 14.
17   C2722.
18   T1686.
19   T842.
20   E2538.
21   M2164; A2464; L2393.
22   G2486; C1405.
23   R227.
24   B1215; L2393; D2739; B1535.

[25]   S2211; W655; B1509.
[26]   L1290; C722.

Chapter 5

[1]   W1813; R1227.
[2]   J2799; N399.
[3]   R1227; T842; G2701.
[4]   C110; D2739.
[5]   C2722; R1418.
[6]   E2538; D826.
[7]   D2051; A2212.
[8]   B2752; H2269; J931.
[9]   M1171; B1989.
[10]   J2187; C110.
[11]   M381; G1803; P2494.
[12]   C2053.
[13]   D2123; J2187; H1709.
[14]   N1484; E743.
[15]   B1771; G2701; S2207.
[16]   H1845; J2799.
[17]   B2066.
[18]   B260; R470.
[19]   N1522.
[20]   K1515.
[21]   C602; A1733.
[22]   T2203; D1602.
[23]   H2637.
[24]   H2637; F1634; R1025.
[25]   C2761.
[26]   J931.
[27]   B1426.
[28]   B1180; J931.
[29]   D2123.
[30]   Directive no. 28, Spring 1989, G2701; H2269.
[31]   B2066.
[32]   P2546.
[33]   D2051.

Chapter 6

[1]   N399.
[2]   S516; A2464.
[3]   S516.
[4]   F1634.

5   N399.
6   S2207; H1703; P1009.
7   Z53.
8   P1978; N399.
9   B2785.
10   R2692; M1171.
11   T1686.
12   C724.
13   R1418; S1540.
14   K2241; B2760; B1426.
15   S2305; S2211.
16   Directive no. 42, Spring 1994, G2134.
17   P416.
18   T2543; C602.
19   B2785.
20   H1709.
21   B1442; W1893; B1426.
22   B2154; P2494.
23   N1484; P1978; R1025.
24   A883; R1478.
25   R1025.
26   N399; D1602.
27   C2722.

Chapter 7

1   D2239.
2   C2761; H1774.
3   H2637.
4   C1405; O2349.
5   R1025; N1592.
6   M1171.
7   W729; T1843.
8   B2810.
9   D2239; H1774.
10   G1241; R2247.
11   C579; S496; B1120.
12   H1263; Z53.
13   R1025; P1009; S2242.
14   G2486; M1171; D826.
15   M1171.
16   O2349; M2290; G2486; M2811.
17   B2760; F1373.
18   H1705; P1730.

[19] N2148.
[20] D826; W1813; C2722.
[21] P2589.
[22] N1522; B1120.
[23] B2810; H2577; W633.
[24] M1171; H1774; T2543; D2239.
[25] R2065; M1381.

Chapter 8

[1] For an early survey of the media's treatment of Aids and homosexuality in the mid-1980s, see Armitage et al. (1987) and latterly and more substantially Miller et al. (1998).
[2] 854; 430; 611. These refer to the NL&GS number allocated to each individual. Their accounts have also been deposited at the University of Sussex archive.
[3] 806; 826; 443.
[4] 805; 367.
[5] 517; 430; 518.
[6] 511; 854.
[7] 602.
[8] 511; 854.
[9] 826.
[10] 518; 611.
[11] 602; 367; 518; 517; 611.
[12] 518; 430; 806.
[13] 517; 826.
[14] 806; 367.
[15] 443; 826; 517.
[16] 806; 611.
[17] 518; 826.
[18] 854; 511.
[19] 826; 517.
[20] 518; 430.

Chapter 9

[1] This is not to say, however, that this influence was not visible as, for example, people reported how their attitudes to Diana became more favourable or they felt upset after watching television tributes. Meanwhile, as this chapter argues, the power of the media could penetrate deep into the individual psyche.
[2] C110.

3   B2785.
4   W633.
5   H266, my emphasis.
6   C110; A2212; H1703; H2410.
7   G1563.
8   D2153.
9   B1989.
10 D2239; T1843.
11 F1634; T1843.
12 For an analysis of the rhetoric of this speech see Fairclough (2000).
13 W2224; B2728; G226; G1241.
14 B1120; T1843.
15 C2053; W1813; H2410.
16 N2148; P2494; O2349.
17 H1705; G1041.
18 S2191; M2132.
19 O2349.
20 C602; B2785; J2187.
21 T2003; J2187.
22 D1602.
23 P1730.
24 B2785; B2258; R2136; M2132.
25 D2123.
26 B2258; Z53; H2140.
27 D2123; C110.
28 G226; W633.

Bibliography

Mass-Observation Primary Sources

Mass-Observation in the 1980s and 1990s Project
Directive 52, Summer 1997, 'Death of Diana', 249 replies.
Directive 42, Spring 1994, 'Death'.
Directive 28, Spring 1989, 'Disasters'.

Original Mass-Observation Project
Famous Persons Survey 1938–1952, Topic Collection 14/1/L, King George
VI – his speech, death and funeral.

National Lesbian and Gay Survey

'Death of a Princess' directive, 12 replies.

Opinion Polls

ICM (1998), 'The Mirror Royal Poll', 17–18 August, published in *Daily Mirror*, 24 August (500 adults interviewed).
MORI (1997a), 'Satisfaction/Future/Diana', ABC, 4–5 September (1,063 adults interviewed).
—— (1997b), 'Satisfaction/Future/Diana', 6–7 September, published in *Sun*, 8 September (602 adults interviewed).
—— (1997c), 'Satisfaction/Future/Diana', 10–11 September (805 adults interviewed).
—— (1998a),'Diana/Royal Family Poll', 5–8 March, published in *Sun*, 6 April (1,000 adults interviewed).
—— (1998b), 'Mail on Sunday – Royal Family Poll', 18–20 August (804 adults interviewed).

—— (1998c), 'Political Attitudes in Great Britain for August 1998', conducted for *The Times*, 21–4 August 1998 (904 adults interviewed).

YouGov Opinion Research (2002), 'Diana, Princess of Wales survey', conducted for *Evening Standard*, 31 July–2 August 2002 (998 adults interviewed, weighted to London population only).

Television, Newspapers and Magazines

BBC, *Class War, Daily Record, Daily Express, Daily Mail, Daily Mirror, Daily Star, Daily Telegraph, Financial Times, Guardian, Independent, Independent on Sunday,* ITV, *The Herald, Mail on Sunday, Morning Star, New Musical Express, New Statesman and Society, Pink Paper, Private Eye, Scotsman, Spectator, Sun, Sunday Express, Sunday Telegraph, Sunday Times, The Times, The Voice, Western Mail.*

Cited Secondary Sources

Abrams, D. (1997), 'Uncertainty and Social Psychological Responses', *The Pyschologist* (November), 500–1.

Abrams, M. (1951), *Social Survey and Social Action*, London, Heinemann.

Addison, P. (1975), *The Road to 1945: British Politics and the Second World War*, London, Jonathan Cape.

Adonis, A. and Pollard, S. (1998), *A Class Act*, London, Penguin.

Aitkenhead, D. (1997), 'This isn't Grief, it's Wanting to Belong', *Guardian* (5 September).

—— (1998), 'Mixed feelings', *Guardian* (16 July).

Alexander, A. (1998), 'Queen of (Some) Hearts', *http://www.bbc.co.uk/ hi/ english/static/ diana_ one_ year_ on/reporters_ refl_.../a_alexandr.st.*

Alibhai-Brown, Y. (2000), *Who do we Think we Are?*, London, Allen Lane.

Anderson, B. (1991), *Imagined Communities*, London, Verso.

Anderson, Bruce (2002), 'The Sober Mourning that Confounds Republican Hopes', *Independent* (8 April).

Appleyard, B. (1997), 'Diana: First Lady of the Global Village', *Sunday Times* (7 September).

Armitage, G., Dickey, J. and Sharples, S. (1987), *Out of the Gutter: A Survey of the Treatment of Homosexuality by the Press*, London, Campaign for Press and Broadcasting Freedom.

Aron, D. and Livingstone, S. (1997), 'A Media Event Interrupts a Global Soap Opera', *The Psychologist* (November), 501–2.

Austin, M. (1998), 'Dons Flood Market with "Dianababble" ', *Sunday Times* (4 April).

Barber, N. (1997), 'Always on the Offensive – As Long as it doesn't Mean Diana', *Independent*, 23 November.

Barcan, R. (1997), 'Space for the Feminine', in Re: Public (ed.), *Planet Diana: Cultural Studies and Global Mourning*, Kingswood, NSW, Research Centre in Intercommunal Studies, University of Western Sydney.

Barnett, A. (1997), *This Time: Our Constitutional Revolution*, London, Vintage.

Baxendale, J. (1999), '"You and I – All of Us Ordinary People": Renegotiating "Britishness" in Wartime', in N. Hayes and J. Hill (eds), *Millions like Us: British Culture in the Second World War*, Liverpool, Liverpool University Press, 295–322.

BBC News (1998), 'TV Fuelled Diana Mourning says Adie', 29 August, *http://news.bbc.co.uk/hi/English/uk/newsid_161000/161029.stm*.

Beniger, J. (1987), 'Toward an Old New Paradigm: The Half Century Flirtation with Mass Society', *Public Opinion Quarterly*, 51, 46–66.

Bennett, C. (2002), 'Good Grief', *Guardian* (11 April).

Bennett, G. and Rowbottom, A. (1998), '"Born a Lady, Became a Princess and Died a Saint": The Deification of Diana in the Press and Popular Opinion in Britain', *Fabula*, 39 (3–4), 197–208.

Benton, S. (1998), 'The Princess, the People and the Paranoia', in M. Merck (ed.), *After Diana: Irreverent Elegies*, London, Verso, 87–101.

Benzie, T. (1997), 'Diana as a Gay Icon', in Re: Public (ed.), *Planet Diana: Cultural Studies and Global Mourning*, Kingswood, NSW, Research Centre in Intercommunal Studies, University of Western Sydney.

Berridge, K. (2001), *Vigor Mortis: The End of the Death Taboo*, London, Profile.

Biddle, L. and Walter, T. (1998), 'The Emotional English and their Queen of Hearts', *Folklore*, 109, 96–9.

Billig, M. (1995), *Banal Nationalism*, London, Sage.

—— (1997a), 'The Princess and the Paupers', *The Psychologist* (November), 505–6.

—— (1997b), *Talking of the Royal Family*, London, Routledge.

—— (1999), 'Conversations on the Diana Moment and its Politics', *Journal of Gender Studies*, 8 (3), 285–8.

Birchall, C. (1999), 'Alt.Conspiracy.Princess-Diana: The Conspiracy of Discourse', *New Formations*, 36, 125–40.

Birnbaum, N. (1955), 'Monarchs and Sociologists: A Reply to Professor Shils and Michael Young', *Sociological Review*, 3, 5–23.

Black, E. and Smith, P. (1999), 'Princess Diana's Meanings for Women: Results of a Focus Group Study', *Journal of Sociology*, 35 (3), 263–78.

Blackman, L. (1999), 'An Extraordinary Life: The Legacy of an Ambivalence', *New Formations*, 36, 111–24.

—— and Walkerdine, V. (2000), *Mass Hysteria: Critical Psychology and Media Studies*, London, Palgrave.

Bloome, D., Sheridan, D. and Street, B. (1993), *Reading Mass-Observation*

Writing: Theoretical and Methodological Issues in Researching the Mass-Observation Archive, M-OA Occasional Paper No. 1, Brighton, University of Sussex.

Blumer, J., Brown, J., Ewbank, A. and Nossiter, T. (1971), 'Attitudes to the Monarchy: Their Structure and Development during a Ceremonial Occasion', *Political Studies*, 19, 149–71.

Bond, M. (1997), 'The Authentic Voice of a Grieving People', *The Times* (31 December).

Bradberry, G. (1998), 'Paying their Respects with Tears and Souvenirs', *The Times* (28 August).

Braidotti, R. (1997), 'In the Sign of the Feminine: Reading Diana', *Theory and Event*, 1 (4), *http://muse.jhu.edu/journals/theory_&_event/v001/1.4braidotti.html*, pp. 1–13.

Brewer's Dictionary of Phrase and Fable (1965), London, Cassell.

Broadcasting Standards Commission (1998), 'Monitoring Report 6', *bsc.org.uk*.

Brunt, R. (1999a), 'Princess Diana: A Sign of The Times', in J. Richards, S. Wilson and L. Woodhead (eds), *Diana*, London, I. B. Tauris, 20–39.

—— (1999b), 'Conversations on the Diana Moment and its Politics', *Journal of Gender Studies*, 8 (3), 279–83.

Bryman, A. (1988), *Quantity and Quality in Social Research*, London, Unwin Hyman.

Bunting, M. (1994), 'Battle of the Royals for a Better Press', *Guardian* (20 May).

Burchill, J. (1992), 'Di Hard: The Pop Princess', in *Sex and Sensibility*, London, Grafton.

—— (1997), 'The People's Destroyer', *Guardian* (2 September).

—— (1998), *Diana*, London, Weidenfeld & Nicolson.

—— (2002), 'Burying our Heads', *Guardian* (20 April).

Byrne, C. (1997), 'BBC Muffles Audience Complaints over Coverage', *Sunday Telegraph* (14 September).

Calder, A. (1969), *The People's War*, London, Jonathan Cape.

—— (1985), 'Mass-Observation 1937–49', in M. Bulmer (ed.), *Essays on the History of British Sociological Research*, Cambridge, CUP, 121–36.

—— (1991), *The Myth of the Blitz*, London, Jonathan Cape.

—— and Sheridan, D. (eds) (1985), *Speak for Yourself: A Mass-Observation Anthology 1937–49*, Oxford, OUP.

Campbell, B. (1997), 'Femme Furious', *Guardian*, 11 September.

—— (1998a), *Diana, Princess of Wales: How Sexual Politics Shook the Monarchy*, London, Women's Press.

—— (1998b), 'Diana and the Sexists', *Guardian* (25 June).

Cannadine, D. (1981), 'War and Death, Grief and Mourning in Modern Britain', in J. Whaley (ed.), *Mirrors of Mortality: Studies in the Social History of Death*, London, Europa.

—— (1983), 'The Context, Performance and Meaning of Ritual: The British

Monarchy and the "Invention of Tradition"', in E. Hobsbawm and T. Ranger (eds), *The Invention of Tradition*, Cambridge, CUP, 101–64.

—— (1997), 'The Making of the Myth of Saint Diana', *Guardian* (6 September), 11.

Cardiff, D. and Scannell, P. (1987), 'Broadcasting and National Unity', in J. Curran, A. Smith and P. Wingate (eds), *Impacts and Influences: Essays on Media Power in the Twentieth Century*, London, Methuen, 157–73.

Cassidy, J. (1997), 'Black to Blighty and a Vision of the Ruling Class on the Run', *Sunday Times* (7 September).

Chaney, D. (2001), 'The Mediated Monarchy', in D. Morley and K. Robins (eds), *British Cultural Studies*, Oxford, OUP, 207–19.

Chirsty, D. (1997), 'Mourning has Broken, Thank God', *Guardian*, 12 September.

Clayton, T. and Craig, P. (2001), *Diana: Story of a Princess*, London, Hodder & Stoughton.

Cohan, A. (1999), 'The Spatial Diana: The Creation of Mourning Spaces for Diana, Princess of Wales', in J. Richards, S. Wilson and L. Woodhead (eds), *Diana*, London, I. B. Tauris, 163–76.

Cohen, N. (1997), 'Hold on a Minute', *Observer* (14 September).

—— (1998), 'Hold on a Minute', *Observer* (14 June).

Cole, R. (1998), 'Feelin's', in M. Merck (ed.), *After Diana*, London, Verso, 169–82.

Colley, L. (1992), *Britons: Forging the Nation*, New Haven, Yale University Press.

Corner, J. (2000), '"Influence": The Contested Core of Media Research', in J. Curran and M. Gurevitch, *Mass Media and Society*, London, Arnold, 376–97.

Couldry, N. (1999), 'The Geography of Celebrity and the Politics of Lack', *New Formations*, 36, 77–91.

—— (2000), *Inside Culture: Re-imagining the Method of Cultural Studies*, London, Sage.

—— (2001), 'Everyday Royal Celebrity', in D. Morley and K. Robins (eds), *British Cultural Studies*, Oxford, OUP, 221–33.

—— (forthcoming), *Media Rituals: A Critical Approach*, London, Routledge.

Coward, R. (1984), 'The Royals', in *Female Desire*, London, Paladin.

Cross, G. (ed.) (1990), *Worktowners in Blackpool: Mass Observation and Popular Leisure in the 1930s*, London, Routledge.

Dahrendorf, R. (1959), *Class and Class Conflict in Industrial Society*, London, Routledge & Kegan Paul.

Davies, C. (1999), 'Jokes on the Death of Diana', in T. Walter (ed.), *The Mourning for Diana*, Oxford, Berg, 253–68.

Davies, D. (1999), 'The Week of Mourning', in T. Walter (ed.), *The Mourning for Diana*, Oxford, Berg, 3–18.

Davies, J. (2001), *Diana, A Cultural History: Gender, Race, Nation and the People's Princess*, London, Palgrave.

Dayan, D. and Katz, E. (1992), *Media Events: The Live Broadcasting of History*, Cambridge, MA, Harvard University Press.

Dodd, V. (1998), 'Prince's Biographer Tells of Hate Campaign', *Guardian* (10 November).

Driscoll, M. (1997), 'Dons Crown Diana Queen of Cultural Icons', *Sunday Times* (9 November).

Dunkley, C. (1997), 'Whatever Happened to Freedom of Choice', *Financial Times* (10 September).

Durez, J. and Johnson, C. (1999), 'Mourning at a Distance; Australians and the Death of a British Princess', in A. Kear and D. Steinberg (eds), *Mourning Diana: Nation, Culture and the Performance of Grief*, London, Routledge, 42–54.

Dyer, R. (1986), *Heavenly Bodies: Film Stars and Society*, London, BFI.

Edgell, S. (1993), *Class*, London, Routledge.

Eldridge, J., Kitzinger, J. and Williams, K. (1997), *The Mass Media and Power in Modern Britain*, Oxford, OUP.

Engel, M. (1997), 'The Grieving', *Guardian* (2 September).

—— (1998a), 'The Joy of Failure', *Guardian* (4 July).

—— (1998b), 'From Sombre to Surreal', *Guardian* (1 September).

—— (1999a), 'Real Lives', *Guardian* (3 November).

—— (1999b), 'Long to Reign over Us (Sigh)', *Guardian* (16 November).

Epstein, S. (1996), *Impure Science: Aids, Activism and the Politics of Knowledge*, Berkeley, University of California Press.

Evans, C. (1997), 'From Military Tears to Cheers from the Crowd', *Sunday Telegraph* (7 September).

Fairclough, N. (2000), *New Labour, New Language?* London, Routledge.

Ferguson, E. (1997), 'A Tragedy, Yes, but Don't Tell Me I Must Cry', *Observer* (7 September).

—— (1998), 'Once More, with Feeling', *Observer* (30 August).

Ferguson, M. and Golding, P. (eds) (1997), *Cultural Studies in Question*, London, Sage.

Fielding, S., Thompson, P. and Tiratsoo, N. (1995), *'England Arise!': The Labour Party and Popular Politics in 1940s Britain*, Manchester, MUP.

Finch, J. (1986), *Research and Policy*, London, Falmer Press.

Flett, K. (1998), 'Thirty Days and Thirty Nights', *Observer* (23 August).

Fountain, N. (1997), 'A Trash Icon for our Times', *Observer* (27 July).

Freedland, J. (1997a), 'To Speak of Emotion Conveys Sincerity', *Guardian* (3 September).

—— (1997b), 'See the New Britain in the Snowfall', *Guardian* (10 September).

—— (1997c), 'More Open and Tolerant, Less Macho and Miserable', *Guardian* (18 September).

—— (1998), 'The Last Flourish of the 20th Century', *Guardian* (19 December).

—— (1999), 'Diana is Dead', *Guardian* (25 August).

Furedi, F. (1998), 'New Britain – a Nation of Victims', *Society* (13 March).

Gauntlett, D. and Hill, A. (1999), *TV Living: Television, Culture and Everyday Life*, London, Routledge/BFI.

Gay Times (1997), 'The Revolution of the Flowers' (October).

—— (1998), 'A Very Modern Gay Icon' (August).

Geertz, C. (1975), *The Interpretation of Culture*, London, Hutchinson.

Gellner, E. (1983), *Nations and Nationalism*, Oxford, Blackwell.

Geraghty, C. (1991), *Women and Soap Opera: A Study of Prime Time Soaps*, Cambridge, Polity.

—— (1998), 'Story', *Screen*, 39 (1), 70–3.

Gerrard, N. (1997), 'Damn this Raging Flood of Emotion', *Observer* (21 September).

Ghosh, P. (1998), 'Mediate and Immediate Mourning', in M. Merck (ed.), *After Diana*, London, Verso, 41–7.

Gibbons, F. (2001), 'Critic Defends Stand over Diana's Death', *Guardian* (29 May).

Giles, D. (2002), 'Parasocial Interaction: A Review of the Literature and a Model for Future Research', *Media Psychology*, 4 (3), 279–302.

—— and Naylor, G. (2000), 'The Construction of Intimacy with Media Figures in a Parasocial Context', paper presented at the BPS London Conference, Institute of Education.

Gilroy, P. (1997), 'Elton's Crooning, England's Dreaming', *Theory and Event*, 1 (4), *http://muse.jhu.edu/journals/theory_&_event/v001/1.4.html*.

Glynn, C., Hayes, A. and Shanahan, J. (1997), 'Perceived Support for one's Opinions and Willingness to Speak out', *Public Opinion Quarterly*, 61 (2), 452–63.

Grant, L. (1997a), 'The People Never Deserted her', *Guardian* (1 September).

—— (1997b), 'Message from the Mall', *Guardian* (9 September).

—— (1999), 'Englishness slips away', *Guardian* (16 September).

Gray, J. (1997), 'Silent Majority Speaks', *Guardian* (3 September).

Greenslade, R. (1997), 'Di's Mourners Turn to Broadsheets', *Guardian* (13 October).

—— (1998), 'Diana: Now the Press gets off its Knees', *Guardian* (6 April).

Griffin, W. (1999), 'An American Paean for Diana, an Unlikely Feminist Hero', in T. Walter (ed.), *The Mourning for Diana*, Oxford, Berg, 241–51.

Gunnell, B. (1998), 'If Mourning Diana isn't your Cup of Tea , is it at Last All Right to Tell Those Tacky Jokes', *Observer* (22 March).

Hall, S. (1992), 'Cultural Studies and its Theoretical Legacies', in L. Grossberg, C. Nelson and P. Treischler (eds), *Cultural Studies*, London, Routledge, 277–94.

Hall, T. (1997), 'The People Led, We Followed', *The Times* (10 September).

Hamilton, A. (2001), 'Militant Mood as Diana Devotees Remember', *The Times*, 1 September.

Harris, L. (1966), *Long to Reign Over us*, London, William Kimber.

Harrison, T. (1940), 'What is Public Opinion', *Political Quarterly*, 11, 368–83.

—— (1947), 'The Future of Sociology', *Pilot Papers*, 2 (1), 10–25.

Hartley, J. (1998), 'Juvenation: News, Girls and Power', in C. Carter, G. Branston and S. Allen, *News, Gender and Power*, London, Routledge, 47–70.

Hawton, K., Harris, L. and Simkin, S. (2000), 'Effect of Diana, Princess of Wales on Suicide and Deliberate Self-Harm', *British Journal of Psychiatry*, 177, 463–6.

Hay, V. (1999), 'Be(long)ing: New Labour, New Britain and the "Dianaization of Politics"', in A. Kear and D. Steinberg, *Mourning Diana*, London, Routledge, 60–76.

Heffer, S. (1997), 'How Diana has Truly United our Kingdom', *Daily Mail* (3 September).

Heller, Z. (1997), 'The Meaning of Diana', *Prospect* (October).

Herman, E. and Chomsky, N. (1994), *Manufacturing Consent: The Political Economy of the Mass Media*, London, Vintage.

Higonnet, M. and Higonnet, P. (1987), 'The Double Helix', in M. Higonnet, J. Jenson, S. Michel and M. Weitz, *Behind the Lines: Gender and the Two World Wars*, New Haven, Yale University Press.

Hill, J. (1999), 'Postscript: A War Imagined', in N. Hayes and J. Hill (eds), *Millions like us: British Culture in the Second World War*, Liverpool, Liverpool University Press, 323–35.

Hilton, E. (1997), 'Royal Reality Check', *Guardian* (2 September).

Hinton, J. (1997), '1945 and the Apathy School', *History Workshop Journal*, 43, 266–72.

Hitchens, C. (1997), 'Throne and Alter', *The Nation* (29 September).

—— (1998), 'Diana: The Mourning After', *Channel 4* (27 August).

Hobson, D. (1980), 'Housewives and the Mass Media', in S. Hall, D. Hobson, A. Lowe and P. Willis, *Culture, Media, Language: Working Papers in Cultural Studies*, London, Hutchinson, 105–14.

Hobson, R. (1997), 'Doubts over Diana Effect', *The Times* (1 December).

Hoggart, R. (1957), *The Uses of Literacy*, London, Chatto & Windus.

Hoggart, S. (1997), 'Cold Stoicism Rules', *Guardian* (5 September).

Holden, A. (2001), 'We will Always Remember Her', *Daily Express* (13 June).

Holt, L. (1998), 'Diana and the Backlash', in M. Merck (ed.), *After Diana*. London, Verso, 183–97.

Howkins, A. (1998), 'A Country at War: Mass-Observation and Rural England', *Rural History*, 9, 75–97.

Hume, M. (1997), 'Blair's Britain AD – After Diana', *Living Marxism*, 104, 4–5.

Humphrys, J. (2000), *Devil's Advocate*, London, Arrow.

Ignatieff, M. (1997), 'The Meaning of Diana', *Prospect* (October), 6–7.

—— (1998), 'A Vast Amount of Unmastered Grief', in B. MacArthur (ed.), *Requiem: Diana, Princess of Wales 1961–1997: Memories and Tributes*, London, Pavilion, 187–90.

Irons, J. (1997), 'This is the Year the British Found their Voice', *The Times* (27 December).

Jack, I. (1997), 'Those who Felt Differently', *Granta*, 60, 9–35.

Jacques, M. (1997a), 'The Floral Revolution', *Observer* (7 September).

—— (1997b), 'New Britain: We've Changed . . . but What will we Become', *Observer* (14 September).

James, O. (1997), 'An Unfulfilled People Clings to its Idol', *Independent* (6 September).

Jefferys, T. (1999), *Mass-Observation: A Short History*, M-OA Occasional Paper No. 10, Brighton, University of Sussex.

Jennings, H. and Madge, C. (1937), *May the Twelfth: Mass-Observation Day Surveys*, London, Faber & Faber.

Jensen, J. (1992), 'Fandom as Pathology: The Consequences of Characterisation', in L. Lewis (ed.), *The Adoring Audience: Fan Culture and Popular Media*, London, Routledge, 2–29.

Johnson, B. (1997), 'Where is this – Argentina?', *Daily Telegraph* (3 September).

Johnson, R. (1999), 'Exemplary Differences: Mourning (and Not Mourning) a Princess', in A. Kear and D. Steinberg (eds), *Mourning Diana*, London, Routledge, 15–39.

Jones, B. (1999), 'Books of Condolence', in T. Walter (ed.), *The Mourning for Diana*, Oxford, Berg, 203–14.

Junor, P. (1998), *Charles: Victim or Villain?* London, Harper Collins.

Karpf, A. (1997), 'Lest We Ignore', *Guardian*, 6 September.

Kay, R. (2000), 'Why We Must Never Forget Princess Diana', *Daily Mail* (31 August).

Kear, A. and Steinberg, D. (eds) (1999), *Mourning Diana: Nation, Culture and the Performance of Grief*, London, Routledge.

Kellner, P. (1997), 'Two in Three Say the Monarchy is Damaged', *Observer*, 7 September.

Kington, M. (1997), 'A Nation in Mourning (and if You weren't You had to Keep Quiet)', *Independent* (7 October).

Kitch, C. (2001), 'A News of Feeling as Well as Fact', *Journalism*, 1 (2), 171–95.

Kitzinger, J. (1999a), 'A Sociology of Media Power: Key Issues in Audience Research', in G. Philo (ed.), *Message Received*, London, Longman, 3–20.

—— (1999b), 'The Moving Power of Moving Images: Television Constructions of Princess Diana', in T. Walter (ed.), *The Mourning for Diana*, Oxford, Berg, 65–76.

Knight, P. (2000), *Conspiracy Culture: From Kennedy to the X Files*, London, Routledge.

Knowsley, J. (1997), 'A Family's Private Grief for Unsung Mary', *Sunday Telegraph* (14 September).

Kuhn, W. (1999), 'The Future of the British Monarchy', *Journal of British Studies*, 38 (2), 267–72.

Bibliography

Langer, J. (1998), *Tabloid Television: Popular Journalism and the 'Other' News*, London, Routledge.

Lawson, M. (1997a), 'Mourning Television', *Guardian* (4 September).

—— (1997b), 'Second Thoughts', *Guardian* (18 September).

—— (2002), 'Diana, the Star that Time Forgot', *Guardian* (27 July).

Lawson, N. (1997a) 'Why the Nation is Right to Share Family's Grief', *The Times* (1 September).

—— (1997b), 'Nothing But Praise for Diana', *The Times* (3 September).

—— (1997c), 'Beware of the Grief Police', *The Times* (10 September).

Lechnowicz, A. (1998), 'Royal Biography', *Contemporary British History*, 12 (4), 170–6.

Lewis, J. (1997), 'What Counts in Cultural Studies', *Media, Culture and Society*, 19, 83–97.

—— (2001), *Constructing Public Opinion: How Political Elites do what they Like and Why we Seem To Go Along With It*, New York, Columbia University Press.

Liebes, T. (1998), 'Television Disaster Marathons: A Danger for the Democratic Process?', in J. Curran and T. Liebes (eds), *Media, Ritual and Identity*, London, Routledge, 71–84.

Lindlof, T. and Grodin, D. (1990), 'When Media Use Can't be Measured', *Journal of Communication*, 40 (4), 8–28.

Linklater, M. (1997), 'Faith, Football and the Day of a Funeral', *The Times* (4 September).

Littlejohn, R. (1997), 'No Disrespect but Scotland should have Played', *Daily Mail* (5 September).

—— (1998), 'Have we All gone Soft over Diana', *Sun* (18 April).

Living Marxism (1997), 'Mourning Sickness' (October), 104, 1–9.

Lloyd, J. (1997), 'How the Left Took over Diana', *The Times* (5 September).

Lukes, S. (1975), 'Political Ritual and Social Integration', *Sociology*, 9, 289–308.

Lumby, C. (1999), *Gotcha: Life in a Tabloid World*, New South Wales, Allen & Unwin.

McAlpine, J. (1997), 'Is the Game up for Unlucky Jim?', *Sunday Times* (14 September).

MacArthur, B. (ed.) (1998), *Requiem: Diana, Princess of Wales 1961–1997: Memories and Tributes*, London, Pavilion.

Macdonald, M. (1995), *Representing Women: Myths of Femininity in the Popular Media*, London, Arnold.

McGann, P. (1997), '"Private Eye" Readers Outflank Diana Threat', *Independent* (25 September).

McGuigan, J. (1992), *Cultural Populism*, London, Routledge.

—— (2000), 'British identity and "the People's Princess"', *Sociological Review*, 48 (1), 1–18.

McIlven, R. and Gross, R. (1999), *Social Influence*, London, Hodder & Stoughton.

McKibbin, R. (1998), 'Mass-Observation in the Mall', in M. Merck (ed.), *After Diana*, London, Verso, 15–24.

McRobbie, A. (1997), 'The E's and the Anti-E's: New Questions for Feminism and Cultural Studies', in M. Ferguson and P. Golding (eds), *Cultural Studies in Question*, London, Sage, 170–86.

Maio, G. and Esses, V. (2001), 'The Need for Affect: Individual Differences in the Motivation to Approach or Avoid Emotions', *Journal of Personality*, 69 (4), 583–615.

Maitland, S (1997), 'We are Not All Part of This', *Independent* (5 September).

Marr, A. (1998), 'The Way we are Now', *Guardian* (22 August).

Marrin, M. (1997), 'Why I Cannot Share the People's Grief', *Sunday Telegraph* (7 September).

Marshall, G. et al. (1988), *Social Class in Modern Britain*, London, Hutchinson.

Mass-Observation (1943a/1987), *The Pub and the People: A Worktown Study*, London, Gollancz.

—— (1943b/1987), *War Factory*, London, Gollancz.

Merck, M. (ed.) (1998), *After Diana: Irreverent Elegies*, London, Verso.

Merrin, W. (1999), 'Crash, Bang, Wallop! What a Picture! The Death of Diana and the Media', *Mortality*, 4 (1), 41–62.

Mestrovic, S. (1997), *Postemotional Society*, London, Sage.

Miller, D., Kitzinger, J., Williams, K. and Beharrell, P. (1998), *The Circuit of Mass Communication*, London, Sage.

Monger, G. and Chandler, J. (1998), 'Pilgrimage to Kensington Palace', *Folklore*, 109, 104–8.

Moore, S. (1993), 'Diana: Her True Colours', *Guardian* (11 December).

—— (1995), 'The New Model Goddess', *Guardian* (22 November).

—— (1997), 'Britain is Unbuttoning, but it will Not Bring the Changes Many Expect', *Independent* (19 September).

Moran, C. (1997), 'Humbug in the Wind', *The Times* (12 September).

—— (1998), 'They are Further Isolating Themselves', in B. MacArthur (ed.), *Requiem*, London, Pavilion, 33–5.

Morley, D. (1992), *Television, Audiences and Cultural Studies*, London, Routledge.

—— (1997), 'Theoretical Orthodoxies: Textualism, Constructivism and the "New Ethnography" in Cultural Studies', in M. Ferguson and P. Golding (ed.), *Cultural Studies in Question*, London, Sage, 170–86.

Morton, A. (1992), *Diana: Her True Story*, London, Michael O'Mara.

—— (1995), *Diana: Her New Life*, London, Michael O'Mara.

—— (1997), *Diana: Her True Story – In Her Own Words*, London, Michael O'Mara.

Muggeridge, M. (1955), 'Royal Soap Opera', *New Statesman* (22 October).

Myers, G. (2000), 'Entitlement and Sincerity in Broadcast Interviews about Princess Diana', *Media, Culture and Society*, 22 (2), 167–85.

Nairn, T. (1988), *The Enchanted Glass: Britain and its Monarchy*, London, Radius.

—— (1994), 'Death of a Great British Romance', *Observer* (3 July).

—— (1998), 'The Departed Spirit', in M. Merck (ed.), *After Diana*, London, Verso, 217–28.

National Lesbian and Gay Survey (1992), *What a Lesbian Looks Like*, London, Routledge.

—— (1993), *Proust, Cole Porter, Michaelangelo, Marc Almond and Me*, London, Routledge.

Neil, A. (1996), *Full Disclosure*, London, Macmillan.

New Formations (1999), *Diana and Democracy*, London, Laurence & Wishart.

Nicoll, R. (1998), 'The Dividend of Diana', *Guardian* (14 January).

Noakes, L. (1996), *Mass-Observation, Gender and Nationhood: Britain in the Falklands War*, M-OA Occasional Paper No. 5, Brighton, University of Sussex.

Noelle-Neumann, E. (1993), *The Spiral of Silence*, Chicago, University of Chicago Press.

O'Hear, A. (1998), 'Diana, Queen of Hearts: Sentimentality Exposed and Canonised', in D. Anderson and P. Mullen (eds), *Faking it: The Sentimentalisation of Modern Society*, London, Social Affairs Unit, 181–90.

Paglia, C. (1995), *Vamps and Tramps*, London, Penguin.

—— (1997), 'A Gift Diana Squandered', *Guardian* (4 September).

Parkin, P. (1987) 'Contested Sources of National Identity: Nation, Class and Gender in the Second World War', Ph.D. thesis, London School of Economics.

Parris, M. (1998), 'I have Become a Stranger in a Once-Familiar Land', *The Times* (31 August).

Parsons, T. (1998), 'Dishing Diana with a Diet of Fat Poison', *Daily Mirror* (20 April).

Paxman, J. (1999), *The English: A Portrait of a People*, London, Penguin.

Pearce, E. (1997), 'Only Adults Deserve a Republic', *Daily Telelegraph* (9 September).

Pearson, A. (1997), 'People Power', *Daily Telegraph* (27 December).

Peukert, D. (1989), *Inside Nazi Germany: Opposition and Conformity in the Third Reich*, London, Penguin.

Philo, G. (1990), *Seeing and Believing*, London, Routledge.

—— (ed.) (1999), *Message Received*, London, Longman.

—— and Miller, D. (eds) (2000), *Market Killing: What the Free Market Does and what Social Scientists can Do about it*, London, Longman.

Pimlott, B. (1997a/2002), *The Queen: A Biography of Elizabeth II*, London, Harper Collins.

—— (1997b), 'The Politics of Cuddling', *Guardian* (1 September).

Plummer, K. (2000), 'Mapping the Sociological Gay: Past, Present and Futures of a Sociology of Same Sex Relations', in T. Sandfort, J. Schuyf,

J. Duyvendak and J. Weeks (eds), *Lesbian and Gay Studies: An Introductory, Interdisciplinary Approach*, London, Sage, 46–60.

Pocock, D. (1987), 'Afterwood', in H. Jennings and C. Madge, *May the Twelfth*, London, Faber & Faber, 415–23.

—— and Sheridan, D. (1985), 'Application to the Nuffield Foundation', M-OA, Brighton, University of Sussex.

Prochaska, F. (2001), *The Republic of Britain 1976–2000*, London, Penguin.

Propp, V. (1968), *Morphology of the Folktale*, Austin, University of Texas Press.

Purvis, J. (1997), 'Diana, Princess of Wales', *Women's History Review*, 6 (3), 315–16.

Quirke, H. (1997), 'Goodbye Yellow Brick Road', *Lesbians on the Loose* (October).

Re: Public (eds) (1997), *Planet Diana: Cultural Studies and Global Mourning*, Kingswood, NSW, Research Centre in Intercommunal Studies, University of Western Sydney.

Reid, J. (1997), 'Hysteria Paving the Way for a Backlash', *Herald* (5 September).

Rennell, T. (2000), 'Do Not Deny Diana Thrice', *Observer* (29 August).

Richards, J. and Sheridan, D. (eds) (1987), *Mass-Observation at the Movies*, London, Routledge.

Richards, J., Wilson, S. and Woodhead, L. (eds) (1999), *Diana: The Making of a Media Saint*, London, I. B. Tauris.

Richardson, R. (1999), 'Disposing with Diana: Diana's Death and the Funeral Culture', *New Formations*, 36, 21–33.

Rose, R. and Kavanagh, D. (1976), 'The Monarchy in Contemporary Culture', *Comparative Politics*, 8, 548–76.

Roseneil, S. (2001), 'A Moment of Moral Remaking: The Death of Diana, Princess of Wales', in F. Webster (ed.), *Culture and Politics in the Information Age*, London, Routledge, 96–114.

Ruddock, A. (2001), *Understanding Audiences: Theory and Method*, London, Sage.

Rushing, J. H. (1998), 'Putting away Childish Things: Looking at Diana's Funeral and Media Criticism', *Women's Studies in Communication*, 21 (2), 150–67.

Savage, J. (1992), *England's Dreaming: Sex Pistols and Punk Rock*, London, Faber & Faber.

Schama, S. (1986), 'The Domestication of Majesty: Royal Family Portraiture 1500–1850', *Journal of Interdisciplinary History*, 17 (1), 155–83.

Scheufele, D. A. and Moy, P. (2000), 'Twenty Five Years of the Spiral of Silence: A Conceptual Review and Empirical Outlook', *International Journal of Public Opinion*, 12 (1), 3–28.

Seaman, W. (1992), 'Active Audience Theory: Pointless Populism', *Media Culture and Society*, 14 (2), 301–12.

Segal, N. (1998), 'The Common Touch', in M. Merck (ed.), *After Diana*, London, Verso, 131–45.

Sewell, B. (1998), 'Diana's Oddly Suitable Death', *Evening Standard* (28 August).

—— (1999), 'How Could we Betray Diana's Legacy so Soon', *Mail on Sunday* (30 May).

Shamir, J. and Shamir, M. (1997), 'Pluralistic Ignorance across Issues and over Time', *Public Opinion Quarterly*, 61, 227–60.

Shaw, J. (1998), *Intellectual Property, Representative Experience and Mass-Observation*, M-OA Occasional Paper No. 9, Brighton, University of Sussex.

Shepherd, D. (ed.) (1993), *Bakhtin: Carnival and Other Subjects*, Amsterdam, Rodopi.

Sheridan, D. (ed.) (1991), *Wartime Women: A Mass-Observation Anthology*, London, Mandarin.

—— (1996), *'Damned Anecdotes and Dangerous Confabulations': Mass-Observation and Life History*, M-OA Occasional Paper No. 7, Brighton, University of Sussex.

——, Street, B. and Bloome, D. (2000), *Writing Ourselves: Mass-Observation and Literary Practices*, Creskill, Hampton.

Shevlin, M., Davies, M., Walker, S. and Ramkalawan, T. (1999), 'A Nation under Stress: The Pyschological Impact of Diana's Death', in T. Walter (ed.), *The Mourning for Diana*, Oxford, Berg.

Shils, E. and Young, M. (1953), 'The Meaning of the Coronation', *Sociological Review*, 1 (2), 63–81.

Showalter, E. (1997a), 'Storming the Wintry Palace', *Guardian* (6 September).

—— (1997b), *Hystories: Hysterical Epidemics in Modern Culture*, London, Picador.

Silverman, D. (2000), *Doing Qualitative Research: A Practical Handbook*, London, Sage.

Silverstone, R. (1998), 'Space', *Screen*, 39 (1), 81–4.

Simmonds, D. (1984), *Princess Di: The National Dish*, London, Pluto.

Smith, A. (1991), *National Identity*, London, Penguin.

Smith, D. (1997), 'Diana: A Gay Times Tribute', *Gay Times*, 229, 7–9, 51–2.

Smith J. (1997a), 'What is the National Mood', *Independent on Sunday* (7 September).

—— (1997b), 'Why do we Pretend we've Forgotten Diana's Faults', *Independent on Sunday* (14 September).

—— (1997c), 'They Gawped for Years, Why would they Stop Now', *Independent on Sunday* (21 September).

—— (1998), 'To Di For: The Queen of Broken Hearts', in *Different for Girls: How Culture Creates Women*, London, Vintage.

Smith, M. (2000), *Britain and 1940: History Myth and Popular Memory*, London, Routledge.

Snow, J. (1997), 'A Death like No Other', *Guardian* (8 September).

Splichal, S. (2000), *Public Opinion: Developments and Controversy in the Twentieth Century*, Lanham, MD, Rowman & Littlefield.

Spurlin, W. (1999), 'I'd rather be the Princess than the Queen! Mourning Diana as a Gay Icon', in A. Kear and D. Steinberg (eds), *Mourning Diana*, London, Routledge, 155–68.

Stanley, L. (1990), *The Archaeology of a 1930s Mass-Observation Project*, University of Manchester, Dept of Sociology, Occasional Paper No. 27.

Stanley, N. (1981), 'The Extra Dimension: A Study and Assessment of the Methods Employed by Mass-Observation in the First Period', Ph.D. thesis, CNAA.

Stanton, G. (1996), 'Ethnography, Anthropology and Cultural Studies: Links and Connections', in J. Curan, D. Morley and V. Walkerdine, *Cultural Sudies and Communications*, London, Routledge, 258–334.

Steel, M. (1998), 'Something Else Di-ed', *Guardian* (17 June).

Sterio, N. (1997), 'New Book on Diana Ignored by the Welsh', *South Wales Echo* (8 December).

Stothard, P. (1997), 'A Perrier with the Princess', *The Times* (2 September).

Summerfield, P. (1985), 'Mass-Observation: Social Research or Social Movement', *Journal of Contemporary History*, 20 (3), 439–52.

Swain, H. (1998), 'Why the Windsors are More than a Tabloid Farce', *The Times Higher Education Supplement* (19 June).

Taylor, A. (1999), *'Down with the Crown': British Anti-monarchism and Debates about Royalty since 1790*, London, Reaktion.

Taylor, J. (2000), *Diana, Self-Interest and British National Identity*, Westport, CT, Praeger.

Teeman, T. (1997), 'Switchboard Flooded with Calls from "Bereaved" Gay Men after Diana's Death', *Pink Paper* (3 October).

Tester, K. (2001), *Compassion, Morality and the Media*, Buckingham, Open University Press.

Thane, P. (2001), 'Old Women in Twentieth-Century Britain', in L. Botelho and P. Thane (eds), *Women and Ageing in British Society since 1500*, London, Pearson, 207–31.

The Princess's People (1998), BBC2 (6 September).

Thomas, J. (2002), *Beneath the Mourning Veil: Mass-Observation and the Death of Diana*, M-OA Occasional Paper No. 12, Brighton, University of Sussex.

Thompson, E. (1991), *The Making of the English Working Class*, London, Penguin.

Toolis, K. (1998), 'The Enforcer', *Guardian* (4 April).

Tunstall, J. (1996), *Newspaper Power: The New National Press in Britain*, Oxford, Clarendon.

Turner, G. (1998), 'Her Candle has Not Survived the Wind', *Spectator* (14 November).

Turner, J. and Sparrow, N. (1997), 'Hearing the Silence: The Spiral of Silence, Parties and the Media', *Media, Culture and Society*, 19 (1), 121–31.

Turner, V. (1969), *The Ritual Process: Structure and Anti-Structure*, New York, Cornell University Press.

Turnock, R. (2000), *Interpreting Diana: Television Audiences and the Death of a Princess*, London, BFI.

Utley, T. (1997), 'The Mourning', *Daily Telegraph* (3 September).

Valentine, G. and Butler, R. (1999), 'The Alternative Fairy Story: Diana and the Sexual Dissidents', *Journal of Gender Studies*, 8 (3), 295–301.

Verba, S. (1965), 'The Kennedy Assassination and the Nature of Political Commitment', in B. Greenberg and E. Parker (eds), *The Kennedy Assassination and the American Public*, Stanford, CA, Stanford University Press, 348–60.

Walter, T. (1991), 'The Mourning after Hillsborough', *Sociological Review*, 39 (3), 599–625.

—— (1999a), 'The Questions People Asked', in T. Walter (ed.), *The Mourning for Diana*, Oxford, Berg, 19–47.

—— (1999b), *On Bereavement: The Culture of Grief*, Buckingham, Open University Press.

——, Littlewood, J. and Pickering, M. (1995), 'Death in the News: The Public Invigilation of Private Emotion', *Sociology*, 29 (4), 579–96.

Waterhouse, K. (1997), 'The Soap is Over and No Repeats', *Daily Mail* (8 September).

—— (2000), 'The Mob and the Mourners – the Same', *Daily Mail* (26 June).

Watts, C. (1999), 'Unworkable Feeling: Diana, Death and Feminisation', *New Formations*, 36, 34–58.

Weeks, J. (2000), 'The Challenge of Lesbian and Gay Studies', in T. Sandfort, J Schuyf, J. Duyvendak and J. Weeks (eds), *Lesbian and Gay Studies: An Introductory, Interdisciplinary Approach*, London, Sage, 1–13.

Wheen, F. (1998), 'Weep and Try Not to Think', *Guardian* (22 April).

Williams, M. (1997), 'The Princess Puzzle', *U.S. News Online* (15 September), *http://www.usnews.com/usnews/issue/970915/15icon.htm*.

Williamson, J. (1988), 'Royalty and Representation', in *Consuming Passions: The Dynamics of Popular Culture*, London, Marion Boyars.

Wilson, A. (1997), 'This Cult of Diana Makes me Shiver', *Evening Standard* (10 September).

Wilson, E. (1998), 'The Unbearable Lightness of Diana', in M. Merck (ed.), *After Diana*, London, Verso, 111–25.

Wolffe, R. (1997), 'Carnival Controversy', *Financial Times*, 8 September.

Worcester, R. (1997), 'The Power of Public Opinion: Diana, Princess of Wales: 1961–1997', *Journal of the Market Research Society*, 19 (4), 527–44.

Yin, R. (1989), *Case Study Research: Design and Method*, London, Sage.

Zelizer, B. (1992), *Covering the Body: The Kennedy Assassination, the Media and the Shaping of Collective Memory*, Chicago, University of Chicago.

Ziegler, P. (1978), *The Crown and People*, London, Collins.

Zoonen, L. van (1994), *Feminist Media Studies*, London, Sage.
Zweiniger-Bargielowska, I. (1993), 'Royal Rations', *History Today*, 431, 13–15.

Index